AL-KAFI

THE EARLIEST & MOST IMPORTANT COMPILATION OF
TRADITIONS FROM PROPHET MUHAMMAD & HIS SUCCESSORS

BOOK I

INTELLECT & FOOLISHNESS

Shaykh Abū Jaʿfar Muḥammad ibn Yaʿqūb al-Kulaynī

COMMENTARY & TRANSLATION
Islamic Texts Institute

UNDER THE DIRECTION OF
Shaykh Rizwan Arastu

TAQWA media

ISBN: 978-1-939420-00-8

Library of Congress Control Number: 2012954729

Layout and Cover Design by:
Islamic Publishing House
Kitchener, ON
www.iph.ca

Published by:
Taqwa Media LLC
Monmouth Junction, NJ
www.taqwamedia.com

Taqwa Media LLC is a print and digital publishing, marketing, and distribution company. Established in September 2012, Taqwa Media's vision is to share the message of God-consciousness *(taqwa)* using state-of-the-art technology. Our company provides an opportunity for independent publishers and authors to disseminate their works using our global distribution network. By the grace of God, Taqwa Media is honored to present *al-Kāfī Book 1: Intellect and Foolishness*. This is the first of a thirty-five-book series that contains the traditions (*ahadith*) of Prophet Muhammad and his family.

Printed in Canada

About the Islamic Texts Institute:

The Islamic Texts Institute (ITI) is a non-profit organization that aims to make Islamic primary sources available to audiences in the West by providing accurate, scholarly translations of major Shīʿī collections of traditions accompanied by sufficient commentary to help readers comprehend and assimilate these teachings. ITI was founded in 2006 by Shaykh Rizwan Arastu, a graduate of Princeton University and of the International Center for Islamic Studies in Qum, Iran.

For more information about ITI, please visit www.islamictexts.org or scan the following QR code:

Contents

Acknowledgements ix
Transliteration x
Preface xi

Shaykh al-Kulaynī's Life xi
His Teachers xiii
  His teachers in Qum xiii
  His teachers in Rayy xiv
  His teachers in Iraq xiv
  His teachers in miscellaneous cities xiv
  His teachers whose places of residence are not known xv
  Elliptical references to his teachers xv
His Students xvii
  His students in Rayy xvii
  His students in Qum xvii
  His students in Iraq xvii
  His students in other places xviii
His Reputation in Academic Circles xviii
His Writings and Compilations xix
His Death xx
Al-Kāfī xx
  Usūl al-kāfī (books 1-8) xxiii
  Furūʿ al-kāfī (books 9-34) xxiii
  Rawḍat al-kāfī (book 35) xxiii
  Al-Kāfī's Authenticity xxiii
  Critique of the Extreme Akhbārī View xxiv
  Critique of the Moderate Akhbārī View xxviii
  The Number of Traditions in *al-Kāfī* xxxvi
  Commentaries on *al-Kafī* xxxvi

ITI's Commentary and Translation xxxviii

Conventions Used in This Work.......xxxix
Introduction.......xlv

Tradition 1.1.1.......1
Tradition 1.1.2.......8
Tradition 1.1.3.......11
Tradition 1.1.4.......13
Tradition 1.1.5.......15
Tradition 1.1.6.......17
Tradition 1.1.7.......20
Tradition 1.1.8.......21
Tradition 1.1.9.......25
Tradition 1.1.10.......26
Tradition 1.1.11.......28
Tradition 1.1.12.......32
Section 1.......32
Section 2.......35
Section 3.......39
Section 4.......47
Section 5.......49
Section 6.......51
Section 7.......53
Section 8.......58
Section 9.......61
Section 10.......63
Section 11.......69
Section 12.......70
Section 13.......73
Section 14.......75
Section 15.......77
Section 16.......79
Section 17.......80
Section 18.......83
Section 19.......85

Section 20 87
Section 21 89
Section 22 91
Section 23 93
Section 24 95
Section 25 97
Section 26 100
Section 27 102
Section 28 106
Section 29 111
Section 30 112
Section 31 114
Section 32 121
Tradition 1.1.13....................124
Tradition 1.1.14....................126
Tradition 1.1.15....................148
Tradition 1.1.16....................151
Tradition 1.1.17....................153
Tradition 1.1.18....................155
Tradition 1.1.19....................158
Tradition 1.1.20....................160
Tradition 1.1.21....................165
Tradition 1.1.22....................167
Tradition 1.1.23....................169
Tradition 1.1.24....................175
Tradition 1.1.25....................176
Tradition 1.1.26....................179
Tradition 1.1.27....................180
Tradition 1.1.28....................183
Tradition 1.1.29....................185
Tradition 1.1.30....................193
Tradition 1.1.31....................195
Tradition 1.1.32....................196
Tradition 1.1.33....................198

Acknowledgements

The research for this book was conducted by Shaykh Muhsin Ahmadi, Shaykh Hamid Ha'iri, and Shaykh Rizwan Arastu.

The English translation and commentary were written by Shaykh Rizwan Arastu.

The content editors were Shaykh Ahmad Nili, Sayyid Sulayman Ali Hasan, and Aun Hasan Ali.

The copy editor was Dara Becker.

Layout and cover design were done by Shaykh Saleem Bhimji of Islamic Publishing House.

Transliteration

Arabic has been transliterated according to the following key:

ء	a, u, or i (initial form)	ط	ṭ
ء	ʾ (medial or final form)	ظ	ẓ
ب	b	ع	ʿ
ت	t	غ	gh
ث	th	ف	f
ج	j	ق	q
ح	ḥ	ك	k
خ	kh	ل	l
د	d	م	m
ذ	dh	ن	n
ر	r	ه	h
ز	z	و	w (as a consonant)
س	s	ي	y (as a consonant)
ش	sh	ة	ah (without iḍāfah)
ص	ṣ	ة	at (with iḍāfah)
ض	ḍ	ال	al-

آ = ءا	ā (initial form)	آ = ءا	ʾā (medial form)
ـَا	ā	ـَوْ	aw
ـُو	ū	ـَوّ	aww
ـِي	ī	ـُوّ	uww
ـَ	a	ـَيْ	ay
ـُ	u	ـَيّ	ayy
ـِ	i	ـِيّ	iyy (medial form)
		ـِيّ	ī (final form)

Preface

By Shaykh Rizwan Arastu

In the name of God, the All-Beneficent, the Ever-Merciful

The mission of the Islamic Texts Institute (ITI) is to produce excellent translations of Islamic primary sources with high-caliber commentary so that non-specialists can access the vast reservoirs of knowledge and spiritual teachings they hold.

From its inception in 2006, ITI has had *al-Kāfī* in its sights because of the pivotal role this book has played in the development of Islamic scholarship and because it is one of the earliest surviving compilations of the traditions of Prophet Muḥammad and the twelve imams who succeeded him, and arguably the most important of them.

In this preface, we shall introduce you to *al-Kāfī* and its author, Shaykh[1] Muḥammad ibn Yaʿqūb al-Kulaynī. At some length, we shall discuss the authenticity of *al-Kāfī*. Finally, we shall mention some points about our commentary on, and translation of, this book.

Shaykh al-Kulaynī's Life[2]

Abū Jaʿfar Muḥammad ibn Yaʿqūb al-Kulaynī[3] (d.328/940 or 329/941)[4] was

---

1. Refer to point three under the heading "Conventions Used in this Work" for an explanation of ITI's usage of honorifics.

2. In writing this preface, we have relied heavily upon an article published by the Computer Research Center of Islamic Studies (CRCIS) within their *Dirāyat al-Nūr* software package. CRCIS in turn relied heavily on the research and findings of Sayyid Mūsā al-Shubayrī al-Zanjānī, a Grand Ayatullah and one of the foremost experts on *rijāl* in the world today. Any citations not mentioned explicitly here can be found in that article.

3. His name is sometimes mistakenly transliterated as "al-Kulīnī" by western academics.

4. All references to dates indicate the Hijrī date followed by the Gregorian date

born in the village of Kulayn in the city of Rayy, which today is nestled in the southern suburbs of Tehran, Iran. Because of his association with Rayy, he is sometimes referred to by the epithet al-Rāzī. Toward the end of his life, he gained the additional epithet of al-Silsilī, since he lived near Darb al-Silsilah, one of the gates of Baghdād, which led toward Kūfah. He has also been referred to as Abū Jaᶜfar al-Aᶜwar ("the One-Eyed"), presumably because he had lost one of his eyes. It was not until many centuries later that Shaykh al-Bahāʾī[5] began referring to him, in his book *Miftāḥ al-falāḥ* and in some of his letters of commendation (*ijāzah*), as Thiqat al-Islām, which means "he upon whom Islam relies." Notwithstanding its late conferral, it is by this honorific title that he is now most commonly referred.

We do not know the specific year of his birth. However, by examining the dates when his teachers in Qum lived, and by assuming that he was between the ages of twenty and thirty when he studied with them, we can guess that he was born between 269/883 and 279/893.

He was from a family of scholars and transmitters of traditions. His maternal grandfather, Muḥammad ibn Ibrāhīm al-Kulaynī, was praised by Shaykh al-Ṭūsī[6] as being "*khayr.*"[7] Shaykh al-Ṭūsī also praised that maternal grandfather's brother, Aḥmad ibn Ibrāhīm al-Kulaynī, as being "*khayr, fāḍil*

---

separated by a forward slash. For instance "328/940" indicates the year 328 A.H., which corresponds to 940 C.E. Generally speaking, the Hijrī dates are accurate; however, there is a margin of error of one year in the Gregorian dates, since every Hijrī date could potentially correspond to two consecutive Gregorian years depending on whether the event happened at the beginning of the year or the end. In converting these dates, we have always assumed that the event took place on Muḥarram 1, simply for ease of conversion.

5. Bahāʾ al-Dīn Muḥammad ibn al-Ḥusayn al-ᶜĀmilī (d.1031/1621)

6. Abū Jaᶜfar Muḥammad ibn al-Ḥasan al-Ṭūsī (d.460/1067), also known as Shaykh al-Ṭāʾifah

7. *Khayr* is a term used to affirm a transmitters's upright character and means "worthy of praise" (Subḥānī, Jaᶜfar. *Uṣūl al-ḥadīth wa aḥkāmuhu*. Qum: Muᶜassasat al-Imām al-Ṣādiq, 1998. 169.).

min ahl al-Rayy."[8] ʿAlī ibn Muḥammad ibn Ibrāhīm al-Kulaynī, known as ʿAllān al-Kulaynī, was his maternal uncle and the most renowned scholar from this family until Shaykh al-Kulaynī's time. Shaykh al-Najāshī[9] praised ʿAllān al-Kulaynī as being "*thiqah, ʿayn*."[10] His book, *Akhbār al-qāʾim*, became one of Shaykh al-Kulaynī's sources for *al-Kāfī*.

His Teachers

We can reconstruct a list of Shaykh al-Kulaynī's teachers (*mashāyikh*) by examining the chains of transmission in *al-Kāfī*. We list here his teachers divided into five groups based on their geographical location.

His teachers in Qum

- ʿAlī ibn Ibrāhīm ibn Hāshim
- Muḥammad ibn Yaḥyā al-ʿAṭṭār
- Aḥmad ibn Idrīs
- al-Ḥusayn ibn Muḥammad ibn ʿĀmir al-Ashʿarī
- ʿAlī ibn Muḥammad ibn ʿAbd Allāh Bundār
- Saʿd ibn ʿAbd Allāh al-Ashʿarī
- ʿAbd Allāh ibn Jaʿfar al-Ḥimyarī
- Muḥammad ibn ʿAbd Allāh ibn Jaʿfar al-Ḥimyarī
- Muḥammad ibn Aḥmad ibn ʿAlī ibn al-Ṣalt al-Ashʿarī
- ʿAlī ibn Mūsā ibn Jaʿfar al-Kumaydhānī

---

8. *Fāḍil* is a term that indicates that he was an eminent scholar. Thus the phrase *fāḍil min ahl al-Rayy* means "an eminent scholar from the city of Rayy."

9. Abū al-Ḥusayn Aḥmad ibn ʿAlī al-Najāshī (d.450/1058)

10. *Thiqah* is a term that indicates either that he is "righteous" in character or "reliable" and "trustworthy" in his transmissions (Subḥānī, Jaʿfar. *Uṣūl al-ḥadīth wa aḥkāmuhu*. Qum: Muʿassasat al-Imām al-Ṣādiq, 1998. 153 and 155-9.). *ʿAyn* is a term that communicates high praise, equivalent to "eminent" (ibid. 162.).

- Dawūd ibn Kūrah
- Aḥmad ibn ʿAbd Allāh ibn Aḥmad ibn Muḥammad al-Barqī
- ʿAlī ibn Ḥusayn al-Saʿdābādhī

His teachers in Rayy

- ʿAlī ibn Muḥammad ibn Ibrāhīm al-Kulaynī, known as ʿAllān al-Kulaynī
- Muḥammad ibn al-Ḥasan al-Ṭāʾī al-Rāzī
- Ḥusayn ibn al-Ḥasan al-Ḥasanī al-ʿAlawī al-Hāshimī
- Muḥammad ibn Abī ʿAbd Allāh al-Asadī al-Kūfī
- Muḥammad ibn ʿAqīl al-Kulaynī

His teachers in Iraq

- Aḥmad ibn Muḥammad al-ʿĀṣimī al-Kūfī
- Aḥmad ibn Muḥammad ibn Saʿīd, known as Ibn ʿUqdah
- Muḥammad ibn Jaʿfar al-Razzāz al-Kūfī
- al-Ḥusayn ibn Aḥmad ibn ʿAbd Allāh al-Mālikī al-Asadī
- ʿAlī ibn Ibrāhīm al-ʿAlawī al-Jawwānī al-Hāshimī
- Ḥabīb ibn al-Ḥasan al-Kūfī
- Ḥumayd ibn Ziyād al-Kūfī

His teachers in miscellaneous cities

- Muḥammad ibn Ismāʿīl al-Naysābūrī
- Muḥammad ibn Aḥmad al-Khaffāf al-Naysābūrī
- Muḥammad ibn ʿAlī al-Jaʿfarī al-Samarqandī
- al-Qāsim ibn al-ʿAlāʾ, from Azerbaijan
- Muḥammad ibn Maḥmūd al-Qazwīnī
- al-Ḥasan ibn ʿAlī al-ʿAlawī al-Hāshimī al-Dīnawarī

His teachers whose places of residence are not known

- Aḥmad ibn Mihrān who was possibly from Rayy
- Abū Dāwūd who was possibly from Qum

Elliptical references to his teachers

Often Shaykh al-Kulaynī refers to his teachers collectively using the phrases, "A number (*ʿiddah*) of our fellow Shīʿah," "A group (*jamāʿah*) of our fellow Shīʿah," or "One (*baʿḍ*) of our fellow Shīʿah." These phrases do not negatively impact the continuity of the chain of transmission, since al-Kulaynī has made clear to whom these collective phrases refer,[11] and in each of these groups some, if not all, of the individuals are reliable. In what follows, we shall list the teachers he refers to by these phrases:

Whenever he says, "A number of our fellow Shīʿah reported from Aḥmad ibn Muḥammad ibn ʿIsā..." the phrase, "a number of our fellow Shīʿah," refers to the following:

- Muḥammad ibn Yaḥyā al-ʿAṭṭār
- ʿAlī ibn Mūsā ibn Jaʿfar al-Kumaydhānī
- Dawūd ibn Kūrah
- Aḥmad ibn Idrīs
- ʿAlī ibn Ibrāhīm ibn Hāshim

Whenever he says, "A number of our fellow Shīʿah reported from Aḥmad ibn Muḥammad ibn Khālid al-Barqī..." the phrase, "a number of our fellow Shīʿah" refers to the following:

- ʿAlī ibn Ibrāhīm ibn Hāshim
- ʿAlī ibn Muḥammad ibn ʿAbd Allāh Bundār
- Aḥmad ibn ʿAbd Allāh ibn Aḥmad al-Barqī
- ʿAlī ibn Ḥusayn al-Saʿdābādhī

---

11. al-Ḥillī, Jamāl al-Dīn Ḥasan ibn Yūsuf. *al-Khulāṣah, "al-fāʾidah al-thālithah."* Qum: Dār al-Dhakhāʾir, 1990. 271.

Whenever he says, "A number of our fellow Shīʿah reported from Sahl ibn Ziyād..." the phrase, "a number of our fellow Shīʿah" refers to the following:

- ʿAlī ibn Muḥammad al-Kulaynī, known as ʿAllān al-Kulaynī
- Muḥammad ibn Abī ʿAbd Allāh al-Asadī al-Kūfī
- Muḥammad ibn al-Ḥasan al-Ṭāʾī al-Rāzī
- Muḥammad ibn ʿAqīl al-Kulaynī

Whenever he says, "One of our fellow Shīʿah reported from Muḥammad ibn ʿAlī or ʿAbd al-ʿAẓīm al-Ḥasanī..." the phrase, "one of our fellow Shīʿah" refers to the following:

- Aḥmad ibn Mihrān

It is clear from the various geographical locations of his teachers that Shaykh al-Kulaynī travelled to several major centers of learning to collect his traditions. As we mentioned, he was born in Rayy and presumably began his studies there. He spent a considerable amount of time in Qum and Iraq. The fact that he transmits traditions from Ḥumayd ibn Ziyād al-Kūfī (d.310/922) shows that he must have travelled to Iraq sometime before 310/922. The Sunnī historian Ibn ʿAsākir[12] reports that he also travelled to Damascus and collected some traditions from there. It is likely that he travelled to Nīshāpūr, since he transmits many traditions from Muḥammad ibn Ismāʿīl al-Naysābūrī and Muḥammad ibn Aḥmad al-Khaffāf al-Naysābūrī. There is no evidence though that he travelled to Qazwīn, Azerbaijan, or Dīnawar.

That Shaykh al-Najāshī extols him as "the elder and dignitary among the scholars of his time in Rayy," suggests that he lived in Rayy during the prime of his life when he had established himself as a first-rate religious authority. It is likely that he lived in Rayy during the years when he compiled *al-Kāfī* and that he first transmitted it to his students in that city. During that time, Rayy was under the rule of the Samanids (203/819–389/999) and then the Buyids (322/934-446/1055), each of whom ruled Rayy during this time with

12. Abū al-Qāsim ʿAlī ibn al-Ḥasan al-Dimashqī (d.571/1177)

the blessing of the Abbasid caliph al-Muqtadir (281/895-319/932). Toward the end of his life, Shaykh al-Kulaynī moved to Baghdād where he finally passed away and was buried.

His Students

Shaykh al-Kulaynī nurtured many students through whom he transmitted his books. As we did with his teachers, we list here his students according to their geographical location.

His students in Rayy

- Muḥammad ibn Aḥmad ibn Muḥammad ibn Sinān al-Zāhirī
- Muḥammad ibn Muḥammad ibn ʿIṣām al-Kulaynī
- Abū Muḥammad al-Ḥasan ibn Aḥmad al-Muʾaddib
- Ḥusayn ibn Ibrāhīm ibn Aḥmad ibn Hishām al-Muʾaddib
- ʿAlī ibn Aḥmad ibn Mūsā al-Daqqāq
- ʿAlī ibn ʿAbd Allāh al-Daqqāq

His students in Qum

- Jaʿfar ibn Muḥammad ibn Qulawayh
- Muḥammad ibn ʿAlī Mājīlawayh
- Muḥammad ibn Mūsā ibn al-Mutawakkil

His students in Iraq

- Aḥmad ibn Ibrāhīm ibn Abī Rāfiʿ al-Ṣumayrī
- ʿAbd al-Karīm ibn ʿAbd Allāh ibn Naṣr al-Bazzāz
- Muḥammad ibn Ibrāhīm al-Nuʿmānī
- Hārūn ibn Mūsā al-Tallaʿukbarī
- Muḥammad ibn ʿAbd Allāh al-Shaybānī
- Muḥammad ibn Aḥmad al-Ṣafwānī

- al-Ḥasan ibn Ḥamzah al-Ṭabarī
- ʿAbd al-ʿAzīz ibn ʿAbd Allāh ibn Yūnus al-Mawṣilī
- ʿAbd al-Waḥīd ibn ʿAbd Allāh ibn Yūnus al-Mawṣilī
- Muḥammad ibn Aḥmad ibn Dāwūd al-Qummī
- Salāmah ibn Muḥammad al-Arzanī
- Isḥāq ibn al-Ḥasan ibn Bakrān
- Aḥmad ibn Aḥmad ibnʿAlī ibn Saʿīd al-Kūfī
- Muḥammad al-Bazzāz
- Aḥmad ibn Muḥammad al-Zurārī
- ʿAlī ibn Muḥammad ibn ʿUbdūs
- Muḥammad ibn al-Ḥusayn al-Bazawfarī

His students in other places

- Aḥmad ibn al-Ḥusayn al-ʿAṭṭār
- ʿAbd Allāh ibn Muḥammad ibn Dhakwān

His Reputation in Academic Circles

Shaykh al-Kulaynī was renowned among Shīʿī and Sunnī scholars and historians for his mastery of the traditions, his juristic prowess, his reliability, and his precision. The first three quotes below are from eminent Shīʿī authorities on the traditions and its related disciplines, while the last two are from prominent Sunnī scholars well known for their biographies on the transmitters of traditions.

> *The elder and dignitary among the scholars of his time in Rayy; he was the most reliable of our scholars of traditions.*[13]
>
> –Shaykh al-Najāshī
>
> *Reliable; an expert on traditions. Of the highest status, a scholar of*

---

13. al-Najāshī, Aḥmad ibn ʿAlī. *al-Rijāl.* Qum: Jāmiʿ al-Mudarrisīn, 1986. 377. Entry 1026.

traditions.[14]

–Shaykh al-Ṭūsī

[Shaykh al-Kulaynī] is one whose righteousness, virtue, and trustworthiness are a point of unanimity.[15]

–Sayyid Ibn Ṭāwūs (d.664/1265)

The Reviver of the Shīʿah for the 4th Century, as a jurist and a leader of the followers of the Prophet's family, a jurist among his sect, eminent, accomplished in their eyes, renowned.[16]

–Ibn al-Athīr (d.606/1209)

He was a leader of the Shīʿah *scholars during the reign of al-Muqtadir.*[17]

–al-Dhahabī (d.748/1348)

His Writings and Compilations

Although Shaykh al-Kulaynī is most famous for *al-Kāfī*, this opus was not his only accomplishment. The following is a list of his known works:

- *al-Kāfī* (extant)
- *Rasāʾil al-aʿimmah*
- *Kitāb al-rijāl*
- *Kitāb al-radd ʿalā al-qarāmiṭah*
- *Kitāb mā qīla fī al-aʾimmah min al-shiʿr*
- *Kitāb taʿbīr al-ruʾyā*

Sadly, of these, only *al-Kāfī* has survived in its entirety. There are explicit

14. al-Ṭūsī, Muḥammad ibn al-Ḥasan. *al-Rijāl*. Najaf: al-Intishārāt al-Haydariyyah, 1961. 439. Entry 6277.

15. Ibn Ṭāwūs, Raḍī al-Dīn. *Faraj al-mahmūm*. Qum: Dār al-dhakhāʾir, 1949. 85.

16. Majd al-Dīn al-Mubārak ibn Muḥammad (d.606/1209)

17. Muḥammad ibn Aḥmad al-Dhahabī (d.748/1348)

references to *Rasāʾil al-aʿimmah* in the works of Sayyid Ibn Ṭāwūs. Shaykh al-Ṣadūq[18] transmits many traditions from Shaykh al-Kulaynī that are not found in *al-Kāfī*. It is thought that he received these traditions through *Rasāʾil al-aʿimmah* and *Kitāb al-radd ʿalā al-qarāmiṭah*. We know of the rest only through indexes that list them.

His Death

Shaykh al-Kulaynī died while he was in residence at Baghdād. Two dates have been transmitted for his death. Shaykh al-Ṭūsī in *al-Fihrist* and Sayyid Ibn Ṭāwūs have said he died in 328/940. Shaykh al-Ṭūsī in *al-Rijāl* and Shaykh al-Najāshī have said he died in the month of Shaʿbān 329/941. Shaykh Muḥammad Taqī al-Tustarī has given preference to 328/940.[19] Others have given preference to 329/941, arguing that Shaykh al-Ṭūsī wrote *al-Rijāl* after he wrote *al-Fihrist* and that his latter opinion overrides his former.[20] Muḥammad ibn Jaʿfar al-Ḥasanī led his funeral prayer. He was buried at the cemetery of the Kūfan Gate in Baghdād.

Al-Kāfī

Al-Kāfī is among the most comprehensive collections of traditions from the formative period of Shīʿī scholarship. It has been held in the highest esteem by generation after generation of Muslim scholars. Shaykh al-Mufīd[21] extolled it as "one of the greatest and most beneficial of Shīʿī books." Shahīd

---

18. Abū Jaʿfar Muḥammad ibn ʿAlī ibn Bābawayh (d.381/991)

19. Al-Tustarī, Muḥammad Taqī. *Qāmūs al-rijāl*. vol. 9. Qum: Muʿassasat al-Nashr al-Islāmī, 2004. 661.

20. *al-Kāfī*. al-Kulaynī, Muḥammad. ed. Dār al-Ḥadīth. vol. 1. Qum: Dār al-Ḥadīth, 2008. 38. Incidentally, 329/941 was also the same year ʿAlī ibn Muḥammad al-Samurī, Imam al-Mahdī's fourth and final deputy, passed away initiating the Major Occultation.

21. Abū ʿAbd Allāh Muḥammad ibn Muḥammad ibn Nuʿmān (d.413/1022)

al-Awwal[22] and Muḥaqqiq al-Karakī[23] have said, "No book has served the Shīʿah as it has." The First Majlisī[24] has said, "Nothing like it has been written for Islām."

The introduction to *al-Kāfī* reads as a personal letter from Shaykh al-Kulaynī to a brother—most likely a fellow believer. This person had complained to Shaykh al-Kulaynī about people's incorrigible ignorance and his own nagging doubts and lack of resources to address them. He had requested Shaykh al-Kulaynī to compile a book addressing all the disciplines of learning, which would be *kāfī* for him (i.e., that would "suffice" him). It took twenty years, but at last, al-Kulaynī writes, "God...has facilitated the compilation of what you requested."

Al-Kāfī actually comprises thirty-five books. What follows is a complete list of these books:

1) *The Book of Intellect and Foolishness*

2) *The Book of Knowledge and its Merit*

3) *The Book of God and his Oneness*

4) *The Book of Divine Guidance*

5) *The Book of Belief and Unbelief*

6) *The Book of Supplication*

7) *The Book of the Qurʾān and its Merit*

8) *The Book of Social Intercourse*

9) *The Book of Purity*

10) *The Book of Menstruation*

11) *The Book of Funeral Rites*

---

22. Muḥammad ibn Makkī al-ʿĀmilī (d.786/1385). Admittedly, the correct form for his title is "al-Shahīd al-Awwal." Again we refer you to point three under the heading "Conventions Used in this Work" for an explanation of ITI's usage of honorifics.

23. ʿAlī ibn ʿAbd al-Āl (d.940/1533)

24. Muḥammad Taqī al-Majlisī (d.1070/1659)

12) *The Book of Prayer*

13) *The Book of Charity*

14) *The Book of Fasting*

15) *The Book of Hajj*

16) *The Book of Jihad*

17) *The Book of Commerce*

18) *The Book of Marriage*

19) *The Book of Animal Sacrifice upon the Birth of a Child*

20) *The Book of Divorce*

21) *The Book of Emancipation*

22) *The Book of Hunting*

23) *The Book of Slaughtering*

24) *The Book of Food*

25) *The Book of Drink*

26) *The Book of Clothing, Beautification, and Honor*

27) *The Book of Domesticated Animals*

28) *The Book of Testaments*

29) *The Book of Inheritance*

30) *The Book of Corporal and Capital Punishments*

31) *The Book of Restitution and Blood Money*

32) *The Book of Testimonies and Depositions*

33) *The Book of Adjudication and Legal Precedents*

34) *The Book of Oaths, Vows, and Penances*

35) *The Book of Miscellanea* (literally a *rawḍah* or "garden" from which one can pick many kinds of flowers)

In recent centuries, these thirty-five books have been divided into three main sections:

Usūl al-kāfī (books 1-8)

The first eight are commonly referred to as *Uṣūl al-kāfī.* The first type-set edition of *al-Kāfī*, which was published in eight volumes, placed *Usūl al-kāfī* in the first two volumes.[25] Generally speaking, *Usūl al-kāfī* contains traditions that deal with epistemology, theology, history, ethics, supplication, and the Qurʾān.

Furūʿ al-kāfī (books 9-34)

Books nine through thirty-four are referred to as *Furūʿ al-kāfī* and are found in volumes three through seven of the first type-set edition. *Furūʿ al-kāfī* contains traditions that deal predominantly with practical and legal issues.

Rawḍat al-kāfī (book 35)

The final book stands alone as *Rawḍat al-kāfī*, which is found in volume eight. *Rawḍat al-kāfī* contains nearly 600 miscellaneous traditions, many of which are lengthy letters and speeches, not arranged in any particular order.

Al-Kāfī's Authenticity

While Shīʿah scholars agree that *al-Kāfī* is a landmark as a collection of traditions, they have historically split along several lines with regard to the authenticity of its traditions. We can summarize these stances as follows:

1) The traditions of *al-Kāfī* are no different from traditions found in other collections. A scholar must evaluate each of its traditions based on many criteria, among which is their chain of transmission, before giving them credence. This was the view of Shaykh al-Ṣadūq, Shaykh al-Mufīd, Sayyid al-Murtaḍā,[26] and Shaykh al-Ṭūsī during the formative period. It

---

25. *al-Kāfī.* al-Kulaynī, Muḥammad. ed. ʿAlī Akbar Ghaffārī. Tehran: Dār al-Kutub al-Islāmiyyah, 1945.

26. ʿAlī ibn al-Ḥusayn ʿAlam al-Hudā (d.436/1044)

has also been the opinion of a majority of our scholars in the past several centuries, particularly those classified as *uṣūlī*.

2) All traditions in *al-Kāfī* are authentic in that they were spoken by an infallible. This was the opinion of Muḥammad Amīn al-Astarābādī (d.1035/1626) and Khalīl al-Qazwīnī (d.1088/1678) among other extreme *akhbārī* scholars.

3) All traditions in *al-Kāfī* are reliable, although we cannot claim that they are all authentic. In other words, we may not be able to say conclusively that they were all spoken by an infallible, but we are justified in relying on them and will be held responsible for their content. This has been the opinion of moderate *akhbārī* scholars.

4) All traditions in *al-Kāfī* are reliable in the same meaning as in the previous viewpoint; however, whenever there is a conflict between two or more traditions, we must use the chain of transmission as a deciding factor. This is the opinion that ʿAllāmah al-Majlisī[27] espouses in his introduction to *Mirʾāt al-ʿuqūl*.

Critique of the Extreme Akhbārī View

As we mentioned, the first opinion is the one espoused by most scholars and represents the most defensible position. The second opinion, that of the extreme *akhbārī* scholars, is clearly weak, and we need not expend any great energy to refute it. It is worthwhile, however, to discuss one of their claims that has found its way into popular thinking. In particular, Khalīl al-Qazwīnī conjectured that *al-Kāfī* was authenticated by Imam al-Mahdī himself through his deputies. He claimed that Shaykh al-Kulaynī sent *al-Kāfī* to the Imam, and he in turn wrote on its cover, "*al-kāfī kafin li shīʿatinā*," meaning, "*al-Kāfī* is sufficient for our followers."

There is no credible evidence to back his conjecture. However, others with similar thinking have argued for his premise based on historical probabilities rather than claiming any concrete evidence. They have based

27. Muḥammad Bāqir al-Majlisī (d.1110/1698)

their argument on the fact that Shaykh al-Kulaynī lived during the Minor Occultation and resided for the latter part of his life in Baghdād, near the deputies of the Imam. Additionally, Shaykh al-Kulaynī is widely regarded to have been extremely cautious with regard to traditions as evinced by the twenty years it took him to compile *al-Kāfī*. He brought his book to Baghdād in 327/939, one to two years before his own death and the death of the fourth and final deputy. Based on all this, they surmise that it is far-fetched, even absurd, to think that Shaykh al-Kulaynī would not have solicited Imam al-Mahdī's stamp of approval for such a monumental work when the Imam's deputy was at an arm's length.

There are numerous problems with this argument. The following points show that it is, in fact, highly unlikely that Shaykh al-Kulaynī presented his book for the Imam's approval:

Point 1: No Exclusive Connection to Deputies

Shaykh al-Kulaynī does not transmit a single tradition in *al-Kāfī* on the direct authority of any of the deputies, and he only transmits a few of their traditions secondhand. This indicates that Shaykh al-Kulaynī had no exclusive connection with the four deputies, much less with Imam al-Mahdī.

Point 2: No Confirmed Access to the Imam While Compiling the Book

There is no evidence that Shaykh al-Kulaynī compiled *al-Kāfī* in Baghdād. As we mentioned earlier, he did apparently visit Baghdād before 309/922. Nonetheless, his permanent residence was in Rayy, and it was there that he compiled and first transmitted *al-Kāfī*. It was only at the end of his life, after he had compiled *al-Kāfī*, that he moved to Baghdād. Thus, we cannot infer that he had access to Imam al-Mahdī while compiling his book, since he only moved to the Imam's vicinity after compiling it.

Point 3: Deputies' Intervention was not Vital

Imam al-Mahdī's four deputies lived under incredibly hostile conditions that forced them to severely limit their activities. The following two incidents graphically illustrate their dire circumstances, which necessitated the strictest form of *taqiyyah* (dissimulation in the face of danger):

- Al-Ḥusayn ibn Rūḥ, the third deputy of Imam al-Mahdī, was in attendance at a gathering of people loyal to al-Muqtadir. Two people began debating the status of the first four caliphs after Prophet Muḥammad. One person argued that Abū Bakr was the best person after the Prophet, then ʿUmar, then ʿAlī, and finally ʿUthmān. The other argued that ʿAlī was greater than ʿUmar. Al-Ḥusayn ibn Rūḥ interjected, "The Prophet's companions were of the opinion that [Abū Bakr] al-Ṣiddīq was best, then [ʿUmar] al-Fārūq, then ʿUthmān Dhū al-Nūrayn, then ʿAlī. The transmitters of traditions also say this, and it is the correct view in my opinion too." His words surprised all who were present, but they praised him for his wisdom and denounced those who accused him of sympathizing with the Shīʿah. The transmitter of the tradition, who was a Shīʿī and was present at the gathering says that he was barely able to control his laughter. He quickly excused himself, but not before al-Ḥusayn ibn Rūḥ saw him. Ibn Rūḥ later visited this man and asked him, "Why did you laugh? In your opinion, was what I said not true?" When the man replied half-heartedly, he continued, "Fear God, old man! I shall not tolerate your insolence when I say such a thing." The man said in his own defense, "Master, you are a man who claims to be a companion of the Imam and his deputy, and then you say something like that! Shall I not be surprised and laugh?" Decisively, al-Ḥusayn ibn Rūḥ told him, "I swear by my life, if you ever repeat these actions, I shall shun you!"[28]
- Al-Ḥusayn ibn Rūḥ was informed that one of his doormen had maligned Muʿāwiyah. He immediately dismissed him from his service and shunned him. He then ignored every attempt the doorman made to approach him and apologize for what he had done.[29]

---

28. al-Ṭūsī, Muḥammad ibn al-Ḥasan. *al-Ghaybah*. Qum: Muʾassasat al-Maʿārif al-Islāmiyyah, 1990. 384.

29. Al-Ḥusayn ibn Rūḥ reacted in this way, not because maligning Muʿāwiyah was

Because of these dire circumstances, they did not speak of, or act on, issues that could be addressed by others through natural means. Only when their intervention was vital, and natural means were insufficient, would they intervene on the Imam's behalf. Accordingly, it is not surprising that they would refrain from involving themselves in the production of a book like *al-Kāfī*, for which natural means were abundantly available.

Point 4: No Strong Precedent from Imams

There was not a strong precedent for presenting books to the imams for approval. The number of books that are known to have been presented to an imam compared to those that have not is negligible.

Point 5: No Strong Precedent from Deputies

There was also not a strong precedent for presenting books to Imam al-Mahdī's deputies for approval. The only book known to have been presented to them was *al-Taklīf*, written by Muḥammad ibn ʿAlī al-Shalmaghānī (d.323/934), known as Ibn Abī al-ʿAzāqir. His book, *al-Taklīf*, was presented to al-Ḥusayn ibn Rūḥ only because of extenuating circumstances surrounding the book and its author's personality. He had been a prominent Shīʿī scholar and an agent of Imam al-Mahdī, but then deviated from the path. His book, *al-Taklīf*, was in high circulation among the Shīʿah as a source of guidance. After his apostasy, his book came under scrutiny, so al-Ḥusayn ibn Rūḥ read it in its entirety and made the following statement: "Everything in it is transmitted from the imams except for two or three places wherein he has falsely attributed something to them." Interestingly, that the book was presented to Imam al-Mahdī's deputy does not necessarily indicate that the opinion given was that of Imam al-Mahdī himself, for, in another similar case, al-Ḥusayn ibn Rūḥ sent a book called *al-Taʾdīb* to Qum to discover what the scholars of that city had to say about it. They replied that its contents agreed with what they knew to be true except in one instance, which they

---

wrong, but because his and Imam al-Mahdī's safety was so critical that it could not be risked for such as this.

mentioned. This interaction demonstrates just how conservative Imam al-Mahdī and his deputies were in intervening where natural means were available. Other than these two books, there is no other known case of a book being presented to the Imam's deputies for approval.

Point 6: No Mention from Shaykh al-Kulaynī

If Shaykh al-Kulaynī had received the Imam's deputy's approval for his book, he would have mentioned this in its introduction, which he did not. Scholars such as Shaykh al-Ṭūsī or Shaykh al-Najāshī, who made special note of this detail when they mentioned *al-Taklīf* and *al-Taʾdīb*, would have mentioned this in their description of *al-Kāfī*, which they did not. The first time such a possibility was even postulated was nearly three centuries later by Sayyid Ibn Ṭāwūs.

Critique of the Moderate *Akhbārī* View

The moderate *akhbārī* scholars have based their opinion on the following key points:

Point 1: Object of Great Praise

Since it was compiled, *al-Kāfī* has been the object of great praise by Shīʿī scholars. In their praise there is latent proof that we should treat all of its traditions as reliable. For instance, as we quoted earlier, the father of ʿAllāmah al-Majlisī said about *al-Kāfī*, "Nothing like it has been written for Islām." If we combine this testimony of his with the testimony of others who have said that *al-Uṣūl al-arbaʿumiʾah*[30] are categorically reliable and that their chains of transmission need not be examined, we can conclude that *al-Kāfī* is also categorically reliable and that its chains of transmission need not be examined, since it must, according to the senior Majlisī's testimony, be better than these "400 source books," which were written before it.

Clearly, this argument is flawed for the following reasons:

30. These are "400 source books" compiled by various companions of the imams, which served as the main source for Shaykh al-Kulaynī's compilation.

- First, the testimony of scholars from latter generations, like the father of ʿAllāmah al-Majlisī, does not carry the same weight as the testimony of scholars from the formative period, since their testimony is not based on firsthand knowledge of the authenticity of the source.
- Second, there is no reason why we must accept the reliability of *al-Uṣūl al-arbaʿumiʾah* hands down; rather, their traditions must also be scrutinized.
- Third, that *al-Kāfī* has been praised repeatedly does not preclude the possibility that it contains traditions with weak chains of transmission. The trait that scholars of traditions have always deemed deplorable was for a transmitter to transmit *numerous* traditions from "weak" individuals. Transmitting *some* traditions from weak individuals was never considered a flaw, especially when those traditions deal with recommended acts (*mustaḥabbāt*); with principles that lie within the jurisdiction of the intellect; and with ideas that comply with known authentic traditions. So it is possible for *al-Kāfī* to contain weak traditions and for scholars to still praise it as an unparalleled book, so their praise is no proof of its categorical reliability. Presumably, it is for this reason that Shaykh al-Kulaynī included the chain of transmission for each tradition: so that coming generations of scholars could evaluate the chain for themselves.
- Fourth, even if we accept the numerous testimonies that *al-Kāfī* is unmatched by any book written before it, we need not concede that it is superior to them in every way. It is possible for another book to excel in one aspect where *al-Kāfī* is lacking and for *al-Kāfī* to still be superior to that book because it is superior in many other ways that outweigh its single inferiority. In conclusion, this argument from the moderate camp among the *akhbārī*s is also unacceptable and fails to establish *al-Kāfī*'s absolute reliability.

Point 2: Shaykh al-Kulaynī is the Most Reliable Transmitter

Like his book, Shaykh al-Kulaynī himself has been praised for being "the most reliable person when it comes to traditions." Assuming this superlative praise is true, he must be more reliable than every other transmitter of traditions. In particular, there are some individuals such as the *aṣḥāb al-ijmāʿ*,[31] Ibn Abī ʿUmayr, Ṣafwān ibn Yaḥyā, and Aḥmad ibn Muḥammad ibn Abī Naṣr al-Bizanṭī, among others, who are reputed to have transmitted traditions only from reliable people. Since Shaykh al-Kulaynī is "the most reliable person when it comes to traditions," he must also share, and even excel in, this trait.

This argument is also flawed for the following reason:

- Even if we concede that Shaykh al-Kulaynī is "the most reliable person" overall, we need not concede that he is superior to all other transmitters in every aspect.

Point 3: Twenty Years to Compile

Shaykh al-Kulaynī took twenty years to compile *al-Kāfī*. The only reason this process would have taken him so long is that he was busy verifying each and every chain of transmission. Thus, the traditions of *al-Kāfī* are all well-researched and therefore, authentic.

This argument is weak because it ignores many other factors that may have prevented Shaykh al-Kulaynī from completing his work sooner. The following are some possible factors:

- We do not know what kind of access Shaykh al-Kulaynī had to books. Perhaps he needed that time to travel and collect the books necessary for his compilation.

---

31. The *aṣḥāb al-ijmāʿ* are an elite group of eighteen companions to the 5th, 6th, 7th, and 8th Imams who had exceptional character and scholarship and about whose reliability our scholars are in "unanimity" (Subḥānī, Jaʿfar. *Kulliyyāt fī ʿilm al-rijāl*. Qum: Muʿassasat al-Nashr al-Islāmī, 2000. 165-8.).

- It might have taken a long time to gather the various versions of these source books and compare them to one another for discrepancies.
- Shaykh al-Kulaynī chose to abandon many conventions of his predecessors and developed a new sequence of books and chapters in al-Kāfī to improve the organization of the traditions. He also sought to homogenize the conventions of how the transmitters were listed. Innovating such a new sequence, inserting traditions into their appropriate place in this sequence, and homogenizing the chain of transmitters each would have taken a significant amount of time. In short, considering all the work that Shaykh al-Kulaynī put into compiling al-Kāfī and our own ignorance of the exact circumstances in which he worked, we cannot say with any certainty that it took him twenty years to compile simply because he was busy verifying each and every chain of transmission.

Point 4: Shaykh al-Kulaynī's Testimony to al-Kāfī's Authenticity

Shaykh al-Kulaynī himself, in his introduction to *al-Kāfī*, says:

> *You said that you would love to have a sufficient book (kitāb kāfin) containing enough of all the religious sciences to suffice the student; to serve as a reference for the disciple; from which those who seek knowledge of the religion and want to act on it can draw authentic traditions from the Truthful [imams]—may God's peace be upon them—and a living example upon which to act, by which our duty to God—almighty is he and sublime—and to the commands of his Prophet—may God's mercy be on him and his progeny—is fulfilled...God—to whom belongs all praise—has facilitated the compilation of what you requested. I hope it is as you desired.*

He recalls that this "brother" of his requested a book from which he could "draw authentic traditions." He then confirms that "God...has facilitated the compilation of what [he] requested." This statement is tantamount to a testimony from Shaykh al-Kulaynī to the authenticity of all the traditions in *al-Kāfī*. Since he has testified thus, we must accept his testimony and accept all its traditions as "authentic," or at least "reliable."

Before we can accept or reject this argument, we must break it down into the following separate issues:

1) What does Shaykh al-Kulaynī mean by "authentic" or *ṣaḥīḥ*?
2) Is Shaykh al-Kulaynī's statement truly a testimony to the authenticity of *al-Kāfī*?
3) Does his testimony apply to every single tradition of *al-Kāfī*?
4) Does his testimony hold any weight for us?

What does Shaykh al-Kulaynī mean by "authentic" or ṣaḥīḥ?

The term *ṣaḥīḥ* did not mean the same thing for Shaykh al-Kulaynī and other scholars from the formative period of Shīʿī scholarship as it has come to mean for later scholars. It was Sayyid Ibn Ṭāwūs (d.664/1265) who first coined the terms *ṣaḥīḥ, ḥasan, muwaththaq,* and *ḍāʿīf* to describe a given tradition based on the relative strength or weakness of the individuals in its chain of transmission. His student ʿAllāmah al-Ḥillī (d.726/1325) popularized his teacher's new system. According to this system, any tradition whose chain of transmission contains only Imāmī Shīʿah who are both righteous and precise, and connects with no missing links to an infallible, is considered *ṣaḥīḥ*. It does not matter if it can be established that the transmitter of the tradition made a mistake and the tradition was never actually spoken by an infallible. It is still called *ṣaḥīḥ*.

Shaykh al-Kulaynī would have been wholly unfamiliar with this usage of the term *ṣaḥīḥ*. For him, as for all scholars of the formative period, *ṣaḥīḥ* referred generally to any tradition that could be confidently attributed to an infallible even if the chain of transmission were weak. For instance if a single weak tradition were repeated in several unrelated sources, a scholar might feel confident that the tradition was indeed spoken by an infallible. Nonetheless, even the scholars from the formative period did not necessarily act on, or issue legal opinions based on, every *ṣaḥīḥ* tradition, since it was possible for an infallible to have said something out of fear or compulsion (*taqiyyah*) and thus not have intended for us to act on it.

In short, there are two different meanings for the term *ṣaḥīḥ*, which overlap but are nonetheless different. According to both definitions, a tradition whose chain of transmission contains only Imāmī Shīʿah who are both righteous and precise, and connects with no missing links to an infallible, and is known to have been spoken by the infallible, is *ṣaḥīḥ*. The scholars from the formative period added to this traditions with weak individuals or disjointed chains of transmission where the tradition could nonetheless be positively attributed to an infallible by other means. Similarly, scholars from the latter period have added traditions that were spoken out of fear or compulsion.

Now that we have clarified what Shaykh al-Kulaynī meant by *ṣaḥīḥ* traditions, we can turn toward the second question.

Is Shaykh al-Kulaynī's statement truly a testimony to the authenticity of al-Kāfī?

As far as his testimony goes, it is clear from his statement, "God... has facilitated the compilation of what you requested," that Shaykh al-Kulaynī believes he has been successful in compiling a book that meets the requirements of the addressee of his introduction. That he then says, "I hope it is as you desired," speaks only to his humility, and cannot reasonably be construed as an indication that he is uncertain of the quality of his work. Thus, Shaykh al-Kulaynī has indeed testified to the authenticity of his book.

Does his testimony apply to every single tradition of al-Kāfī?

We cannot reasonably conclude this. Two examples from *al-Kāfī* will illustrate why this is the case.

1) In Book 4, *The Book of Divine Guidance*, we find chapters comprising traditions that confirm the legitimacy of each of the twelve imams. Upon further examination, we find that some of the traditions in each chapter contain names of individuals who are wholly unknown, individuals who, in some cases, occur in no other chain of transmission. It is highly unlikely that Shaykh al-Kulaynī believed every one of these traditions to be *ṣaḥīḥ*, positively attributable to an infallible. However, to be fair, it

is not necessary that he believe every single one to be authentic, since all the traditions of that chapter speak to a single idea: the legitimacy of a given imam. If he includes some traditions whose authenticity is doubtful along with others whose authenticity he accepts, all of which convey the same message, he has not contradicted his purpose or reneged on his testimony. However, with this knowledge, we cannot reasonably construe his testimony as being a testimony to the authenticity of every single tradition.

2) There are many traditions in *al-Kāfī* that pertain to recommended (*mustaḥabb*) and disliked (*makrūh*) acts. In many cases, these traditions do not have solid chains of transmission, and it is reasonable to assume that Shaykh al-Kulaynī did not have certain knowledge of all of their authenticity. Nevertheless, he was justified in including these traditions, if only on the basis of what are known as *akhbār man balagh*, such as "*Ṣaḥīḥat Hishām ibn Sālim*," which tells us that Imam al-Ṣādiq said, "If any [promise of] reward reaches a person from the Prophet, and he acts on it, he shall get the reward for that act even if the Prophet of God did not [in fact] say it."[32] Acting on such traditions, Shaykh al-Kulaynī may have included traditions whose authenticity he could not confirm because he knew people were justified in acting on them. Once again, while he was justified in including these traditions, and we are justified in acting on them, we cannot reasonably construe his testimony as being a testimony to the authenticity of every one of these traditions.

Does his testimony hold any weight for us?

Even if we concede that Shaykh al-Kulaynī's testimony does speak to the authenticity of every one of the traditions in *al-Kāfī*, the question remains: Does his testimony hold any weight for us? The answer is no. At most, Shaykh al-Kulaynī's statement in his introduction tells us that he believed he had successfully compiled a book of *ṣaḥīḥ* traditions. Keeping in mind the meaning of the term *ṣaḥīḥ* to him, we can conclude only that he believed

32. *Wasāʾil al-shīʿah* 1.1.18.184

its traditions to have been spoken by an infallible. But without knowing exactly what his criteria were for arriving at this belief, we cannot accept his testimony at face value. In particular, it is possible that he held this belief, not because he had firsthand knowledge of each tradition's veracity, but because of any of a number of factors including the following:

- He might have seen a given tradition repeated in several of the source books from which he drew.
- He might have seen a particular chain of transmission repeated several times within a particular source book, leading him to believe that the book's author had confidence in the chain.
- He might have found a particular tradition in one of the source books compiled by one of the *aṣḥāb al-ijmāʿ*.
- He might have found a particular tradition in one of the books that is known to have been presented to, and approved of, by Imam al-Mahdī's deputies.
- He might have found a particular tradition in a book that was otherwise considered authentic, regardless of the theological leanings of its compiler.
- He might have considered the text of the tradition to be characteristic of authentic traditions.
- He might have considered the tradition to be corroborated by the human intellect.

In conclusion, Shaykh al-Kulaynī's testimony does not hold any weight for us, and even if it did, it would not speak to the authenticity of each individual tradition in *al-Kāfī*. Thus, it is up to a scholar to evaluate each of *al-Kāfī's* traditions as he would with any other book's traditions and exercise his independent judgment before giving them credence or not. As a rule, the opinion of a scholar, no matter how eminent he may be, is not to be automatically accepted by later generations.

The Number of Traditions in *al-Kāfī*

There have been several attempts to count the number of traditions contained in *al-Kāfī*. Shaykh Yūsuf al-Baḥrānī (d.1185/1772) counted 16,199 traditions.[33] Another effort has yielded 15,508 traditions.[34] The reason for these discrepancies in counting is a difference in standards of what constitutes a separate tradition. For instance, after transmitting some traditions, Shaykh al-Kulaynī mentions a second chain of transmission, sometimes to allude to a difference in wording, and sometimes simply to mention an additional chain. Whether one counts such instances as additional traditions or simply corroborations of the previous traditions affects the overall count, but has no substantive repercussions.

Commentaries on *al-Kafī*

Al-Kāfī has long held the attention of Shīʿī scholars. Jurists have drawn from its traditions to derive their juridical opinions. Some, especially in the 11th/17th Century, systematically studied every tradition and wrote voluminous commentaries on it. The most extensive of these were written by Mullā Muḥammad Ṣāliḥ al-Māzandarānī (d.1081/1670 or 1086/1675) and ʿAllāmah Muḥammad Bāqir al-Majlisī (d.1111/1699). The latest publication of the former is in eleven volumes and of the latter is in twenty-six volumes. Below is a list of all extant commentaries on *al-Kāfī*.

1	*Mirʾāt al-ʿuqūl fī sharḥ akhbār āl al-rasūl*	Muḥammad Bāqir al-Majlisī	d.1191/1680
2	*al-Wāfī*	Muḥsin al-Fayḍ al-Kāshānī	d.1111/1699

33. al-Baḥrānī, Yūsuf. *Luʾluʾat al-baḥrayn*. 394-395.

34. Attributed to *Maʿ al-kulaynī wa kitābihi al-kāfī* in *al-Kāfī*. al-Kulaynī, Muḥammad. ed. Dār al-Ḥadīth. vol. 1. Qum: Dār al-Ḥadīth, 2008. 40.

3	*al-Taʿlīqah ʿalā uṣūl al-kāfī*	Muḥammad Bāqir al-Dāmād	d.1041/1631
4	*Sharḥ uṣūl al-kāfī*	Muḥammad Ṣadr al-Dīn al-Shīrāzī	d.1050/1640
5	*Sharḥ al-kāfī: al-uṣūl wa al-rawḍah*	Muḥammad Ṣāliḥ al-Māzandarānī	d.1081/1670 or 1086/1675
6	*al-Kashf al-wāfī fī sharḥ uṣūl al-kāfī*	Muḥammad Hādī Āṣif al-Shīrāzī	d.1081/1670
7	*al-Shāfī fī sharḥ al-kāfī*	Khalīl al-Qazwīnī	d.1089/1678
8	*al-Dharīʿah ilā ḥāfiẓ al-sharīʿah*	Rafīʿ al-Dīn Muḥammad al-Jīlānī	d.11th/17th c.
9	*al-Hadāyā*	Sharaf al-Dīn Muḥammad al-Tabrīzī	d.1093/1682
10	*al-Ḥāshiyah ʿalā uṣūl al-kāfī*	Muḥammad Amīn al-Astarābādī	d.1036/1626
11	*al-Ḥāshiyah ʿalā uṣūl al-kāfī*	Aḥmad al-ʿĀmilī	d.11th/17th c.
12	*al-Ḥāshiyah ʿalā uṣūl al-kāfī*	Badr al-Dīn al-ʿĀmilī	d.11th/17th c.
13	*al-Durr al-manẓūm min kalām al-maʿṣūm*	ʿAlī al-ʿĀmilī	d.1103/1691 or 1104/1692
14	*Sharḥ furūʿ al-kāfī*	Muḥammad Hādī al-Māzandarānī	d.1120/1708
15	*al-Biḍāʿah al-muzjāh*	Muḥammad Ḥusayn ibn Qār Yāghdī	d.1089/1678

ITI's Commentary and Translation

The edition before you represents, in part, a synthesis of centuries of research and deliberation over the text of *al-Kāfī*. More importantly, it represents a very modern effort to update this rich tradition of scholarship by addressing the needs, as we see them, of western Muslims in the 21st Century. In researching each tradition of this book, ITI's team has painstakingly combed through the fifteen extant commentaries and annotations on *al-Kāfī*, all of which were written around the 11th/17th Century. Where we found their literary analysis and exegesis to be sound and relevant to the modern reader, we simply narrated and, at most, refined their work. Where we found their work to be wanting, or more often, where they had not addressed issues that are now vital to our understanding, we endeavored to fill the void by writing our own original commentary. We believe this book to be a testament to the continued vibrancy and rigor of Islamic scholarship among the Shīʿah, the followers of Prophet Muḥammad and his twelve successors.

We have been greatly aided in our work by certain advances in technology. Simple and free "Voice over Internet Protocol" (VoIP) and screen-sharing software have allowed the researchers of ITI to do their work across continents and oceans. The Computer Research Center of Islamic Sciences and certain other institutions have placed tens of thousands of volumes at our fingertips through their sophisticated software. We are now able to refer to books that are out of print, perform complex search operations, and compare and contrast multiple texts with great ease. We can refer to dozens of lexicons in a fraction of the time it used to take using conventional books. In some cases we were even able to define words that had been overlooked by generations of lexicographers simply by searching out instances of their usage through this software with a facility unique to the computer age.

We have also been aided in our work by the tireless efforts of ʿAlī Akbar Ghaffārī who was responsible for the first type-set edition of *al-Kāfī* in eight volumes more than sixty-five years ago.[35] More recently, Dār al-Ḥadīth with

---

35. *al-Kāfī*. al-Kulaynī, Muḥammad. ed. ʿAlī Akbar Ghaffārī. Tehran: Dār al-Kutub

the help of Sayyid Mūsā al-Shubayrī al-Zanjānī published, in fifteen volumes, what is, by all accounts, the most accurate and well-researched version of *al-Kāfī* to date, for they have taken into account all extant manuscripts of the book.[36] We have made their version of *al-Kāfī* the starting point for our work. In a few instances, where we have had reason to disagree with their text or vowelization, we have documented our reasons for doing so.

Conventions Used in This Work

What follows are some of the conventions ITI has adopted for this work.

1) As Muslims, it is customary to offer a prayer for God's mercy and peace whenever we mention the name of Prophet Muḥammad, his family, or any of God's prophets, angels, or saints. While many Islamic books use the abbreviations "S.A." (for *ṣallā Allāhu ʿalayhi wa ālihi*), "A.S." (for *ʿalayhi al-salām*), and others to remind the reader to invoke these prayers, we have decided not to do so. This decision should not be misconstrued as a sign of disrespect to these great personalities. The only reason for leaving them out is to remove any hindrance to the fluency of the text, especially for non-Muslims who are wholly unfamiliar with these conventions. In following with tradition, the reader is still encouraged to make his invocations while reading these names just as the writers have done while writing them.

2) We have broken with another convention by not capitalizing pronouns referring to "God." We have done this partly to conform to western standards of style[37] and partly to remove a crutch that the capitalized "He" often creates.[38] To compensate, we have made every effort to

al-Islāmiyyah, 1945.

36. *al-Kāfī*. al-Kulaynī, Muḥammad. ed. Dār al-Ḥadīth. Qum: Dār al-Ḥadīth, 2008.

37. *The Chicago Manual of Style*, 15th Edition. Chicago: University of Chicago Press, 2003. 348 paragraph 8.102.

38. Nida, Eugene A. and Charles R. Taber. *The Theory and Practice of Translation*. Leiden: E.J. Brill, 1982. 29.

structure our sentences to clearly indicate pronouns that refer to God without having to depend on this convention.

3) We have struggled to find the best way to refer to important Islamic personalities: prophets, imams, and scholars. We refer to prophets who are known in the Judeo-Christian tradition by their anglicized names (e.g., Adam, Noah, Jesus). We refer to all other prophets by transliterating their Arabic or Arabicized names (e.g., al-Khiḍr, Hūd, Muḥammad). We refer to each of the twelve imams by his most common name or epithet (e.g., Imam ʿAlī, Imam al-Ḥasan, Imam al-ʿAskarī). We are fully aware that this form of their names is grammatically incorrect in Arabic and that it should rather be "al-Imām al-ʿAskarī." However, because "imam" has been assimilated into the English language, and the correct form simply feels awkward in English, we feel justified in referring to them by what we believe has become the vernacular for English-speaking Shīʿah. We refer to scholars by an honorific such as *shaykh, sayyid, ʿallāmah*, or the like along with their most common descriptive title (e.g., Shaykh al-Kulaynī, Sayyid al-Murtaḍā, ʿAllāmah al-Majlisī). Like "imam," honorifics such as "shaykh" have been assimilated into the English language; however, many others have not. Nonetheless, for the sake of consistency and ease of pronunciation, we have decided to leave off the "al-" from all honorifics, contrary to correct Arabic form. Additionally, at the first mention of each scholar's name, we have offered a footnote detailing his complete name and death date.

4) In keeping with Islamic scholarly tradition, we have made every effort to find support for our interpretations and assertions from Islamic primary sources and the works of widely accepted Islamic scholars. However, we have left out many of these citations in the English version of our work for two reasons. First, the vast majority of these sources are not available in English, so there is little probability that our English readers will refer back to them. Second, we did not want our commentary to become inundated with parenthetical citations, which would have greatly hindered its fluidity. If God wills, ITI will be publishing the Arabic

version of this commentary, which is more than twice as long, through which interested readers will be able to benefit from these citations.

5) The citations that we have given for traditions generally consist of the title of the compilation in which they are found followed by three or four numbers separated by periods. Where there are three numbers, they refer respectively to the *kitāb* number, the *bāb* number, and the tradition number. For instance, "*al-Kāfī* 2.2.1" represents a tradition found in *al-Kāfī*, *kitāb* 2, *The Book of Knowledge and its Merit*, *bāb* 2, "On the Characteristics of Knowledge, its Virtue, and the Virtue of Scholars," tradition 1. Where there are four numbers, they refer respectively to the volume number, the *kitāb* number, the *bāb* number, and the tradition number. In a few instances, we have had to resort to volume and page numbers. In those instances, the numbers refer to the same edition of the text used by the Noor software series produced by the Computer Research Center of Islamic Sciences. All citations for *Nahj al-balāghah* are according to the numbering of Ṣubḥī al-Ṣāliḥ.

6) We have made every effort to translate the text of *al-Kāfī* such that the overall effect on its English reader is the same as the overall effect on its Arabic reader. We have also taken care to distinguish what corresponds directly to the Arabic text from what we have inferred from the Arabic text by enclosing the latter in square brackets ([ ]). Generally, the translation makes sense with or without what is in brackets; however, we believe the intended meaning is more clearly expressed *with* the brackets.

7) We have not evaluated the chains of transmission (*sanad*, pl. *asnād*) for *al-Kāfī's* traditions. Although evaluating chains of transmission is a primary means of authenticating *aḥādīth* in the Sunnī scholarly tradition, in the Shīʿī tradition other factors are no less important. Authors like Shaykh al-Kulaynī looked at the totality of evidence to determine whether a particular tradition was reliable. In some cases, he would prefer a better edition of a tradition with a weak chain of transmission over a poorer

edition of the same with a stronger chain of transmission if there was strong evidence that the tradition itself was authentic. In addition to the chain of transmission, he would look at the context of a tradition's origin; its transmitters' level of, and area of, competence; the tradition's breadth of circulation; and the differences among its various written versions among other factors. For later generations of scholars, many of these factors were less accessible, and the chain of transmission became increasingly important.

Nonetheless, we can say with confidence that the vast majority of *al-Kāfī's* traditions are reliable and were, in fact, spoken by an infallible primarily because *al-Kāfī* is an outstanding book compiled by an outstanding scholar. At the very least, the repetition of a single concept in multiple traditions, collected under the banner of a single chapter title, gives us confidence that the concept itself was, in fact, taught by an infallible. On the basis of this confidence, we have proceeded to explain each tradition in the best possible light. If, occasionally, a matter is mentioned in a single tradition and never mentioned in another, we have treated the matter in one of two ways. If we felt confident that the matter was false—because it contradicts the Qurʾān, other traditions, or the intellect for example—then we have proceeded to explain our reasoning for rejecting it based on its content. If we had no reason to believe it was false, we have assumed that it was in fact spoken, and we have proceeded to explain it in the best possible light.

To be clear, our methodology in this regard should not be mistaken for a blanket authentication of all of *al-Kāfī's* traditions or as a disparagement of the science of *rijāl*, which is, without doubt, an essential component in the study of traditions, albeit outside the scope of this commentary. Rather, we have given weight to the greatness of the book and the author, to Shaykh al-Kulaynī's own testimony to the caliber of his book, and to the attention every generation of Shīʿī scholars has given it. We refer those who are interested in discussions about the chains of transmission to the commentaries of Mullā Ṣāliḥ al-Māzandarānī and ʿAllāmah al-

Majlisī as well as to the work of Sayyid Mūsā al-Zanjānī, which is the basis for the *Dirāyat al-Nūr* software package produced by the Computer Research Center of Islamic Studies (CRCIS).

We beg God to bless the Prophet and his family; to reward those he has graced to be his agents in making this publication possible; and to reward those whom he graces to benefit from what lies herein.

Shaykh Rizwan Arastu
Director of the Islamic Texts Institute
May, 2012

Introduction

By Shaykh Abū Jaʿfar Muḥammad ibn Yaʿqūb al-Kulaynī

In the name of God, the All-Beneficent, the Ever-Merciful

All praise is for God who is extolled for his blessings, who is worshipped for his power, who is obeyed in his dominion, who is feared for his majesty, who is desired for what [rewards] he possesses, whose command holds authority over all his creatures. He is high, thus he has [rightfully] declared his highness; he is near [to everything], thus he is almighty. He has risen above [the field of view of] every faculty of sight. [It is he] whose precedence has no beginning and whose everlastingness has no end. He exists before all things. He is the Everlasting through whom all things subsist. He is the Dominant who is not burdened by protecting his creatures. He is the Omnipotent who has sole control over his vast dominion through his greatness, who has sole power over his realm through his might, who has made his proofs manifest for his creatures by his wisdom.

He originated all things with [nothing save] his power, and initiated their creation for [no purpose save the dictates of] his wisdom. [He did] not [originate them] from any preceding matter, which would have contradicted "origination," nor [did he initiate their creation] for any [external] purpose, which would have contradicted "initiation." Rather, he created what he wished, how he wished, single-handedly to make manifest his wisdom and the true nature of his lordship.

Neither can intellects contain him, nor can minds perceive him, nor can eyes behold him, nor can any measure encompass him. Words fall short of [describing] him. Eyes fall short of [beholding] him. Every permutation of attributes fails [to praise him sufficiently].

He is concealed without any veil to conceal him. He is hidden without any screen to hide him. He is known without being seen. He is described without any image. He is defined without any figure. There is no god but him, the Great, the Most High. Minds fall short of reaching his essence. Intellects are overwhelmed in their [vain] attempts to reach the ends of his infinity. The limits of no mind can reach him. The penetration of no eye can behold him. Yet he is the All-Hearing, the All-Knowing.

He has sealed his case against his creatures through his messengers. He has clarified all matters through his guidance. He has raised, among them, prophets as bearers of glad tidings and as warners "so that those who perish do so despite clear evidence, and those who live do so based on clear evidence;"[1] and so that his servants may know of their Lord what they knew not, and thus know him as their Lord after having known him not; and so that they know him as their singular God after having attributed to him partners.

I praise him in a way that brings solace to the soul, pleases him, and conveys gratitude for what has come to us of his copious blessings, plentiful gifts, and beautiful trials.

I testify that there is no god but God, alone, who has no partner, who is one, unique, and self-sufficient. Neither has he a spouse nor a child. And I testify that Muḥammad—may God shower him and his family with mercy—is his chosen servant, his appointed messenger, whom he sent after a hiatus in [the chain of] messengers and a lengthy slumber in human civilization; when ignorance had spread throughout, when strife had blocked [the path to truth], when all that had been sturdy had crumbled, when people were blind to the truth, when they had resorted to iniquity and false religion.

He revealed to him a book of exposition and clarification "as an eloquent book with no crookedness so that people should fear God."[2] He clarified it for people through a body of knowledge expressed in various ways, through a religion he explained, through a canon of laws he made obligatory on them, and matters that he revealed to his creatures. In all this, there are guides to

---

1. Qurʾān 8:42

2. Qurʾān 39:28

salvation and signposts calling to guidance.

The Prophet, in turn—may God shower him and his family with mercy—conveyed the message with which he was sent, and made known that to which he had been ordered, and fulfilled the duties of the prophethood with which he had been charged. He persevered for his Lord's sake, and struggled in his path, and sought what was in the best interest of his people, and called them to salvation, and encouraged them to remember God, and showed them how they could remain on the path of guidance after he was gone by following the Callers whom he installed, the Beacons of Light that he erected, so that they should not stray after him, for he was kind and compassionate to them.

When his time was up and his days were complete, God took his soul, while his deeds were pleasing to God, his share [of paradise] was abundant, and his station was great. He—may God shower him and his family with mercy—passed on and bequeathed to his people the book of God and his successor, the Commander of the Faithful, the Imam of the God-fearing [ʿAlī ibn Abī Ṭālib]—may God shower him with mercy. These two [the Qurʾān and his successor] were inseparable companions, each corroborating the other. The Imam would speak on God's behalf of what God had made binding upon all people in his book: of obedience to himself and to the Imam and of the Imam's authority, and of those rights that God has [over his creatures], which he intends [for them to fulfill]: that they [do their part to] perfect [the practice of] his religion, that they [do their part to] make his religion prevail [over all religions], that they debate [with others] using [the teachings of] his guides, and that they become enlightened with his divine light, which [he has placed] in the depths of his chosen people, in the elect of this righteous servants.

Thus, did God explain his religion through his guided imams from the family of our Prophet—may God shower him and his family with mercy. He showed us through them the way to reach him. He tapped through them into the innermost recesses of the springs of his knowledge. He made them the path for us to know him, the signposts to guide us to his religion, the intermediaries between him and his creation, and the gateways leading to true knowledge. He granted them access to his most treasured secrets.

Whenever one of those imams would pass away, God would appoint another from his progeny for [the guidance of] his creatures as a clearly appointed leader, an enlightened guide, a responsible leader. They would lead with truth and justice, as God's proofs and his callers, his shepherds over his flocks, so that his servants should live by their example, and the land should be resplendent with their light. God made them a source of life for man, lanterns in the darkness, keys to [unlock] God's word, and pillars of Islam.

He made submitting to them in what we know [of their teachings], and referring to them for what we do not know, the foundation of all our acts of obedience to him and the means for us to complete what he has made incumbent upon us. He forbade everyone other than them to hastily accept ideas of whose veracity they are ignorant, as he also forbade them to reject ideas of whose falsehood they know nothing. [He has done all this] to save whomever he wishes from among his creatures from the strife that inevitably befalls them and the confusion that threatens to blind them.

May God shower his blessings upon Muḥammad and on the righteous members of his household from whom he has staved off all filth and whom he has purified thoroughly.

Thereafter, I say the following: I have understood, my brother, that of which you have complained to me: that the people of our time have joined hands in the cause of ignorance and have endeavored to pave the paths that leads to it; that they have distanced themselves from knowledge and scholars to such an extent that knowledge in its entirety has nearly dried up and been cut off from its source, for people are content to rely on ignorance and to let knowledge and scholars waste away.

You asked me, "Is it permissible for people to remain in ignorance and devote themselves to religious practice without knowledge, when they are people of faith who concede all its tenets and practices, albeit on the basis of personal taste or because they have grown up with religion or because they want to follow in the footsteps of their forebears or because they rely on pure reason in all things great and small [without any attention to religion]?"

Thus, you should know [the answer], my brother—may God have mercy on you. God—almighty is he and good—has created humankind different from beasts in that he has placed keenness and intellect in them, and thus they can bear the burden of being commanded and forbidden. In turn, he divided them into two groups: one group comprises those with healthy intellects, while the other contains those with blinded and impaired intellects. He exclusively commanded and forbade those with healthy intellects after having given them [their intellects, which serve as] the means by which they can bear the burden of accountability. On the other hand, he lifted this burden from those with blinded and impaired intellects because he created them in such a way that they could not bear discipline and learning. The only reason he lets them remain is the presence of those with healthy intellects,[3] while the reason those with healthy intellects are allowed to remain is for the sake of discipline and learning. So if it were permissible for those with healthy intellects to remain ignorant, it would be possible to lift the burden of responsibility from them. And if that were possible, then there would be no purpose in [sending] divine books, messengers, or ethics. And if divine books, messengers and ethics ceased to exist, the order [of human society] would go to chaos, and we would have to concede that what atheists say

3. The purpose of creation was to create a being that would serve God of his own free will. This purpose can only be fulfilled by those with intellect. Children, the mentally handicapped, and the insane do not fulfill this purpose—albeit through no fault of their own. The whole world exists only to aid those with intellect to fulfill the ultimate purpose of creation. If it were not for them, God would not have created the rest of the world. In this way, the continued existence of those with little or no intellect is tied to the existence of those with healthy intellects.

is right.[4] Thus, it must be, according to God's justice and wisdom, that he specially charged those among his creatures whom he has created with the potential to bear commandments and injunctions, with commands and injunctions so that they are not left idle, and so that they aggrandize him; know him as the One God; concede that he is their Lord; and that he is their creator and provider. For the evidence for his lordship is a clear indicator, his arguments are brilliant and clear, his signs are lucid. These signs call people to belief in his oneness—almighty is he and sublime. They testify [before these people] that their creator is Lord and God, for these signs contain the traces of the act of creation and the wonders of his management. Thus, he has called them to know him because it would not be permissible for them to be ignorant of him or of his religion and his laws, for God, the Wise, does not allow himself and his religion to remain unknown. He has said, "Has the [following] covenant not been made with them [and recorded] in their book: that they not attribute to God anything except what is true?"[5] And he has said, "Rather [than answering our challenge,] they have repudiated what they have not comprehended."[6] Through these verses, those with healthy intellects alone have been commanded and forbidden: commanded to speak the truth; forbidden to remain in ignorance. He commanded them to ask and to gain a deep understanding of the religion when he said, "Why do not some from every group of them go off to gain a deep understanding of the religion and to warn their people when they return to them?"[7] And he said, "So ask those who remember if you do not know."[8] If it were permissible for those with healthy intellects to remain in ignorance, he would not have

4. What they say is that there is no overarching purpose to our existence and that there is no accountability or judgment.

5. Qurʾān 7:169

6. Qurʾān 10:39

7. Qurʾān 9:122

8. Qurʾān 16:43

commanded them to ask, and there would have been no need of sending messengers with books and ethics. They then would have been at the level of beasts and at the level of those with blinded and impaired intellects. If they had been like that, they would not have remained in existence for even a blink of an eye.

Since their very existence depends on ethics and learning, every person with a sound intellect and a complete means [of understanding] must have a teacher, a guide, an advisor, one to command him and forbid him, [from whom to acquire] discipline, learning, and [to whom to address his] questions. For this reason, the most appropriate thing for one with intellect to assimilate, for one who is reflective and clever to seek, for one who is successful and heading in the right direction to endeavor toward, is knowledge of religion, knowledge of the things that God has demanded of his creatures: his oneness, his laws, what he has commanded and forbidden, his injunctions, and ethics. For the arguments are solid, your responsibility is affirmed, life is short, and procrastination is unacceptable. Additionally, God's condition—sublime is his name—for the duties he has demanded of his creatures is that they fulfill all of them with knowledge, conviction, and insight, so that he who fulfills his duty may be praiseworthy in his Lord's eyes and worthy of his great reward. The one who fulfills these duties without knowledge or insight, knows not what he does, nor does he know for whom he does it. And if he is ignorant of these things, he cannot be sure he has fulfilled his duty properly, nor can he confirm [what he has done], since one cannot confirm something unless he knows what he is confirming without the slightest uncertainty or doubt. One with doubt does not possess the same passion, fear, humility, and drive to attain God's proximity that one with knowledge and conviction possesses. God—almighty is he and sublime—has said, "Except for him who testifies truthfully and knows."[9] In this verse, their testimony is accepted because of their knowledge of the testimony; if it were not for their knowledge of the

9. Qurʾān 43:87

testimony, their testimony would not be accepted. On the other hand, the judgment of one who fulfills his duty with uncertainty, without knowledge or insight, is up to God—sublime is his name: if he wills, he may grace him and accept his deeds; and if he wills, he may reject him. For God's condition was that duties be fulfilled with knowledge, conviction, and insight so that people avoid being among those whom God has described in the following verse: "There are among people those who worship God on the fringes [of faith]: if good fortune befalls him, he is content with it; but if an ordeal befalls him he turns on his heels. He has lost [the gain of] this life and the next. That is clear loss."[10] [This person lives on the fringes] because he practices the religion without knowledge or conviction. Accordingly, he may [as easily] leave the religion without knowledge or conviction. In this vein, one of the knowledgeable imams has said, "He remains constant in faith who enters it with knowledge, and his faith shall benefit him. Whereas, he who enters the faith without knowledge leaves it just as he entered it." He also said, "Mountains will crumble before the faith of one who takes his religion from the book of God and the example of his Prophet—may God's mercy be on him and his progeny. Whereas, the faith of one who takes his religion from the mouths of men will be destroyed by men." He also said, "He who does not know our mission by means of the Qur'ān will not avoid strife." It is for this reason that this flood of deviant religions and sects, which fulfill all the conditions of disbelief has swamped the people of our times.

[Whether one takes his religion from the book of God and the example of his Prophet or from the mouths of ignorant laymen] is a factor of God's grace or desertion: if God wishes to grace someone such that his faith should be solid and sturdy, he facilitates the means by which he can take his religion from the book of God and the example of his Prophet—may God's mercy be on him and his progeny—with knowledge, conviction, and insight. Such a person is more firm in his faith than the sturdy mountains. However, if God

10. Qur'ān 22:11

wishes to desert someone such that his faith should be [fleeting] like a thing on loan (we seek refuge in him from that), he facilitates the means for him to act according his personal tastes, to follow blindly, and to interpret without knowledge or insight. The lot of such a person is contingent on God's will: if God—almighty and good is he—wishes, he may reinforce his faith, and if he wishes, he may strip him of it. There is no guarantee for him against waking up as a believer and sleeping as an unbeliever, or sleeping as a believer and waking up as an unbeliever, since every time he sees an influential person, he inclines toward him, and every time he sees something that seems on its surface to suit his taste, he accepts it. One of the knowledgeable imams has said, "God—almighty is he and sublime—created the prophets with prophethood, thus they cannot be anything else. And he created their successors as successors, thus they cannot be anything else. And he has lent [all other] people faith. If he wishes, he completes it for them, and if he wishes he strips them of it." Then he said, "The following words apply to [the two groups of] people: 'Some have hearts with firm faith and some have hearts with faith on loan.'"[11]

You mentioned that some issues are unclear to you: that you do not know the truth concerning them for the disparity in the traditions about them; that you know that the disparity in the traditions about them is for various reasons; that you do not have anyone at hand whose knowledge of these things you can trust and with whom you can discuss these things. You said that you would love to have a sufficient book (*kitāb kāfin*) containing enough of all the religious sciences to suffice the student; to serve as a reference for the disciple; from which those who seek knowledge of the religion and want to act on it can draw authentic traditions from the Truthful [imams]—may God's peace be upon them—and a living example upon which to act, by which our duty to God—almighty is he and sublime—and to the commands of his Prophet—may God's mercy be on him and his progeny—may be fulfilled.

---

11. Qurʾān 6:98

You also said, "If this could be, I hope it could be a means by whose help, and through whose compilation, God fortifies our brothers in faith and leads them to guidance."

Thus, you should know, my brother—may God [continue to] guide you—that nobody can resolve any of the disparities in the traditions of the scholars [i.e., the imams]—may God's peace be upon them—using his own opinion. Rather [these can only be resolved] according to the methods stated by one of the knowledgeable imams—may God's peace be upon him—when he said, "Compare them to the book of God. Take whichever of them concurs with the book of God—almighty is he and sublime—and reject whichever of them contradicts the book of God;" and when he said, "Abandon whatever concurs with the majority [i.e., Sunnīs], for guidance is found in opposing them;" and when he said, "Take what is unanimously agreed upon, for there is no [room to] doubt in what is unanimously agreed upon." However, [despite these methods,] we only know a few instances where [true] resolution is possible. Thus, we find no path more prudent, or easier, than to refer the knowledge of all this back to the knowledgeable Imam of our time—may God's peace be upon him—and to accept the freedom of choice that he gave to us when he said, "Any one that you act on out of submission is fine."[12]

God—to whom belongs all praise—has facilitated the compilation of what

---

12. The majority of contemporary scholars of the fundamentals of jurisprudence (*uṣūl al-fiqh*) believe that a jurist must decide between two contradictory traditions using standards (*murajjiḥāt*), many of which are enumerated by the imams in various traditions (see *al-Kāfī* 2.22.1-12). If these standards are not effective in bringing about a resolution, both traditions lose their credibility, and he must refer to a set of principles (*uṣūl ʿamaliyyah*) that determine our practical duty in such cases. Others believe that it is not necessary that he decide between them and that he may choose freely (*takhyīr*) whichever he wishes (al-Khurāsānī, Muḥammad Kāẓim. *Kifāyat al-uṣūl*. Qum: Āl al-Bayt Institute, 1988. 445). In this paragraph, Shaykh al-Kulaynī reveals that he believes the jurist may choose freely (*takhyīr*) only after none of the standards (*murajjiḥāt*) proves effective in choosing one over the other. (al-Khūʿī, Abū al-Qāsim. *Miṣbāḥ al-uṣūl*. Qum: Dāwarī, 1996. vol.3 p.412).

you requested. I hope it is as you desired. Whatever shortcomings may lie herein, it is not for a lack in my goodwill, for I took it as a duty to my brethren in faith. Additionally, I desired to share [in its reward] with everyone who benefits from it and acts upon what is in it, in our age, and in the future, until the end of the temporal world. [And we must act on it] because our Lord—almighty is he and sublime—is one; his messenger, Muḥammad, the Seal of the Prophets—may God's mercy and peace be upon him and his progeny—is one; the law is one, and what Muḥammad has sanctioned is sanctioned, and what he has forbidden is forbidden, until the Day of Resurrection; [thus, we have nowhere to turn but to these traditions].

I have made the *Book of Divine Guidance* (i.e., *Kitāb al-ḥujjah*) extensive so as not to miss out on all of its benefits, though I did not complete it as was its due.

I hope that God will approve of my intention. If he delays my death, I shall write a more expansive and more complete book in which I do it justice, if God wills. He alone is the source of strength, and in him alone do I seek additional succor. May God's mercy be on our master, Prophet Muḥammad and on his immaculate and righteous progeny.

I shall begin my book with a book on intellect and [another on] the merit of knowledge, the lofty station of those possessed of it, the deplorability of ignorance and the lowliness of those bereft of knowledge. [I begin with the intellect] because the intellect is the axis around which all else turns: through it does one argue; for it is one given reward; and according to it is one punished. And God is the Grantor of success.

—Abū Jaʿfar Muḥammad ibn Yaʿqūb al-Kulaynī

Tradition 1.1.1

أَخْبَرَنَا أَبُو جَعْفَرٍ مُحَمَّدُ بْنُ يَعْقُوبَ قَالَ حَدَّثَنِي عِدَّةٌ مِنْ أَصْحَابِنَا مِنْهُمْ مُحَمَّدُ بْنُ يَحْيَى الْعَطَّارُ عَنْ أَحْمَدَ بْنِ مُحَمَّدٍ عَنِ الْحَسَنِ بْنِ مَحْبُوبٍ عَنِ الْعَلَاءِ بْنِ رَزِينٍ عَنْ مُحَمَّدِ بْنِ مُسْلِمٍ عَنْ أَبِي جَعْفَرٍ عليه السلام قَالَ:

Abū Jaʿfar Muḥammad ibn Yaʿqūb informed us[1] that a number of our fellow Shīʿah, among whom was Muḥammad ibn Yaḥyā al-ʿAṭṭār, reported from Aḥmad ibn Muḥammad from al-Ḥasan ibn Maḥbūb from al-ʿAlāʾ ibn Razīn from Muḥammad ibn Muslim that Abū Jaʿfar [al-Bāqir] said:

لَمَّا خَلَقَ اللَّهُ الْعَقْلَ اسْتَنْطَقَهُ ثُمَّ قَالَ لَهُ: أَقْبِلْ، فَأَقْبَلَ. ثُمَّ قَالَ لَهُ: أَدْبِرْ، فَأَدْبَرَ. ثُمَّ قَالَ: وَ عِزَّتِي وَ جَلَالِي مَا خَلَقْتُ خَلْقاً هُوَ أَحَبُّ إِلَيَّ مِنْكَ وَ لَا أَكْمَلْتُكَ إِلَّا فِيمَنْ أُحِبُّ. أَمَا إِنِّي إِيَّاكَ آمُرُ وَ إِيَّاكَ أَنْهَى وَ إِيَّاكَ أُعَاقِبُ وَ إِيَّاكَ أُثِيبُ.

"When God created intellect[2], he gave it the faculty of language and said, 'Come forward,' whereupon it came forward. Then he said to it, 'Go back,' whereupon it went back.[3] Then he said, 'By my might and my majesty, I have not created a creature more beloved to me than you, and I have not perfected you except in whom I love.[4] Let it be known! You alone do I command, and you alone do I forbid.[5] [According to] you alone do I punish, and [according] to you alone do I confer reward.'"[6]

---

1. After compiling *al-Kāfī*, Shaykh al-Kulaynī, in keeping with tradition, would have conveyed his book to his students, such as Muḥammad ibn Ibrāhīm al-

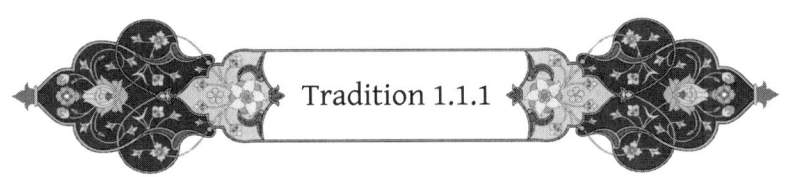

Nuʿmānī and Muḥammad ibn Aḥmad al-Ṣafwānī, either through dictation (*qirāʾah*) or by consigning it to them (*munāwalah*) so that they could make copies for themselves. At the beginning of their copies, they would have included the phrase, "Abū Jaʿfar Muḥammad ibn Yaʿqūb informed us..." to announce that they had received the entire text of the book as well as the authority to transmit it from Shaykh al-Kulaynī himself. They would then have transmitted the book in its entirety through dictation or by consigning their copies to others. This third generation would also have transcribed the phrase, "Abū Jaʿfar Muḥammad ibn Yaʿqūb informed us..." presumably as part of their effort to meticulously transmit the book without the slightest adulteration. We now find this phrase at the beginning of each book of *al-Kāfī* as an artifact of that ancient system. Other than this phrase, we can safely assume that every other word in *al-Kāfī* was part of Shaykh al-Kulaynī's original work.

2. Muslim scholars use the word *ʿaql* to mean many different things. However, the traditions of Prophet Muḥammad and the imams use it to mean only four things. In one sense it is a human faculty while in the other three it connotes an infinitive that represents the relationship of that faculty to the one endowed with it. The four meanings of *ʿaql* are as follows:

The first meaning of ʿaql

It is the faculty of "intellect" or "reason" by which human beings understand all things—among which are good and evil—and by which they differentiate among them. When a person possesses the critical level of intellect, he becomes accountable before God for his beliefs and actions. Below this critical level, he is not accountable; above this critical level, God's expectations of him are commensurate with his intellectual capacity, such that, with increased intellect, the obligations for which he is held responsible are concomitantly greater in number and more difficult. According to the traditions, it is possible to strengthen this intellectual capacity by, among other things, abstaining from sin, learning and teaching, exercising discipline, learning from experience, and submitting to truth. The absence of this faculty is termed *jahl* or "foolishness," which we must differentiate from *jahl* or "ignorance," which is the opposite of *ʿilm* or "knowledge."

It is important to emphasize that the intellect understands things through a process of ratiocination, reasoned thinking. This statement stands in stark contrast to the opinion of those who subscribe to the Perennialist School (e.g., Syed Hossein Nasr), which looks cynically upon ratiocination as a means for knowing truth and uses the term "intellect" to refer to something beyond the realm of reason and logic. In other words, our usage of the term "intellect" as a translation for *ʿaql* should not be construed as an endorsement of the Perennialist School's usage of this term.

The second meaning of ʿaql

It is an infinitive meaning "to have an intellect." In this sense, an *ʿāqil* is anyone to whom God has given sufficient intellect to fairly hold him responsible for his beliefs and actions. The equivalent of *ʿāqil* in this sense is "sane" or "rational." Its opposite, *jāhil*, is anyone to whom God has not given sufficient intellect and from whom he appropriately expects nothing. A *jāhil* in this sense comprises those who are mentally handicapped (*safīh*), those who are insane (*majnūn*), as well as children whose intellects have not yet reached maturity.

The third meaning of ʿaql

It is an infinitive meaning "to use one's intellect." Whenever *ʿaql* is used to mean "to think" or "to understand," it is being used in this sense. Thus, an *ʿāqil* in this sense is anyone who not only has an intellect, but uses it to understand things, and a *jāhil* is one who has sufficient intellectual capacity but fails to use it. We must be aware though that in many traditions the term *jāhil* is used even for people who use their intellect but do not act according to what their intellect has helped them understand, since understanding something and not acting accordingly is tantamount to not understanding at all.

The fourth meaning of ʿaql

It is an infinitive meaning "to use one's intellect for a right purpose." In this sense, an *ʿāqil* is someone, like the prophets, imams, and other righteous individuals, who uses his intellect to further God's purpose. A *jāhil* on the other hand is one who satanically uses his intellectual capacity to machinate against truth, to satisfy his lust, and to spread evil. It is in this sense that Imam al-Ṣādiq says that Muʿāwiyah ibn Abī Sufyān lacks intellect (see *al-Kāfī* 1.1.3).

3. This tradition shares elements with traditions 1.1.14, 1.1.26, and 1.1.31. The word "intellect" in all four traditions is used in the first sense of the word to refer to the faculty of reason. There are two prevalent interpretations for these traditions. The first—and stronger of the two—says that they allegorically describe the function for which God created the intellect: to comprehend truth, and in particular, to comprehend that obeying God is good. We will present a full justification of this view in our commentary on tradition 1.1.14. Suffice it to mention here that some Qurʾānic verses and many traditions describe in similar terms how God created and then spoke to various parts of creation as an allegorical expression of their subservience to his will. For instance, the Qurʾān says, "Then God turned to the sky, when it was yet smoke-like, and he said to it and to the earth, 'Come, willingly or unwillingly!' They answered, 'We come willingly'" (41:11). In examples from the traditions, Prophet Muḥammad said, "When God created the world, he commanded it to obey him, so it obeyed its Lord" (*Biḥār al-anwār* 67.58.20). Imam al-Ṣādiq said, "When God created paradise he said to it, 'Speak.' So it said, 'The believers have surely succeeded'" (*Tafsīr al-Qummī* in the commentary on Qurʿān 23:1). Again Prophet Muḥammad said, "When God created the heavens and the earth he called to them and they answered" (*Biḥār al-anwār* 17.13.24).

The second interpretation says that God actually created an independent creature called "Intellect" as a sentient being and then gave it the power of language and spoke to it and commanded it to move forward and backward, and it obeyed, though we may not understand exactly how all this played out. Accordingly, the relationship between that intellect, which was created as an independent being and the intellect created in every person is that the latter is a watered down form of the former. They are both the same intellect, only one is more complete, possessing all the attributes of intellect in perfection, and the other is a lower form of the same. This relationship may be something like the relationship between "all things" and the "treasuries" from which they descend as described in the following verse of the Qurʾān: "The treasuries of every single thing are with us, and we only send it down in due portion" (15:21). We say that these two intellects must be "the same thing" because the phrase, "I have not perfected you except in whom I love" clearly indicates that the intellect to which God spoke is the very same intellect that he created in all people and perfected in whom he loves.

In any case, whether the tradition is an allegory or a narration of an actual event, its unequivocal purpose is to show that the faculty of intellect perfectly comprehends that obeying God is good. For an explanation of the significance of "coming forward" and "moving back," see our commentary on tradition 1.1.14.

4. There are three plausible meanings for the sentence, "I have not perfected you except in whom I love." "Perfection" in its literal sense refers to a singular level above which there is no level. A person either has a perfect intellect or an imperfect one; there are no gradations of lesser or greater perfection. According to this literal meaning of "perfection," the sentence, "I have not perfected you except in whom I love," could refer specifically to Prophet Muḥammad, who was the best and most beloved of God's creatures. This would mean that only he possessed a perfect intellect and that all other creatures' intellects have been, and will be, less than perfect. It could alternatively refer to all the divine guides: the prophets, messengers, and imams. This would mean that all of them have had perfect intellects, and that the elevated status of some above others is due, not to a difference in intellect, but to some other virtues they possess in varying degrees. The tradition of Prophet Muḥammad, "God did not send a single prophet or messenger until he perfected his intellect," (*al-Kāfī* 1.1.11) corroborates this latter interpretation, since it indicates that all the divine guides possessed perfect intellects. According to both of these possible meanings, the "love" to which God alludes is a special love he reserves for his infallible guides.

If, on the other hand, we construe "perfection" figuratively to mean any increase in intellect, the sentence, "I have not perfected you except in whom I love," would more aptly be translated, "I have not increased you except in whom I love." This sentence would then indicate that there is a direct correlation between God's love for a person and the intellect he gives him. Naturally, the prophets, messengers, and imams, who are most beloved to God, would be given the most intellect while other people would be given varying degrees of intellect commensurate with the love God has for them.

5. When God commands or forbids a person, it is the intellect within him to whom he speaks. It is the intellect that has the ability to comprehend the command. It is the intellect that determines that obeying is the right thing to do.

6. The last two sentences of this tradition describe an oft-repeated theme in this section of *al-Kāfī*: the degree of intellect one is given determines the standard by which God will judge him (see 1.1.7-9). It should be noted that we have inferred the phrase "according to" when it does not exist in the Arabic for two reasons. First, it contradicts what we know about reward and punishment to say that intellect alone is rewarded or punished. It is the human body and soul as a whole that receives reward and punishment, not just the intellect, which is merely a *trait* of the human being, not the human being himself. Second, other narrations of this same tradition include the Arabic equivalent of "according to" (see *al-Kāfī* 1.1.32 and *Man lā yaḥḍuruhu al-faqīh* 4.4.176.1).

TRADITION 1.1.1 TEACHES THE FOLLOWING:

- The intellect comprehends that obedience to God is good.
- The intellect is God's most beloved creature.
- Perfect intellect is found only in Prophet Muḥammad or in all of the prophets, messengers, and imams (this is based on the literal interpretation of "perfection").
- The dearer one is to God, the stronger his intellect (this is based on the figurative interpretation of "perfection").
- God's command only applies to a person to the extent of his intellect; likewise, he is only rewarded and punished to the extent of his intellect.

Tradition 1.1.2

ʿAlī ibn Muḥammad reported from Sahl ibn Ziyād from ʿAmr ibn ʿUthmān from Mufaḍḍal ibn Ṣāliḥ from Saʿd ibn Ṭarīf from al-Aṣbagh ibn Nubātah that ʿAlī said:

عَلِيُّ بْنُ مُحَمَّدٍ عَنْ سَهْلِ بْنِ زِيَادٍ عَنْ عَمْرِو بْنِ عُثْمَانَ عَنْ مُفَضَّلِ بْنِ صَالِحٍ عَنْ سَعْدِ بْنِ طَرِيفٍ عَنِ الْأَصْبَغِ بْنِ نُبَاتَةَ عَنْ عَلِيٍّ عليه السلام قَالَ:

"Gabriel descended upon Adam[1] and said, 'Adam, I have been commanded to offer you the choice of one of three [traits], so choose one, and leave two.'[2] Adam asked him, 'Gabriel, and what are these three [traits]?' He answered, '[They are] intellect, decency, and devotion.'[3] Adam said, 'I most certainly choose intellect.' Gabriel told decency and devotion, 'Go away and leave intellect [with Adam].' Thereupon they said, 'Gabriel, we have been ordered to remain with intellect wherever he may be.'[4] Gabriel said, 'As you wish.' Then he ascended."

هَبَطَ جَبْرَئِيلُ عَلَى آدَمَ عليه السلام، فَقَالَ: يَا آدَمُ، إِنِّي أُمِرْتُ أَنْ أُخَيِّرَكَ وَاحِدَةً مِنْ ثَلَاثٍ، فَاخْتَرْهَا وَ دَعِ اثْنَتَيْنِ. فَقَالَ لَهُ آدَمُ: يَا جَبْرَئِيلُ، وَ مَا الثَّلَاثُ؟ فَقَالَ: الْعَقْلُ وَ الْحَيَاءُ وَ الدِّينُ. فَقَالَ آدَمُ: إِنِّي قَدِ اخْتَرْتُ الْعَقْلَ. فَقَالَ جَبْرَئِيلُ لِلْحَيَاءِ وَ الدِّينِ: انْصَرِفَا وَ دَعَاهُ. فَقَالَا: يَا جَبْرَئِيلُ، إِنَّا أُمِرْنَا أَنْ نَكُونَ مَعَ الْعَقْلِ حَيْثُ كَانَ. قَالَ: فَشَأْنَكُمَا، وَ عَرَجَ.

---

1. This tradition's detailed account of the interaction and conversation between Gabriel and Adam prevents us from consigning it to allegory. However, the three personified human attributes mentioned here are problematic: how can human attributes that cannot exist independently of their possessor stand before Adam and speak? In traditions about purgatory and the hereafter, it is not uncommon for good and bad traits to appear in the form of beautiful and ugly figures. In fact, even in this temporal life, realities appear to some people in the form of visions. In the story of Joseph, for example, God depicts the ultimate reunion of Joseph and his family and his noble standing among them as eleven stars, the sun, and the moon prostrating before Joseph in a dream (Qurʾān 12:4). The king and Joseph's two cellmates also see similar visions that represent future events (Qurʾān 12:36 and 12:43). Thus, in the tradition at hand, there is nothing far-fetched about Gabriel's teaching Adam the nature of three human traits in tangible form. If it seems unusual, it is because we are used to dealing with mental concepts and words, not symbolic representations. However, because it is extremely important that a prophet of God know reality intimately, God chose to leave aside weaker, conventional methods of teaching with words and concepts and personified the three traits as figures to give Adam an unforgettable lesson about intellect's role in guiding decency and devotion.

2. Obviously, Adam possessed these three traits—especially intellect—before Gabriel's offer. Accordingly, perhaps Gabriel was asking him which of the three he would like to keep or which of the three he would like perfected in him.

3. Understanding this tradition requires an understanding of these three human traits and their interactions with one another. Intellect—in the first sense of the word—is the human capacity to understand reality. Decency (*ḥayāʾ*) is a trait that makes a person recoil from anything he deems bad—whether it be bad in reality or not. Devotion (*dīn* in the sense of *diyānah*) is a trait that compels a person to do anything he deems good—whether it be good in reality or not. A person's intellect, inasmuch as it understands reality, realizes that decency and devotion are good in and of themselves and that he should acquire them. Once he acquires them, his intellect guides his decency so that it makes him recoil only from what is *truly* bad. Similarly, his intellect guides his devotion so that it compels him to do only what is *truly* good. It follows that if Adam had chosen decency or devotion instead of intellect, he would have been like a fledgling child whose misguided decency causes him to shy away from asking a question or conversing with an adult; or like the pagans of Mecca or the Khawārij, who devoted themselves to a religion founded on fantasies and misconceptions. However, by choosing intellect, he acquired a torch by which to guide his other two faculties.

4. God's commands are of two types. One, called a legal command (*amr tashrīʿī*), is similar to human commands in that, when they are issued, the recipient can choose to obey or refuse. The second, called an existential command (*amr takwīnī*), simply reflects God's will for something to be. No word is spoken; no refusal is possible. It is as God says, "If we want something to exist, all we say to it is 'be,' and it is" (Qurʾān 16:40). Considering that the personified traits, decency and devotion, are not sentient beings capable of obeying or refusing a divine command, the command referred to here is necessarily of the latter kind: a reflection of God's will that they remain forever inextricably coupled with intellect.

TRADITION 1.1.2 TEACHES THE FOLLOWING:

- The intellect is inextricably coupled with decency and devotion.
- A person who shies away when he should be bold or devotes himself when he should remain aloof has a weak intellect.
- The intellect, when put to use, guides decency and devotion.
- Adam—and all the prophets—can be shown reality in a tangible form.

Tradition 1.1.3

أَحْمَدُ بْنُ إِدْرِيسَ عَنْ مُحَمَّدِ بْنِ عَبْدِ الْجَبَّارِ عَنْ بَعْضِ أَصْحَابِنَا رَفَعَهُ إِلَى أَبِي عَبْدِ اللَّهِ عليه السلام قَالَ: قُلْتُ لَهُ: مَا الْعَقْلُ؟ قَالَ:

Aḥmad ibn Idrīs reported from Muḥammad ibn ʿAbd al-Jabbār from one of our fellow Shīʿah from [the time of] Abū ʿAbd Allāh [al-Ṣādiq without mentioning his source, from a man who] said, "I asked Abū ʿAbd Allāh [al-Ṣādiq], 'What is intellect?' He replied:

مَا عُبِدَ بِهِ الرَّحْمَنُ وَ اكْتُسِبَ بِهِ الْجِنَانُ.

'It is that by which [God,] the All-Beneficent is worshipped[1] and the gardens are earned.'"[2]

قَالَ: قُلْتُ: فَالَّذِي كَانَ فِي مُعَاوِيَةَ؟ فَقَالَ:

"I asked him, 'Then [what was] the trait in Muʿāwiyah?' He answered:

تِلْكَ النَّكْرَاءُ، تِلْكَ الشَّيْطَنَةُ، وَ هِيَ شَبِيهَةٌ بِالْعَقْلِ وَ لَيْسَتْ بِالْعَقْلِ.

'That was cleverness. That was devilry. It is similar to intellect, but it is not intellect.'"[3]

---

1. The intellect is the means by which God is worshipped in three distinct ways:

- It is the means of knowing God;
- It is the means of knowing one's duty to God;
- It is the means of knowing the best way to fulfill that duty to him.

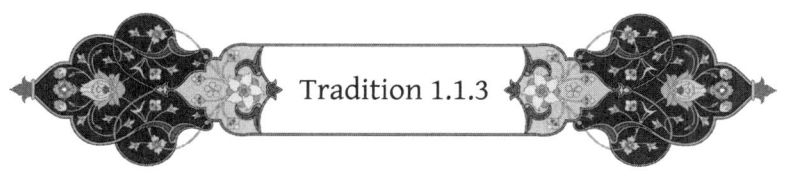

2. Apparently, the transmitter of this tradition has heard people speak of the "intellect" and wants the imam to define it for him. The Imam's response, however, is narrower than the transmitter had expected and thus seems not to apply to some faculties he previously thought to be intellect. This is why he asks about the faculty in Muʿāwiyah.

On another note, this tradition conveys the same message as tradition 1.1.6. If they are read together, each one helps us understand the other.

3. Imam al-Ṣādiq uses intellect here in the fourth sense of the word (i.e., to use one's intellect for a right purpose). When he says that devilry is similar to intellect, he means that they both require that a person have a strong intellectual capacity—in the second sense of the word—and they both require him to use that capacity—in the third sense of the word. However, the difference is that this faculty ought to be used for good, so if he uses it for evil, it is as though he has no intellect, since he has not used it for what it was intended. Thus, the likes of Muʿāwiyah, despite having a strong intellect and putting it to use, are devils because they use that faculty for evil, and it can be said that, in reality, they have no intellect whatsoever.

TRADITION 1.1.3 TEACHES THE FOLLOWING:

- The intellect is the means of knowing God, worshipping him, and reaching paradise.
- One who does not use his intellect for these purposes has not used it properly and is practically devoid of intellect.
- The likes of Muʿāwiyah, who use the divine gift of intellect for evil, are devils.

Tradition 1.1.4

Muḥammad ibn Yaḥyā reported from Aḥmad ibn Muḥammad ibn ʿĪsā from Ibn Faḍḍāl from al-Ḥasan ibn al-Jahm that he said, "I heard al-Riḍā say:

مُحَمَّدُ بْنُ يَحْيَى عَنْ أَحْمَدَ بْنِ مُحَمَّدِ بْنِ عِيسَى عَنِ ابْنِ فَضَّالٍ عَنِ الْحَسَنِ بْنِ الْجَهْمِ قَالَ: سَمِعْتُ الرِّضَا عليه السلام يَقُولُ:

'Every man's friend is his intellect,[1] and his enemy is his foolishness.'"[2]

صَدِيقُ كُلِّ امْرِئٍ عَقْلُهُ، وَ عَدُوُّهُ جَهْلُهُ.

---

1. It might seem strange that Imam al-Riḍā would say that man's friend is his intellect and his enemy is his foolishness, thereby limiting friendship to intellect and enmity to foolishness, as though man has no other friend or enemy. However, if we examine the role of friends and enemies, we see that his message warrants hyperbole. A friend is one who acts in our best interest and defends us against harm. This is precisely the role intellect plays in our lives. In fact, it is more fitting that we call intellect a friend than any other because, by allowing us to comprehend the existence of God, helping us to worship him, and leading us to everlasting happiness in paradise, it benefits us more than any other friend can. Likewise, an enemy is one who harms us. This is precisely the effect that foolishness—the failure to use our intellect—has on our lives. In fact, since the harm inflicted by our own foolishness is far greater than the harm inflicted by anyone else, it is more fitting that it be called an enemy. It is to convey this message that Imam al-Riḍā phrases his sentence as he does, not to negate the existence of other friends and enemies.

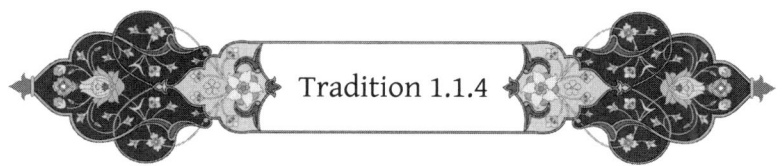

2. Our intellect is only our friend to the extent that we use it. If we leave our intellect idle, we are said to be foolish. Thus, foolishness is not a faculty that exists in parallel with intellect; rather, it is the failure to use our intellect.

TRADITION 1.1.4 TEACHES THE FOLLOWING:

- We should befriend a person who employs his intellect because if his intellect is *his* friend, then it is the friend of his friend as indicated by the proverb of Imam ʿAlī, "Your friends are three...your own friend, your friend's friend, and your enemy's enemy" (*Nahj al-balāghah* proverb 295). Likewise, we should be the enemy of a fool, for if his foolishness is *his* enemy, then it is the enemy of his friend as indicated by the proverb of Imam ʿAlī, "Your enemies are three...your own enemy, your friend's enemy, and your enemy's friend" (*Nahj al-balāghah* proverb 295).
- We should act according to the perceptions of our intellect since it serves our best interest.
- The intellect is more beneficial than a friend is.

Tradition 1.1.5

[Muḥammad ibn Yaḥyā] reported from Aḥmad ibn Muḥammad from Ibn Faḍḍāl from al-Ḥasan ibn al-Jahm that he said, "I told Abū al-Ḥasan [al-Riḍā], 'Among us are those who love [the Prophet's family dearly] and believe as we believe [in your teachings]; however, they do not have that [great] resolve [to act according to your teachings. What is to become of them? Will they be punished for not acting according to their beliefs?]'[1] He replied:

وَ عَنْهُ عَنْ أَحْمَدَ بْنِ مُحَمَّدٍ عَنِ ابْنِ فَضَّالٍ عَنِ الْحَسَنِ بْنِ الْجَهْمِ قَالَ: قُلْتُ لِأَبِي الْحَسَنِ عليه السلام: إِنَّ عِنْدَنَا قَوْماً لَهُمْ مَحَبَّةٌ، وَ لَيْسَتْ لَهُمْ تِلْكَ الْعَزِيمَةُ، يَقُولُونَ بِهَذَا الْقَوْلِ. فَقَالَ:

'They are not among those whom God has reproved.[2] God has only said, "*Take heed, O possessors of insight!*"'"[3]

لَيْسَ أُولَئِكَ مِمَّنْ عَاتَبَ اللَّهُ. إِنَّمَا قَالَ اللَّهُ: ﴿فَاعْتَبِرُوا يَا أُولِي الْأَبْصَارِ﴾.

---

1. We have inferred the questioner's intent through an analysis of the Imam's response and by comparing this tradition to tradition 1.1.32, which narrates what seems to be the same incident through a different chain of transmission. Al-Kulaynī most likely included both narrations because both have a strong chain of transmission and because each one reveals details left out by the other.

2. The Imam's response makes it clear that the people about whom the questioner is asking are not normal people endowed with sufficient intellect to discern good and evil, otherwise they would definitely be reproved by God—

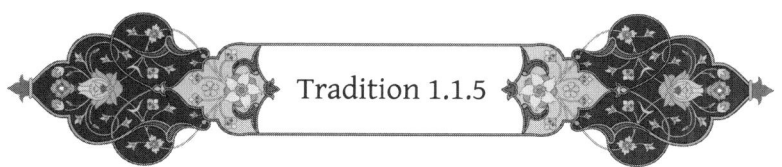

and worse—for their lack of resolve. Rather they are members of a group called *mustaḍʿafūn*, people who have been "made weak" by circumstances beyond their control. In particular, the intellectual capacity of these *mustaḍʿafūn* has not developed fully because of the environment in which they grew up, or because of a lack of education and training, or because of congenital defects like mental retardation. Because God is just and he knows that these people do not have the ability to make sound judgments, he will not punish them more than the extent that their intellectual capacity warrants.

3. This statement is an allusion to Qurʾān 59:2. The message of this verse is as follows: "O you with insight! Take heed of the punishment God meted out to the Jewish tribe Banū al-Naḍīr for breaking their treaty with the Prophet, and know that you may also expect a similar punishment if you betray the Prophet as they did." Imam al-Ṣādiq mentions verse 59:2 to explain why the people in question are not the object of God's reproof in the Qurʾān despite their lack of resolve and obedience. According to this verse, God commanded only those with insight—which is a faculty of the intellect—to "take heed." If they do not take heed, then God is justified in reproving them. On the other hand, he has not commanded those without insight to "take heed," since they do not have the faculty to do so; thus, he is not justified in reproving them, much less punishing them.

TRADITION 1.1.5 TEACHES THE FOLLOWING:

- God has not burdened the weak of intellect with obligations and thus does not hold them accountable for those obligations except to the extent of their intellect.
- Love of the Prophet and his family is separable from obedience to them, so all who love them are not necessarily obedient to them.

Tradition 1.1.6

أَحْمَدُ بْنُ إِدْرِيسَ عَنْ مُحَمَّدِ بْنِ حَسَّانَ عَنْ أَبِي مُحَمَّدٍ الرَّازِيِّ عَنْ سَيْفِ بْنِ عَمِيرَةَ عَنْ إِسْحَاقَ بْنِ عَمَّارٍ قَالَ: قَالَ أَبُو عَبْدِ اللَّهِ عليه السلام:

Aḥmad ibn Idrīs reported from Muḥammad ibn Ḥassān from Abū Muḥammad al-Rāzī from Sayf ibn ʿAmīrah from Isḥāq ibn ʿĀmmār that Abū ʿAbd Allāh [al-Ṣādiq] said:

مَنْ كَانَ عَاقِلًا كَانَ لَهُ دِينٌ، وَ مَنْ كَانَ لَهُ دِينٌ دَخَلَ الْجَنَّةَ.

"He who employs his intellect shall be devoted to [the true] religion,[1] and he who is devoted to [the true] religion shall enter the garden."[2]

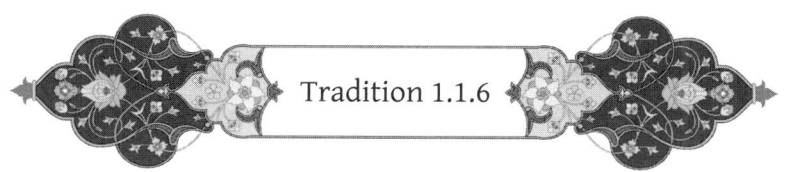

1. We have inferred the qualifier "true" even though it does not exist in the words of the Imam. It is not uncommon for such a qualifier to be omitted in Arabic where contextual clues serve as a replacement. For instance, when al-Khiḍr explains to Moses why he knocked a hole in the hull of the boat in which they were sailing, he says there was a king approaching them who confiscated "every boat" he could find, apparently to strengthen his naval fleet (Qurʾān 18:79). The question arises: Why would the king forgo this boat just because it had a hole in it? Is a boat with a hole in it not a boat? The answer is that he did not confiscate "*every* boat," rather every *sound* boat. However, the verse does not mention the qualifier "sound" because it is clear that al-Khiḍr's unconventional service would have been pointless had the king really been after *every* boat, even those with holes in them. Similarly, in this tradition, the Imam speaks only of "religion" and does not specify whether he means the *true* religion, Islam, or any religion. What clues us in to the existence of such a qualifier is his statement, "he who is devoted to religion shall enter the garden," for it is clear to anyone who knows the Qurʾān that God has no tolerance for those who are devoted to idolatry or any other religion and would not allow them into paradise. He states unequivocally, "Should anyone follow a religion other than Islam, it shall never be accepted from him" (Qurʾān 3:85). Thus, it is clear that Imam al-Ṣādiq intended the *true* religion, Islam, not just *any* religion.

2. Imam al-Ṣādiq has used a perfect syllogism whose logical conclusion is, "He who employs his intellect shall enter the garden (i.e., paradise)." This unqualified statement applies to non-Muslims and Muslims alike.

If a non-Muslim uses his intellect, he will discern the truth that is Islam from the falsehood in every other religion and—assuming he acts on his newfound understanding—will become Muslim. For this reason, the intellect is called a guide for all people (*al-Kāfī* 1.1.23), and for this reason, the Qurʾān repeatedly calls on the unbelievers to use their intellect. For instance, Abraham tells the people of Kūthā Rubā, when they admit that their gods can neither speak in their own defense nor harm nor benefit their devotees, "Fie on you and what you worship besides God. Will you then not employ your intellect?" (Qurʾān 21:67).

Likewise, if a Muslim uses his intellect, he will discern the overwhelming benefit of devotion to the tenets of Islamic faith and practice and—assuming he acts on his newfound understanding—will become a *devout* Muslim. For this reason, intellect is called a guide for the believer (*al-Kāfī* 1.1.24). Thus, we see that anyone who uses his intellect, whether he be Muslim or non-Muslim—assuming he acts on what his intellect tells him—will enter paradise.

TRADITION 1.1.6 TEACHES THE FOLLOWING:

- If a non-Muslim uses his intellect, it will guide him to Islam.
- If a Muslim uses his intellect, it will guide him to be more devout.
- The intellect alone cannot lead us to paradise except by means of the divine guidance embodied in true religion.

- This tradition only indicates that the intellect leads to devoutness. It does not imply that devoutness is necessarily an indicator of intellect.

Tradition 1.1.7

A number of our fellow Shīʿah reported from Aḥmad ibn Muḥammad ibn Khālid from al-Ḥasan ibn ʿAlī ibn Yaqṭīn from Muḥammad ibn Sinān from Abū al-Jārūd that Abū Jaʿfar [al-Bāqir] said:

عِدَّةٌ مِنْ أَصْحَابِنَا عَنْ أَحْمَدَ بْنِ مُحَمَّدِ بْنِ خَالِدٍ عَنِ الْحَسَنِ بْنِ عَلِيِّ بْنِ يَقْطِينٍ عَنْ مُحَمَّدِ بْنِ سِنَانٍ عَنْ أَبِي الْجَارُودِ عَنْ أَبِي جَعْفَرٍ عليه السلام قَالَ:

"God will be exacting with his servants at the reckoning on the Day of Resurrection only to the extent that he gave them intellect in the temporal world."

إِنَّمَا يُدَاقُّ اللَّهُ الْعِبَادَ فِي الْحِسَابِ يَوْمَ الْقِيَامَةِ عَلَى قَدْرِ مَا آتَاهُمْ مِنَ الْعُقُولِ فِي الدُّنْيَا.

TRADITION 1.1.7 TEACHES THE FOLLOWING:

- The severity of a person's judgment does not exceed his intellectual capacity.
- Different people have different intellectual capacities.
- God's clemency is not necessarily an indication of one's virtue; rather it could indicate one's deficient intellectual capacity.

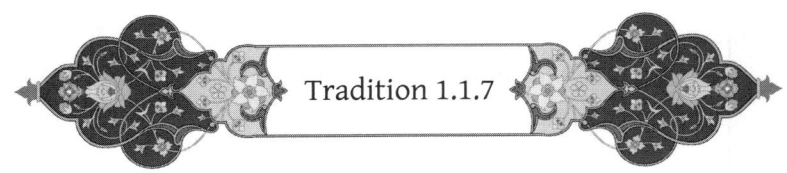

Tradition 1.1.8

ʿAlī ibn Muḥammad ibn ʿAbd Allāh reported from Ibrāhīm ibn Isḥāq al-Aḥmar from Muḥammad ibn Sulaymān al-Daylamī from his father that he said, "I told Abū ʿAbd Allāh [al-Ṣādiq], 'So and so[1] [is outstanding] in worship, devotion, and virtue!' He asked:

عَلِيُّ بْنُ مُحَمَّدِ بْنِ عَبْدِ اللَّهِ عَنْ إِبْرَاهِيمَ بْنِ إِسْحَاقَ الْأَحْمَرِ عَنْ مُحَمَّدِ بْنِ سُلَيْمَانَ الدَّيْلَمِيِّ عَنْ أَبِيهِ قَالَ قُلْتُ لِأَبِي عَبْدِ اللَّهِ عليه السلام : فُلَانٌ مِنْ عِبَادَتِهِ وَ دِينِهِ وَ فَضْلِهِ! فَقَالَ:

'How is his intellect?'

كَيْفَ عَقْلُهُ؟

I replied, 'I do not know.' Then he said:

قُلْتُ: لَا أَدْرِي. فَقَالَ:

'Reward [for goodness and virtue] is proportional to intellect [as indicated by the following story.] A man from the Israelites used to worship God on an oceanic island that was lush green, covered with trees, with a panoramic view of the water. One of the angels passed by him [and witnessed his acts of piety and wished to know his reward,] so he said, "My Lord, show me the reward of this servant of yours." God, the Exalted, showed it to him, and the angel considered it a pittance

إِنَّ الثَّوَابَ عَلَى قَدْرِ الْعَقْلِ. إِنَّ رَجُلًا مِنْ بَنِي إِسْرَائِيلَ كَانَ يَعْبُدُ اللَّهَ فِي جَزِيرَةٍ مِنْ جَزَائِرِ الْبَحْرِ خَضْرَاءَ نَضِرَةٍ، كَثِيرَةِ الشَّجَرِ، ظَاهِرَةِ الْمَاءِ. وَ إِنَّ مَلَكاً مِنَ الْمَلَائِكَةِ مَرَّ بِهِ فَقَالَ: يَا رَبِّ، أَرِنِي ثَوَابَ عَبْدِكَ هَذَا. فَأَرَاهُ اللَّهُ تَعَالَى ذَلِكَ فَاسْتَقَلَّهُ الْمَلَكُ. فَأَوْحَى اللَّهُ تَعَالَى إِلَيْهِ أَنِ اصْحَبْهُ. فَأَتَاهُ الْمَلَكُ فِي صُورَةِ إِنْسِيٍّ، فَقَالَ لَهُ: مَنْ أَنْتَ؟ قَالَ: أَنَا رَجُلٌ عَابِدٌ بَلَغَنِي مَكَانُكَ

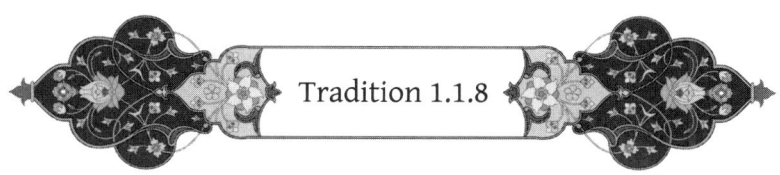

[compared to his great acts of piety].[2] So God, the Exalted, communicated to him saying, "Spend some time with him." The angel came to him in the form of a man. The Jewish man asked, "Who are you?" The angel replied, "I am a pious man. News reached me of this place of yours and of your acts of worship in this place, so I have come to worship God with you."[3] He remained with him that whole day. When morning came, the angel said to him, "This place of yours is most pristine and ought to be used for nothing but worship." The pious man said, "This place of ours does have a flaw." The angel asked, "And what is it?" He said, "Our Lord does not have any animals. If only he had a donkey, we could graze it on this land, for this pasture is being wasted." The angel asked him, "[You say] your Lord does not have a donkey?" He said, "If he had a donkey, this pasture would not be wasted." Thereat God communicated to the angel saying, "I shall only reward him in proportion to his intellect.""'[4]

وَ عِبَادَتُكَ فِي هَـذَا الْمَكَانِ، فَأَتَيْتُكَ لِأَعْبُدَ اللَّهَ مَعَكَ. فَكَانَ مَعَهُ يَوْمَهُ ذَلِكَ. فَلَمَّا أَصْبَحَ قَالَ لَهُ الْمَلَكُ: إِنَّ مَكَانَكَ لَنَزِهٌ وَ مَا يَصْلُحُ إِلَّا لِلْعِبَادَةِ. فَقَالَ لَهُ الْعَابِدُ: إِنَّ لِمَكَانِنَا هَذَا عَيْباً. فَقَالَ لَهُ: وَ مَا هُوَ؟ قَالَ: لَيْسَ لِرَبِّنَا بَهِيمَةٌ. فَلَوْ كَانَ لَهُ حِمَارٌ رَعَيْنَاهُ فِي هَذَا الْمَوْضِعِ. فَإِنَّ هَذَا الْحَشِيشَ يَضِيعُ. فَقَالَ لَهُ ذَلِكَ الْمَلَكُ: وَ مَا لِرَبِّكَ حِمَارٌ؟ فَقَالَ: لَوْ كَانَ لَهُ حِمَارٌ مَا كَانَ يَضِيعُ مِثْلُ هَذَا الْحَشِيشِ. فَأَوْحَى اللَّهُ إِلَى الْمَلَكِ: إِنَّمَا أُثِيبُهُ عَلَى قَدْرِ عَقْلِهِ.

---

1. Most likely Sulaymān mentioned the person's name when he originally praised him before Imam al-Ṣādiq; however, when he recounted the story for his son, he replaced it with the generic "so-and-so" because he did not see any use in mentioning the name of someone unknown to his son.

2. The angel's reaction to the man's reward and the subsequent lesson he is taught indicate that this angel is fallible in his understanding. However, we should note that his devaluation of God's reward is not an objection to divine justice, for that would contradict the sinless nature of all angels. Rather he simply wishes to know the reason for God's decision. In this way, this tradition is similar to the story of the angels in the Qurʾān who question why God wishes to create a being "who will cause corruption and spill blood" (2:30).

3. All three statements made by the angel are apparently false, for he is not a man, but an angel; news of the pious man did not *reach* him; rather, he passed by and saw him himself; and he did not come to worship with him, but to learn firsthand of the wisdom in God's judgment. Since angels are infallible, we must consider either of the following justifications for his false statements.

- He might have used double entendre (*tawriyah*), saying one thing and meaning another, as Abraham did—according to one justification—when he told his townspeople, "I am ill," (Qurʾān 37:89), or when he said about the sun, "This is my Lord; this is greater" (Qurʾān 6:78).
- Alternatively, he might have lied because he correctly deemed his duty before God to visit this man and regain his conviction in divine justice more important than his duty to speak the truth, and he saw that he could not accomplish the former without sacrificing the latter.

4. Three points in this story illustrate this pious man's weak intellectual capacity:

- He believes God to have a physical body and that he needs a donkey for transportation.

- He believes God has created the island's pasture in vain.
- He thinks the only use for green grass is to graze one's animals.

If he had greater powers of intellect:

- he would realize that God is incorporeal and needs nothing, least of all a donkey;
- he would realize that God creates nothing without purpose;
- he would stretch his imagination to see that green grass has so many more purposes than only fodder for animals.

TRADITION 1.1.8 TEACHES THE FOLLOWING:

- Intellect, and not the apparent virtue of an act, is the standard for reward.
- The external form of a deed done by one with intellect and one without is the same, while the reality of each one's deed is vastly different.
- A pious person with scant intellect does not deserve much praise.
- God does not disregard even the acts of people like the Jewish man from this story; rather, he rewards them in proportion to their intellectual capacity.
- Angels can appear in human form and talk with people.
- We must not think the wisdom behind God's creation is limited to what our deficient minds can comprehend.
- The best place for worship is a pristine place.
- The angel's comment that such a pristine place "ought to be used for nothing but worship" shows that those with intellect strive to use God's blessings for the best purposes.

Tradition 1.1.9

عَلِيُّ بْنُ إِبْرَاهِيمَ عَنْ أَبِيهِ عَنِ النَّوْفَلِيِّ عَنِ السَّكُونِيِّ عَنْ أَبِي عَبْدِ اللَّهِ عليه السلام قَالَ:

ʿAlī ibn Ibrāhīm reported from his father from al-Nawfalī from al-Sakūnī that Abū ʿAbd Allāh [al-Ṣādiq] said:

قَالَ رَسُولُ اللَّهِ صلى الله عليه وآله : إِذَا بَلَغَكُمْ عَنْ رَجُلٍ حُسْنُ حَالٍ فَانْظُرُوا فِي حُسْنِ عَقْلِهِ، فَإِنَّمَا يُجَازَى بِعَقْلِهِ.

"The Messenger of God said, 'If news reaches you of a man's favorable disposition [in deeds and character], then examine the level of his intellect, for he shall only be rewarded according to his intellect.'"

TRADITION 1.1.9 TEACHES THE FOLLOWING:

- The standard for God's judgment is intellect.
- One's apparent disposition is no indication of the strength of one's intellect.
- One's apparent disposition is no indication of one's reward.
- We should evaluate others—as far as possible—based on real, not superficial, traits.

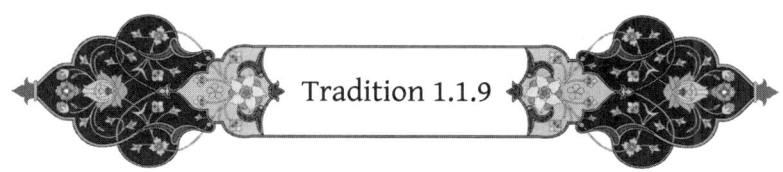

Tradition 1.1.10

Muḥammad ibn Yaḥyā reported from Aḥmad ibn Muḥammad from Ibn Maḥbūb from ʿAbd Allah ibn Sinān [that] he said, "I mentioned to Abū ʿAbd Allāh [al-Ṣādiq] a man who suffered from [incessant doubts about his] ablutions and prayers, and [as I described the man's circumstances,] I said, 'He is a rational man.' Abū ʿAbd Allāh retorted:

مُحَمَّدُ بْنُ يَحْيَى عَنْ أَحْمَدَ بْنِ مُحَمَّدٍ عَنِ ابْنِ مَحْبُوبٍ عَنْ عَبْدِ اللَّهِ بْنِ سِنَانٍ قَالَ: ذَكَرْتُ لِأَبِي عَبْدِ اللَّهِ عليه السلام رَجُلًا مُبْتَلًى بِالْوُضُوءِ وَ الصَّلَاةِ، وَ قُلْتُ: هُوَ رَجُلٌ عَاقِلٌ. فَقَالَ أَبُو عَبْدِ اللَّهِ:

'What kind of reason does he have when he obeys Satan?'[1]

وَ أَيُّ عَقْلٍ لَهُ وَ هُوَ يُطِيعُ الشَّيْطَانَ؟

I asked him, 'How does he obey Satan?' He replied:

فَقُلْتُ لَهُ: وَ كَيْفَ يُطِيعُ الشَّيْطَانَ؟ فَقَالَ:

'Just ask him where these [doubts] that enter his mind come from, and he will tell you, "[They are] the work of Satan."'"

سَلْهُ هَذَا الَّذِي يَأْتِيهِ مِنْ أَيِّ شَيْءٍ هُوَ؟ فَإِنَّهُ يَقُولُ لَكَ: مِنْ عَمَلِ الشَّيْطَانِ.

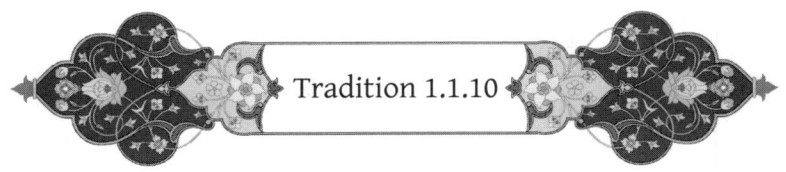

1. This companion understands that the man's doubts are a sickness and has come to the Imam to ask how to treat one who is suffering from them. As he describes the man, he mentions that he is generally a rational person who employs his intellect. At this point, the Imam interjects and says that such a man practically has no intellect, since he fails to act according to the dictates of his intellect. If only he would use his intellect and act accordingly, he would realize that he is in Satan's clutches and would deliver himself by refusing to obey his satanic insinuations.

TRADITION 1.1.10 TEACHES THE FOLLOWING:

- One with intellect must not pay heed to baseless doubts.
- Paranoia (*waswasah*) about acts of worship is the work of Satan.
- To pay heed to one's baseless doubts is to act in collusion with Satan and, thus, is prohibited.

Tradition 1.1.11

A number of our fellow Shīʿah reported from Aḥmad ibn Muḥammad ibn Khālid from one of his teachers that he recounted [without mentioning his source] that the Messenger of God said:

عِدَّةٌ مِنْ أَصْحَابِنَا عَنْ أَحْمَدَ بْنِ مُحَمَّدِ بْنِ خَالِدٍ عَنْ بَعْضِ أَصْحَابِهِ رَفَعَهُ قَالَ: قَالَ رَسُولُ اللَّهِ ﷺ:

"God has not apportioned anything for his servants better than the intellect. Thus, the sleep of one who employs his intellect is better than a fool's vigil, and for one who employs his intellect to remain homebound and sedentary is better than the journeying of a fool [in God's service].[1]

مَا قَسَمَ اللَّهُ لِلْعِبَادِ شَيْئاً أَفْضَلَ مِنَ الْعَقْلِ، فَنَوْمُ الْعَاقِلِ أَفْضَلُ مِنْ سَهَرِ الْجَاهِلِ، وَ إِقَامَةُ الْعَاقِلِ أَفْضَلُ مِنْ شُخُوصِ الْجَاهِلِ.

"God did not send a single prophet or messenger[2] until he perfected his intellect and his intellect became better than the combined intellectual capacities of his people. The [mere] intention of a prophet is better than the tireless efforts of all others.[3]

وَ لَا بَعَثَ اللَّهُ نَبِيّاً وَ لَا رَسُولًا حَتَّى يَسْتَكْمِلَ الْعَقْلَ وَ يَكُونَ عَقْلُهُ أَفْضَلَ مِنْ جَمِيعِ عُقُولِ أُمَّتِهِ. وَ مَا يُضْمِرُ النَّبِيُّ فِي نَفْسِهِ أَفْضَلُ مِنِ اجْتِهَادِ الْمُجْتَهِدِينَ.

"A servant [of God] cannot fulfill his obligations to God unless he knows

وَ مَا أَدَّى الْعَبْدُ فَرَائِضَ اللَّهِ حَتَّى عَقَلَ

God [as he has described himself].[4]

عَنْهُ.

"The devotions of all worshippers combined [if they lack intellect] cannot reach the station attained by a [single] person with intellect [through his devotions].[5]

وَ لَا بَلَغَ جَمِيعُ الْعَابِدِينَ فِي فَضْلِ عِبَادَتِهِمْ مَا بَلَغَ الْعَاقِلُ.

"People with intellect are those [about] whom God has said, *'Nobody heeds reminders except the possessors of intellect.'*"[6]

وَ الْعُقَلَاءُ هُمْ أُولُو الْأَلْبَابِ الَّذِينَ قَالَ اللَّهُ تَعَالَى : ﴿وَ مَا يَتَذَكَّرُ إِلَّا أُولُوا الْأَلْبَابِ﴾.

---

1. A characteristic of a person who employs his intellect is that he considers all available options and chooses the one that is most important and most beneficial. If he chooses to sleep rather than observe the night vigil in worship, it is because he has weighed his options and concluded that under his current circumstances, the former holds more benefit for him than the latter. A fool on the other hand, insofar as he does not use his intellect, chooses his course based on whims and fancies without any consideration for priorities. If he chooses to forgo sleep and spend the night in worship, it is not because he has weighed his options, but simply because he is acting on impulse or because it is his habit. Whether or not his sleepless night and his consequent fatigue will prevent him from fulfilling his worldly and Godly obligations the next day is irrelevant to him. Thus, the meaning of this portion of the tradition is that intellect is the best faculty God has given man because it is the tool by which man chooses the best course of action, even though his choice may seem to be the lesser of two options, as is the case with sleep and remaining homebound. Likewise, the fool who fails to make use of God's gift of intellect chooses according to habit and fancy what may, in and of itself, seem to be the better of two choices like prayer and journeying in God's service. Accordingly, there is nothing special about the four actions mentioned in the tradition; rather, they are simply examples that illustrate the greatness of this blessing. If anything, sleep and vigil represent one's choices with regard to acts of worship, and remaining homebound and journeying represent one's choices with regard to other human activities such as going out to earn a living.

2. For a detailed discussion of the differences between a prophet and messenger, see *al-Kāfī* 4.3.1-4.

3. This segment of the tradition is analogous to the tradition's first segment where one person's sleep was compared to another's vigil. Because a prophet has perfect powers of intellect, he carefully considers all his options and evaluates the outcome of each. Appropriately, whatever he decides, or simply intends, to do is the best possible action under the circumstances. This tradition tells us that such a solid and deliberate intention—despite the fact that making an intention is an effortless act of the mind—far outweighs all the tireless exertion of all people combined if their actions are not based on such exercise of intellect.

4. We find the phrase "*ʿaqala ʿan Allāh*" four times in *The Book of Intellect and Foolishness*. While no explanation of this phrase is found in Arabic lexicons, we can deduce its meaning from its usage in this book and in other traditions of the Prophet and imams. The phrase indicates knowledge of God as he has described himself, not as we may imagine him or as people may describe him. Imam al-Ḥasan uses this phrase to describe the mission of the prophets in the following tradition: "God raised the prophets among them as bearers of glad tidings and as warners so that those who perish do so despite clear evidence, and those who live do so based on clear evidence; and so his servants may know of their Lord what they knew not, and thus know him as their Lord after having known him not" (*Biḥār al-anwār* 43.1.17.6).

5. The Prophet's statement here offers a clear justification for another tradition that is attributed to him. It is reported that he said, "ʿAlī's single blow to ʿAmr ibn ʿAbd Wadd in the Battle of the Trench (*al-khandaq*) was better than the worship of all [other] humans and jinn combined" (*Iqbāl al-aʿmāl* p.466).

6. Qurʾān 2:269

At first glance, it seems that the sentences of this tradition are unrelated except that they all extol intellect. However, there are three main ideas that serve to unify its various parts. The tradition's crux is that intellect is the greatest of God's gifts to humankind. It goes on to explain two reasons for its greatness. First, God's greatest act with respect to humankind, the guidance he offers them through his prophets, depends on the perfection of the faculty of intellect in his prophets. Second, humankind's greatest act, which is the fulfillment of their duty to God, cannot happen if they do not possess the faculty of intellect.

TRADITION 1.1.11 TEACHES THE FOLLOWING:

- Every choice a person with intellect makes is better than every choice a foolish person makes.
- One must know God as he has described himself to fulfill one's duties to him.
- Intellect is what gives value to worship.
- Only a person with intellect heeds a reminder.
- Prophets have the strongest intellects of all people, and it is because of this strength that they are chosen as prophets and sent to guide people.
- Every prophet is better than all members of his community combined.

Tradition 1.1.12

أَبُو عَبْدِ اللَّهِ الْأَشْعَرِيُّ عَنْ بَعْضِ أَصْحَابِنَا رَفَعَهُ عَنْ هِشَامِ بْنِ الْحَكَمِ قَالَ: قَالَ لِي أَبُو الْحَسَنِ مُوسَى بْنُ جَعْفَرٍ عليه السلام:

Abū ʿAbd Allāh al-Ashʿarī reported from one of our scholars that he reported [without mentioning his source] from Hishām ibn al-Ḥakam[1] that he said, "Abū al-Ḥasan Mūsā ibn Jaʿfar [al-Kāẓim] said to me:

Section 1

يَا هِشَامُ، إِنَّ اللَّهَ تَبَارَكَ وَتَعَالَى بَشَّرَ أَهْلَ الْعَقْلِ وَالْفَهْمِ فِي كِتَابِهِ، فَقَالَ: ﴿فَبَشِّرْ عِبَادِ الَّذِينَ يَسْتَمِعُونَ الْقَوْلَ فَيَتَّبِعُونَ أَحْسَنَهُ، أُولَئِكَ الَّذِينَ هَدَاهُمُ اللَّهُ، وَأُولَئِكَ هُمْ أُولُوا الْأَلْبَابِ﴾.

'O Hishām! God—exalted and good—has given glad tidings in his book to the possessors of intellect and comprehension saying,[2] "*So give glad tidings to those servants of mine who listen to what is said and then follow the best of it.*[3] *Those are the ones whom God has guided, and those alone are the possessors of intellect.*"

---

1. Hishām ibn al-Ḥakam was a devoted disciple of Imam al-Ṣādiq and Imam al-Kāẓim. His faith was firm, his knowledge vast, and he was renowned as an eloquent, quick-witted debater who challenged and defeated the best scholars of his time. For these qualities, Imam al-Kāẓim shared with him the wisdom entailed in this tradition.

2. Qurʾān 39:17-8

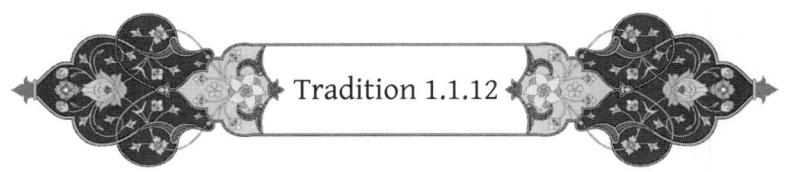

3. Some commentators have construed the word *qawl* ("what is said") as a specific reference to the Qurʾān. Others have construed it to mean anything that is said by anyone with regard to anything. There is no evidence for restricting this phrase to the Qurʾān. However, it is also inappropriate to broaden its meaning to include *anything* that is said by *anyone* with regard to *anything*. Rather, there are clues within the verse that provide us with two qualifiers for "what is said." First, since the people in the verse "listen to what is said and then follow the best of it," "what is said" must be something that can be "followed." This includes statements related to religious belief and practice. But it excludes statements that cannot be "followed" through belief or action; for instance, things that are said about historical events that have no clear relation to a person's religious belief and action. Second, it must be possible for the intellect to independently evaluate the relative goodness of "what is said," for the verse praises these people for listening to "what is said," evaluating its strengths and weaknesses, and then following the best. This praise, therefore, presupposes that we are talking about something that the intellect can independently evaluate. Divine laws, on the other hand, are outside the jurisdiction of intellect. Once we identify the correct source of divine law using our intellect, we must simply take the law at face value. Our intellect has no power, for instance, to determine whether, in *wuḍūʾ* (ablutions before prayer), it is better to wash our arm from the elbow to the fingertips or vice versa.

Taking all this into consideration, we can identify the following examples for this verse. An example in the realm of beliefs is for a person to listen to the arguments for the existence of only one god and the arguments for atheism or polytheism. A person with a strong intellect would weigh the arguments, determine that the former is better (i.e. it is supported by rational arguments and empirical evidence) and follow it to the exclusion of the latter. An example in the realm of action is for a person to listen to the arguments for and against *taqlīd* (the practice of referring to a qualified jurist in religious matters of practical importance). Again, a person with intellect will weigh the arguments, determine that the arguments *for taqlīd* are more sound than those *against* it, and follow it as a means of determining his duty before God.

It is important to note that this verse is not trying to encourage all people to listen to all that is said. It only praises those who "listen to what is said" insofar as they can "follow the best of it." That they follow the best of "what is said" presupposes that they possess the requisite intellect to determine what is best. If they do not, then listening to all that is said is foolhardy, since it could lead to their confusion and ultimately to their misguidance.

SECTION 1 OF TRADITION 1.1.12 TEACHES THE FOLLOWING:

- God holds those with a strong intellect in high esteem, for he calls them "my servants" and conveys tidings to them through his Prophet.
- The reason for God's high esteem for those with a strong intellect is that they listen to various things that are said, use their intellects to determine which is best, and then follow the best.
- Those with weaker intellects should not listen to everything that is said, for they do not possess the ability to determine which among them is best.

Section 2

'O Hishām! God—exalted and good—has perfected [the efficacy of] his divine guides[1] for people's benefit by [endowing people with] intellect;[2] has aided his prophets with [the power of] eloquent speech; and has guided people to know that he is their Lord through verses [in his book].[3] For he has said,[4] "*Your god is one; there is no god but him;*[5] *[he is] the All-Beneficent, the Ever-Merciful. In the creation of the sky and the earth, and the alternation of night and day,*[6] *and the ships that sail at sea for people's benefit, and [in] the water that God sends down from the sky—by which he revives the earth after its death and scatters therein every kind of animal; [in] the changing of the winds, and [in] the clouds, which have been subjugated [by the wind] between the sky and the earth, are signs for people who use their intellect.*"[7]

يَا هِشَامُ، إِنَّ اللَّهَ تَبَارَكَ وَتَعَالَى أَكْمَلَ لِلنَّاسِ الْحُجَجَ بِالْعُقُولِ، وَنَصَرَ النَّبِيِّينَ بِالْبَيَانِ، وَدَلَّهُمْ عَلَى رُبُوبِيَّتِهِ بِالْأَدِلَّةِ، فَقَالَ: ﴿وَإِلٰهُكُمْ إِلٰهٌ واحِدٌ، لا إِلٰهَ إِلَّا هُوَ، الرَّحْمٰنُ الرَّحِيمُ. إِنَّ فِي خَلْقِ السَّماواتِ وَالْأَرْضِ وَاخْتِلافِ اللَّيْلِ وَالنَّهارِ وَالْفُلْكِ الَّتِي تَجْرِي فِي الْبَحْرِ بِما يَنْفَعُ النَّاسَ وَما أَنْزَلَ اللَّهُ مِنَ السَّماءِ مِنْ ماءٍ فَأَحْيا بِهِ الْأَرْضَ بَعْدَ مَوْتِها وَبَثَّ فِيها مِنْ كُلِّ دابَّةٍ وَتَصْرِيفِ الرِّياحِ وَالسَّحابِ الْمُسَخَّرِ بَيْنَ السَّماءِ وَالْأَرْضِ لَآياتٍ لِقَوْمٍ يَعْقِلُونَ﴾.

---

1. The word *ḥujjah* literally means "proof" or "evidence." A *ḥujjah* is literally evidence used to argue against someone. God's prophets and imams are called *ḥujaj* (the plural of *ḥujjah*) for two reasons. First, God will argue on the Day of Judgment against those who rejected his religion by calling on these divine guides and establishing that they fulfilled their mission by communicating God's guidance to all people, thereby leaving no room for anyone to say, "We did not know." Second, in the temporal world, the believers use the character and teachings of these divine guides to argue against the unbelievers. Thus, because God and the believers use these divine guides as evidence against the unbelievers they are known as *ḥujaj*. While the terms *ḥujjah* and *ḥujaj* clearly refer to God's divine guides for most Shīʿah who are familiar with this terminology, the English words "proof" and "argument" do not convey this meaning clearly at all. For this reason, we have translated the word *ḥujjaj* simply as "divine guides."

2. Clearly, all the divine guides in the world, no matter how convincing they may be, could not guide a single one of us if it were not for the faculty of intellect that God has placed in each of us. Thus, the intellect complements the role of the divine guides by allowing us to comprehend their teachings.

3. Up to here, this section of the tradition has outlined the key components of God's system of guidance. On the one hand, he has sent divine guides endowed with the power of eloquent speech and with divine scripture. On the other, he has endowed human beings with the intellect necessary to comprehend this guidance and conclude from it that God is indeed their Lord.

4. Qurʾān 2:163-4

5. We might think saying, "Your god is one" is a sufficient statement of God's oneness, and that there is no need to follow it with, "There is no god but him." On the contrary, the first phrase specifies only that *our* god is one. It does not preclude the possibility that *others* may have multiple gods. The phrase, "There is no god but him," serves to preempt this possibility and establish that there is only one god *for all people*.

6. The "alternation of night and day" is a sign of God's lordship insofar as it is caused by the perpetual rotation of the earth on its axis. The forces involved in this rotation, the precise timing of night and day, and the vital role they play in the proper functioning of the world as we know it should all give us pause to think of him who made it so.

This phrase could alternately be translated as "the variations in the night and day," for the systematic elongation of summer days and winter nights and the proportionate shortening of summer nights and winter days is also a sign of God's lordship.

7. Imam al-Kāẓim introduces these two verses (2:163-4) as an example of verses in which God has guided us to know that he is our Lord. To understand why he has cited these verses, we must uncover the connection between the subject of these verses and God's lordship. Verse 163 makes the assertion that there is only one *ilāh* or "god worthy of worship." People only worship, through service and prayer, what they believe has the power to control their circumstances and has taken on the management of their affairs. It is these two components that define a *rabb* or "lord." As a result, by claiming that there is only one *ilāh* or "god worthy of worship," verse 163 is, by the same token, claiming that there is only one *rabb* or "lord."

Up to here, we are presented with an assertion but no supporting evidence. Verse 164 provides the missing evidence. It encourages us to look at the natural world around us. Since these phenomena are "signs for people who use their intellect," we should ponder over them with an analytical mind. What we see is that the water in the sea is turned to vapor by the heat of the sun; the water vapor rises and condenses forming clouds; the clouds are pushed inland by the wind until they pour down rain on the surface of the earth; the rain and sun allow plants to grow; animals graze on the fresh herbage, and human beings feast on both plant and animal. In short, every part of the world around us is intrinsically interconnected with every other part forming a single natural system. A single system, if it is to function as seamlessly as the world around us, must be managed by a single lord, for a lord, by definition, has absolute sovereignty over his subjects and provides for all their needs. In the example above, the sea needs the sun to make its water evaporate, and then the wind to push its clouds inland. The plants need the rain borne by these clouds, along with the sun, to grow. Animals in turn need the plants, and human beings need plants and animals. We can conclude that the lord of all of these components is one, for they are all parts of one seamless system. If, on the other hand, each component were under the auspices of a separate lord, we would expect a total lack of coordination in the management of these parts: the god of the sea would bar the god of the sun from stealing his water; the god of the sun might decide not to shine on the sea anymore; the god of the wind might make his wind blow in another direction preventing rain from reaching inland; without rain the god of agriculture would not be able to make his plants grow, and so on. In a similar way, every natural phenomenon that is part of this single, seamless, interconnected system is necessarily under the lordship of the one Lord, the one God. Thus, these two verses first assert that our Lord is one, and then invite us to prove this to ourselves by appealing to our intellect and guiding it to parts of the natural world from which we can confirm that he is indeed one.

SECTION 2 OF TRADITION 1.1.12 TEACHES THE FOLLOWING:

- The divine guides could not guide people if people were not endowed with intellect.
- The intellect would be ineffectual in guiding man if it were not for the divine guides.
- God gave all his prophets the gift of articulate speech.
- Human intellect is mentioned here as the perfect complement to divine guidance. This implies that the dictates of pure intellect are infallible and perfect; otherwise, it would not complete and perfect the circle of guidance.
- The intellect plays a vital role in helping us to know our Lord, since the Qurʾān has relied upon our intellect to draw the correct conclusion from the pieces of evidence in 2:164.
- The natural phenomena mentioned in 2:164, and by extension, all other natural phenomena, contain evidence for those with intellect to recognize that God is the manager of all affairs of the cosmos.

Section 3

'O Hishām! God has made such verses a guide [for people] to know him, by knowing that there is someone managing their affairs, [and that he is that someone]. For he has said,[1] "He has subjugated night, day, the sun, and the moon for your benefit;[2] and the stars have been subjugated by his command. Indeed, there is a sign in this for people who use their intellect."

يَا هِشَامُ، قَدْ جَعَلَ اللَّهُ ذَلِكَ دَلِيلًا عَلَى مَعْرِفَتِهِ بِأَنَّ لَهُمْ مُدَبِّراً، فَقَالَ: ﴿وَسَخَّرَ لَكُمُ اللَّيْلَ وَالنَّهَارَ وَالشَّمْسَ وَالْقَمَرَ وَالنُّجُومُ مُسَخَّرَاتٌ بِأَمْرِهِ، إِنَّ فِي ذَلِكَ لَآيَاتٍ لِقَوْمٍ يَعْقِلُونَ﴾.

He has also said,[3] "He is the one who created you from dust,[4] then from a sperm, then from a clinging mass, then he brings you forth as infants, then [he nourishes you] so that you reach your prime and then grow old. However, among you are those who die before [reaching some of] these stages. [In all cases, we sustain you] until you reach an age specified [for you]. [We do all this] in hopes that you may use your intellect."[5]

وَقَالَ: ﴿هُوَ الَّذِي خَلَقَكُمْ مِنْ تُرَابٍ ثُمَّ مِنْ نُطْفَةٍ ثُمَّ مِنْ عَلَقَةٍ ثُمَّ يُخْرِجُكُمْ طِفْلًا ثُمَّ لِتَبْلُغُوا أَشُدَّكُمْ ثُمَّ لِتَكُونُوا شُيُوخاً. وَمِنْكُمْ مَنْ يُتَوَفَّى مِنْ قَبْلُ. وَلِتَبْلُغُوا أَجَلًا مُسَمًّى وَلَعَلَّكُمْ تَعْقِلُونَ﴾.

He has also said,[6] "In the alternation of night and day, and the provision[7] that God sends down from the sky—by which he revives the earth after its death; and [in] the changing of the winds, and [in] the clouds, which have been subjugated [by the wind] between the sky and the earth are signs for people who use their

وَقَالَ: ﴿إِنَّ فِي اخْتِلَافِ اللَّيْلِ وَالنَّهَارِ وَمَا أَنْزَلَ اللَّهُ مِنَ السَّمَاءِ مِنْ رِزْقٍ فَأَحْيَا بِهِ الْأَرْضَ بَعْدَ مَوْتِهَا وَتَصْرِيفِ الرِّيَاحِ وَالسَّحَابِ الْمُسَخَّرِ بَيْنَ السَّمَاءِ وَالْأَرْضِ لَآيَاتٍ لِقَوْمٍ يَعْقِلُونَ﴾.

intellect."

He has also said,[8] *"He revives the earth after its death. We have made our signs clear to you in hopes that you will use your intellect."*

وَقالَ: ﴿يُحْيِ الْأَرْضَ بَعْدَ مَوْتِها. قَدْ بَيَّنّا لَكُمُ الْآياتِ لَعَلَّكُمْ تَعْقِلُونَ﴾.

He has also said,[9] *"[On earth there are neighboring parcels of land, and on them there are] vineyards, farms, and date palms—growing with offshoots and without offshoots[10]—[all] irrigated by the same water, yet we distinguish the fruit of some over [the fruit of] others. There are signs in this for those who use their intellect."*[11]

وَقالَ: ﴿وَجَنّاتٌ مِنْ أَعْنابٍ وَزَرْعٌ وَنَخِيلٌ صِنْوانٌ وَغَيْرُ صِنْوانٍ، يُسْقى بِماءٍ واحِدٍ وَنُفَضِّلُ بَعْضَها عَلى بَعْضٍ فِي الْأُكُلِ، إِنَّ فِي ذٰلِكَ لَآياتٍ لِقَوْمٍ يَعْقِلُونَ﴾.

He has also said,[12] *"And among his signs is that he shows you lightning to arouse fear and hope, and he sends down water from the sky with which he revives the earth after its death. There are signs in that for those who use their intellect."*[13]

وَقالَ: ﴿وَمِنْ آياتِهِ يُرِيكُمُ الْبَرْقَ خَوْفاً وَطَمَعاً وَيُنَزِّلُ مِنَ السَّماءِ ماءً فَيُحْيِي بِهِ الْأَرْضَ بَعْدَ مَوْتِها، إِنَّ فِي ذٰلِكَ لَآياتٍ لِقَوْمٍ يَعْقِلُونَ﴾.

He has also said,[14] *"Say: 'Come, that I may recount for you that from which your Lord has prohibited you: Do not ascribe any partners to him; and be good to your parents;*[15] *and do not kill your children due to poverty, for we shall provide for you and for them;*[16] *and do not [even] approach acts of [sexual]*

وَقالَ: ﴿قُلْ: تَعالَوْا أَتْلُ ما حَرَّمَ رَبُّكُمْ عَلَيْكُمْ: أَلَّا تُشْرِكُوا بِهِ شَيْئاً وَبِالْوالِدَيْنِ إِحْساناً وَلا تَقْتُلُوا أَوْلادَكُمْ مِنْ إِمْلاقٍ، نَحْنُ نَرْزُقُكُمْ وَإِيّاهُمْ، وَلا تَقْرَبُوا الْفَواحِشَ ما ظَهَرَ مِنْها وَما بَطَنَ، وَلا تَقْتُلُوا النَّفْسَ

indecency—whether in public or in private;[17] *and do not kill a person, whose [murder] God has prohibited, except with due cause.*[18] *This is what he has charged you with in hopes that you may understand."*[19]

الَّتِي حَرَّمَ اللَّهُ إِلَّا بِالْحَقِّ. ذٰلِكُمْ وَصَّاكُمْ بِهِ لَعَلَّكُمْ تَعْقِلُونَ﴾.

He has also said,[20] *"Do you have among your slaves any partners who share equally with you in that with which we have provided you such that you fear [displeasing] them as you fear [displeasing] those [partners] who are [free] like you?*[21] *In this way do we elaborate our verses for people who use their intellect."*[22]

وَقَالَ: ﴿هَلْ لَكُمْ مِنْ ما مَلَكَتْ أَيْمانُكُمْ مِنْ شُرَكاءَ فِي ما رَزَقْناكُمْ فَأَنْتُمْ فِيهِ سَواءٌ تَخافُونَهُمْ كَخِيفَتِكُمْ أَنْفُسَكُمْ؟ كَذٰلِكَ نُفَصِّلُ الْآياتِ لِقَوْمٍ يَعْقِلُونَ﴾.

---

1. Qurʾān 16:12

2. Both verses 2:164 and 16:12 mention "night and day" as signs that help "people who use their intellect" to know God. However, each verse focuses on a different aspect of these signs. Verse 2:164 presents the intricate interdependence of night, day, and various other phenomena, as evidence of God's lordship. Verse 16:12, on the other hand, mentions night and day, along with several other phenomena, as blessings created by the Lord for our benefit. Thus, one verse focuses on the seamless functioning of the system itself, while the other focuses on the inordinate benefit the system brings to humankind. Both aspects guide us toward God, but in different ways.

3. Qurʾān 40:67

4. This may refer to God's creation of Adam, the ancestor of all humans, from dust (Qurʾān 3:59). It could also refer to the fact that the material that comprises the sperm and the egg is derived from the food that the parents eat, which in turn comes from the earth, referred to here as "dust."

5. This verse shows that human beings are under the management of a higher power in their prenatal development; throughout their life; in their parabolic progression from the feebleness of childhood to the prime of life to the feebleness of old age; and at the time of their death.

6. What is cited here is taken from Qurʾān 45:5 with several notable discrepancies. Since verse 45:5 does not stand alone as a complete sentence, but continues from verses 45:3 and 45:4, it seems that Imam al-Kāẓim wanted to complete the sentence by carrying over some particles from those verses. Additionally, the phrase, "and [in] the clouds, which have been subjugated [by the wind] between the sky and the earth," has been added to the middle of the verse. Most likely, the scribes of *al-Kāfī* accidentally added it because it is so similar to 2:164, located only a few lines above.

7. The word "provision" has been used figuratively for "water" since the water that descends as rain inevitably supplies crops and livestock, which are our major sources of provisions.

8. Qurʾān 57:17

9. Qurʾān 13:4

10. Some species of date palms grow offshoots during a part of their life cycle. These offshoots are cut and used for propagation, since date palms grown of seedlings apparently do not grow very well or produce consistent fruit. This verse refers to the presence and absence of these offshoots in date palms that draw all their nourishment from a single source.

11. Imam al-Kāẓim clearly intended for this verse to support his thesis: God is the manager of all the affairs of the cosmos. We can reconstruct his argument as follows. The verse tells us that the difference between the fruits of two species, and between two individuals of the same species, is not necessarily due to a difference in the water used to irrigate them or the soil upon which they grow, for the verse assumes that these two factors are controlled. Thus, something else must cause the difference. The verse encourages those with strong intellects to research and unveil these factors, for they will find in the course of their research that the system that governs these things is extremely intricate. Consequently, because of their strong intellect, they will conclude that such a complex system is necessarily the work of an intelligent being, a supreme "manager" of these plants' affairs.

12. Qurʾān 30:24

13. When we see lightning we may feel frightened at its terrible power, but we also feel hopeful that the lightning is a harbinger of life-giving rain. Thus, one of the purposes of lightning is to foster in man the emotions of fear and hope, which form the backbone of his ethical system. Imam al-Kāẓim mentions this verse in this paragraph to show us that God, as our Lord, not only manages our existential affairs, but also nurtures our ethical development.

14. Qurʾān 6:151

15. It may seem out of place, in a list of things that "your Lord has prohibited," to mention a commandment to do good to one's parents. It seems it would have been more appropriate to say, "And do not be bad to your parents." However, our obligation to our parents is so immense that it is not good enough to simply "not be bad to them." Rather, we must in addition "be good to them."

16. A close comparison of this sentence and a similar sentence in 17:31 reveals a prime example of the Qurʾān's scrupulous attention to detail. Here, in 6:151, God is addressing poor people, as evinced by the phrase, "due to poverty." Since a person feeling the crunch of poverty is primarily concerned with his own survival, and only secondarily with the survival of his children, God reassures him by first promising to provide for his needs, then for his children's needs. Verse 17:31, on the other hand, is addressing those who are currently well off, but fear the sting of poverty if they were to have children as evinced by the phrase, "for fear of poverty." Such a person is not currently concerned with his own provision—since he is well-off—but with the fulfillment of his children's needs if he were to have children. Thus, God first promises to provide for his children, then for him.

17. Examples of public acts of sexual indecency include dressing indecently, publicly displaying affection, flirting, and dating. Private acts of sexual indecency include adultery, fornication, and masturbation, which are all usually conducted in private.

18. The following are examples of due cause for killing a person:

- *qiṣāṣ*: A murderer can be executed at the request of certain heirs of his victim
- *ḥadd*: For certain crimes, such as rape, a criminal may be executed.

19. To understand this verse and why it is included in this paragraph, we must study it in the context in which it appears in the Qurʾān. Verses 6:138-150 earmark some of the baseless superstitions of the pagan Arabs whereby they would declare prohibitions against certain animals for certain people. Following this, 6:151 enumerates some major prohibitions God has imposed on us and then encourages us to use our intellect to examine those prohibitions. He hopes we will realize that his prohibitions are based on real harm that exists in those actions, unlike arbitrary superstitions. This realization should fortify our certainty in God as the wise and knowledgeable manager of our legal affairs.

20. Qurʾān 30:28

21. This parable calls polytheists to examine their belief in a pantheon of gods by calling to mind their own relationship to their slaves. The verse asks them, "Are you as slaveholders willing to share your possessions equally with your slaves, to make them your partners, such that you would need to attain their consent before using your things? Of course, you would never agree to such a thing. Then what makes you think that God, the supreme master, would be willing to share his dominion with the angels and jinn—who are, after all, his slaves—by making them his equal partners?"

22. This final verse cited in section three of 1.1.12 adds an additional dimension to God's role as manager. Not only does he manage the existential world around us, our ethical development, and the affairs of life through legislation, he also manages our ideological affairs by correcting mistaken beliefs through admonishment and parables.

SECTION 3 OF TRADITION 1.1.12 TEACHES THE FOLLOWING:

- There exists one who manages all the affairs of humankind in the existential realm by creating all that we need to flourish; in the realm of ethics, by fostering ethical development; in the legal realm by issuing laws to guide us; and in the intellectual realm by elucidating the truth in such a way as to leave no reasonable room for us to fall into ideological error.
- The day, night, sun, moon, and stars, among other natural phenomena, have been created for the benefit of humankind.
- One of the purposes of natural phenomena is for people to use them to know that God is the manager of all their affairs.
- A given natural phenomenon, such as the night or day, can convey more than one message for those willing to use their intellect.
- The intellect does not err in its judgment.

- Being bad to one's parents is a major sin.
- Being good to one's parents is one of the greatest virtues, second only to belief in one God.
- Murder is prohibited except in the cause of justice.
- Murdering one's children is illegal, even for fear of poverty.

Section 4

'O Hishām! God has also admonished those with intellect and enticed them to [seek] the hereafter. For he has said,[1] *"The temporal life is but sport and amusement,*[2] *whereas the abode of the hereafter is certainly better for those who fear God. Why then do you not use your intellect?"*

يَا هِشَامُ، ثُمَّ وَعَظَ أَهْلَ الْعَقْلِ وَرَغَّبَهُمْ فِي الْآخِرَةِ، فَقَالَ: ﴿وَمَا الْحَيَاةُ الدُّنْيَا إِلَّا لَعِبٌ وَلَهْوٌ، وَلَلدَّارُ الْآخِرَةُ خَيْرٌ لِلَّذِينَ يَتَّقُونَ، أَفَلَا تَعْقِلُونَ؟﴾.

---

1. Qur'ān 6:32

2. We have translated *la'ib* as "sport" and *lahw* as "amusement." *Lahw* refers to any activity that has no sensible purpose and distracts a person from what is important. An example is reading a book of fiction for no other purpose than to pass time. *La'ib* is a kind of *lahw* that has a specific form, organized movements, and an imaginary purpose: winning the game. It is true that many games facilitate improved health—which is a "sensible purpose" and not simply an "imaginary goal." However, exercise is not the goal of these games insofar as they are games; rather, it simply happens to be one positive component of these games. This is not to say that games and amusement are necessarily bad. The legal rulings for specific games and forms of amusement are a separate issue altogether that can be found in books of Islamic jurisprudence.

Having said this, it may seem strange that the Qur'ān should denigrate life in the temporal world as nothing but "sport and amusement." This statement seems to deny the possibility of living a moral, religious, and purposeful life in this world. The secret to this riddle lies in an acute understanding of the term *dunyā*, which literally means "nearer" and refers to the temporal life, which is "nearer" than the *ākhirah* or "hereafter." The temporal life is nothing more than the time and place that serve as the setting for the life that we live between birth and death. There is nothing inherently pejorative or positive about it. For this reason, Imam Zayn al-ʿĀbidīn has said, "The temporal world is of two kinds: one that helps you reach [happiness in the hereafter] and one that is bereft of God's mercy" (*al-Kāfī* 5.61.11). If we use life in this world as we ought to and accomplish the goals that God has set for us, it becomes a noble and meaningful life that acts as a stepping stone to reach eternal happiness in the hereafter. It is in this sense that Imam ʿAlī has said, "The *dunyā* (temporal world) is an honest abode for him who is honest with it; an abode of well-being for him who understands it; an abode of plenty for him who packs his provisions with its stores; and an abode full of good advice for him who will take it. [It is] the place where God's beloveds prostrate, where God's angels pray; the place where God's revelation descends, and the bazaar of God's friends: in it they earn God's mercy and gain paradise" (*Nahj al-balāghah* proverb 131). If, on the other hand, the frills of the world divert our attention from these goals, it becomes reprehensible, and life in it becomes nothing but "sport and amusement." It is in this sense that verse 6:32 refers to it.

SECTION 4 OF TRADITION 1.1.12 TEACHES THE FOLLOWING:

- It is possible to admonish someone by simply telling him facts without necessarily telling him what he should or should not do, just as God has "admonished those with intellect" here by simply informing them of the true nature of life in the temporal world.
- Those who fear God avoid mere sport and amusement.
- The intellect dictates that one should favor the hereafter over the temporal world.

Section 5

'O Hishām! God has also frightened those who do not use their intellect [by warning them] of his punishment. For he—the Exalted—has said,[1] "*Then [after delivering Lot and his family] we destroyed all the others. And you [O Quraysh!] pass by them [or rather what is left of their civilization] morning and night. Why then do you not use your intellect?*"

يَا هِشَامُ، ثُمَّ خَوَّفَ الَّذِينَ لَا يَعْقِلُونَ عِقَابَهُ، فَقَالَ تَعَالَى: ﴿ثُمَّ دَمَّرْنَا الْآخَرِينَ، وَإِنَّكُمْ لَتَمُرُّونَ عَلَيْهِمْ مُصْبِحِينَ وَبِاللَّيْلِ، أَفَلَا تَعْقِلُونَ﴾.

He has also said,[2] "*[The angels told Lot,] 'We are going to send down upon the people of this city*[3] *a punishment from the sky because of their habitual transgressions.' And [when we punished them,] we left a manifest sign [in the ruins] of their city for people who use their intellect.*"[4]

وَقَالَ: ﴿إِنَّا مُنْزِلُونَ عَلَى أَهْلِ هٰذِهِ الْقَرْيَةِ رِجْزاً مِنَ السَّمَاءِ بِمَا كَانُوا يَفْسُقُونَ. وَلَقَدْ تَرَكْنَا مِنْهَا آيَةً بَيِّنَةً لِقَوْمٍ يَعْقِلُونَ﴾.

---

1. Qur'ān 37:136-8

2. Qur'ān 29:34-5

3. In other words, the people of Sodom.

4. The ruins of Sodom, their crimes, and their fate, were familiar to Arabs (see Qur'ān 11:89). The verses cited in this section indicate that the wisdom behind preserving these ruins was to remind Arabs—and by extension, all people—of the consequence of defying God and his prophets. However, only those with intellect contemplate history and learn its lessons as they should.

SECTION 5 OF TRADITION 1.1.12 TEACHES THE FOLLOWING:

- The purpose of travelling to and studying the ruins of ancient civilizations ought to be to learn the lessons implied by their actions and consequent fate.
- The story of Lot's people and the ruins of Sodom were familiar to the pre-Islamic Arabs of Mecca.

Section 6

'O Hishām! Use of the intellect goes hand in hand with knowledge.[1] For God has said,[2] *"We draw these comparisons[3] for all people, but no one [fully] comprehends them except those possessed of knowledge."*[4]

يا هِشَامُ، إِنَّ الْعَقْلَ مَعَ الْعِلْمِ، فَقَالَ: ﴿وَتِلْكَ الْأَمْثَالُ نَضْرِبُهَا لِلنَّاسِ، وَما يَعْقِلُهَا إِلَّا الْعَالِمُونَ﴾.

---

1. Several traditions in the *Book of Intellect and Foolishness* mention the interaction between knowledge and intellect. The sentence we are now studying first indicates that the two simply go hand in hand, but goes on to cite verse 29:43, which indicates that knowledge is the cause of intellection and comprehension. Tradition 1.1.23, on the other hand, says, "From intellect alone [does]...knowledge issue," indicating that intellect is the source and cause for knowledge. Tradition 1.1.34, in turn, says, "The depths of wisdom (which is a type of knowledge) can only be extracted by the intellect, and the depths of the intellect can only be extracted by wisdom," thereby indicating that their causality is reciprocal.

2. Qurʾān 29:43

3. "[T]hese comparisons" refers to the comparison of polytheism to a spider's web, which is mentioned in 29:41, and other such comparisons mentioned throughout the Qurʾān.

4. If you have ever endeavored to understand the Qurʾān's comparisons, you will have noticed how difficult they can be to grasp. This verse indicates that there is a prerequisite for understanding them firsthand and for correctly applying them to real-life examples. That prerequisite is knowledge. In particular, one must have intimate knowledge of the subjects of these comparisons, which include natural phenomena, God's various creatures, the history of past civilizations, and the biographies of important historical figures. Only those possessed of knowledge, who are accustomed to contemplating all that passes before them, fulfill this prerequisite. This is not to say that others cannot benefit from these comparisons once those with knowledge have uncovered the meaning and explained it to them. After all, they are comparisons God draws "for *all* people."

SECTION 6 OF TRADITION 1.1.12 TEACHES THE FOLLOWING:

- We cannot make full use of our intellect without knowledge.
- Only those with knowledge can comprehend firsthand the crux of the Qurʾān's comparisons and apply them correctly to real-life examples.

Section 7

'O Hishām! God has also censured those who do not use their intellect. For he has said,[1] *"When they are told, 'Follow what God has sent down,' they say, 'We would rather follow what we have found our ancestors believing in.' What, even if we suppose that their ancestors comprehended nothing[2] and did not avail themselves of guidance?"*[3]

يا هِشامُ، ثُمَّ ذَمَّ الَّذِينَ لا يَعْقِلُونَ، فَقالَ: ﴿وَإِذا قِيلَ لَهُمُ: اتَّبِعُوا ما أَنْزَلَ اللَّهُ قالُوا: بَلْ نَتَّبِعُ ما أَلْفَيْنا عَلَيْهِ آباءَنا. أَوَلَوْ كانَ آباؤُهُمْ لا يَعْقِلُونَ شَيْئاً وَلا يَهْتَدُونَ؟﴾.

He has also said,[4] *"[One who invites] such unbelievers [to faith and submission] is like a shepherd who shouts at his sheep, which hear nothing but a mere call and a cry.*[5] *[These unbelievers are] deaf, dumb, and blind,*[6] *so they do not use their intellect."*[7]

وَقالَ: ﴿وَمَثَلُ الَّذِينَ كَفَرُوا كَمَثَلِ الَّذِي يَنْعِقُ بِما لا يَسْمَعُ إِلَّا دُعاءً وَنِداءً. صُمٌّ بُكْمٌ عُمْيٌ فَهُمْ لا يَعْقِلُونَ﴾.

He has also said,[8] *"Among them are those who [halfheartedly] listen to you, [Muḥammad.] Do you think you can make the deaf hear, even if they do not use their intellect?"*[9]

وَقالَ: ﴿وَمِنْهُمْ مَنْ يَسْتَمِعُ إِلَيْكَ، أَفَأَنْتَ تُسْمِعُ الصُّمَّ وَلَوْ كانُوا لا يَعْقِلُونَ؟﴾.

He has also said,[10] *"Moreover, do you suppose that most of them hear or use their intellect?*[11] *They are just like cattle; rather they are further astray from the path."*[12]

وَقالَ: ﴿أَمْ تَحْسَبُ أَنَّ أَكْثَرَهُمْ يَسْمَعُونَ أَوْ يَعْقِلُونَ؟ إِنْ هُمْ إِلَّا كَالْأَنْعامِ بَلْ هُمْ أَضَلُّ سَبِيلاً﴾.

He has also said,[13] *"They will not fight*

وَقالَ: ﴿لا يُقاتِلُونَكُمْ جَمِيعاً إِلَّا فِي قُرىً

against you, [though they stand] unified, except from fortified townships or from behind walls. Their ferocity is intense only within their own ranks; [but when they fight you, their ferocity evaporates]. You deem them united while their hearts are asunder. This [disunity of theirs] is because they are a people who do not use their intellect."[14]	مُحَصَّنَةٍ أَوْ مِنْ وَراءِ جُدُرٍ. بَأْسُهُمْ بَيْنَهُمْ شَدِيدٌ. تَحْسَبُهُمْ جَمِيعاً وَقُلُوبُهُمْ شَتَّى. ذلِكَ بِأَنَّهُمْ قَوْمٌ لا يَعْقِلُونَ﴾.
He has also said,[15] *"[Do you (i.e., Jewish leaders) bid others to do good] yet forget [to bid] yourselves [to do good] while you recite the book (i.e., the Torah)? Do you not use your intellect?"*	وَقالَ: ﴿وَتَنْسَوْنَ أَنْفُسَكُمْ وَأَنْتُمْ تَتْلُونَ الْكِتابَ، أَ فَلا تَعْقِلُونَ؟﴾.

---

1. Qurʾān 2:170

2. This statement screams of hyperbole. Of course, pre-Islamic Arabs comprehended much of the world around them. However, because they failed to engage their intellectual powers in matters of real importance, the Qurʾān treats all they knew as naught.

3. The purpose of this verse is to make pagan Arabs aware that blindly submitting to the religion of their forebears is absurd. A rational person would only follow forebears who were either possessed of a strong intellect and had learned the teachings of the prophets firsthand through their own efforts or had learned those teachings by following a scholar possessed of intellect and correct knowledge. This verse reminds pagan Arabs that their forebears were neither. It poses the following question to them: "Would you follow your ancestors under any circumstances, even if they neither possessed intellect and knowledge nor availed themselves of a scholar's knowledge?" In other words, "Do you follow your ancestors simply because they are your ancestors or because of their intellect or the guidance they follow?" If they respond with the former, it is clear that they themselves are fools and do not seek the truth. If they respond with the latter, they have taken one positive step toward the truth, and must then prove that their ancestors' beliefs—in particular their belief in a pantheon of gods—were rationally sound, a task they will never be able to do.

4. Qurʾān 2:171. Imam al-Kāẓim broke these two contiguous verses up because each is a sufficient reason to censure those who fail to use their intellect.

5. Regardless of what the shepherd says, his sheep understand nothing but the rise and fall of his voice. Likewise, people who are stubborn and closed-minded hear nothing of the content of what is said to them.

6. Because they do not pay heed to the guidance they hear, they are as good as deaf. Because they do not answer the call of the Prophet or ask him their sincere questions, they are as good as dumb. Because they act as though they never saw his miracles, they are as good as blind.

7. The intellect is merely a faculty for processing information. Without the necessary information, it has nothing to process. In this vein, Imam al-Ṣādiq has said, "[H]e shall not use his intellect who does not have knowledge" (*al-Kāfī* 1.1.29). Those to whom this verse refers do not use their intellect because they, of their own fault, do not have the necessary knowledge to do so, for they have sealed their own eyes, ears, and hearts to the teachings of the Prophet.

8. Qurʾān 10:42. In all well-known recensions (*qirāʾāt*) of the Qurʾān, this verse appears with the word "*yastamiʿūn*" (3rd person plural form). Imam al-Kāẓim, on the other hand, has quoted it with the word "*yastamiʿu*" (3rd person singular form). One possible explanation for this discrepancy is that Imam al-Kāẓim intended to paraphrase the verse without necessarily quoting its exact wording. Another possible explanation is that he wished to make the point that the plural form of the verb is not authentic and that the singular form is the way it should be read. This second possibility is strengthened by the presence of the verb "*yanẓuru*" (3rd person singular form) in the next verse. Since the structure of both verses is parallel, it makes sense that the verbs should be in the same person. Whichever possibility we favor, we must reaffirm that this level of variation among recensions (*qirāʾāt*) of the Qurʾān—whether among the seven or ten famous recensions or lesser-known recensions like this one—in no way indicates that the Qurʾān has been altered. In this instance in particular, both the singular and plural verbs can be easily justified from a grammatical point of view, and choosing one verb form over the other has no significant bearing on the meaning of the verse.

9. Many pagan Arabs would listen to the Prophet's preaching without taking what he said to heart. To console the Prophet, God compares these unbelievers to deaf people. He asks the Prophet rhetorically, "Do you think you are able to make the deaf hear, even if, in addition to their loss of hearing, they have lost their ability to think?" If a deaf person's intellect is intact, he may decipher what you are trying to communicate to him using his intellect. However, if he also has no intellect, or refuses to use what intellect he has, then your hopes for communicating with him are unfounded. Similarly, these unbelievers who pay no heed to what they hear from you are as good as deaf. If, in addition to their hearing, their intellects are also impaired—since they fail to use them—then your hopes for guiding them are unfounded.

10. Qurʾān 25:44

11. The problem with such people is that they do not hear what is said to them. Worse yet, even if they hear, they do not think about what they have heard.

12. These people are worse off than cattle because they fail to think despite their faculty of intellect, whereas cattle fail to think because they have no such faculty.

13. Qurʾān 59:14

14. The point of this sentence is not to encourage the unbelievers to leave off their differences with one another and unify against Islam. Rather it seeks to point out that they do not and cannot truly unite because each of them is seeking his own selfish goals instead of the truth. If only they would use their intellect, they would realize that the greatest good is to be found in the pursuit of truth, and they would unite, not against you, but with you in its pursuit.

15. Qurʾān 2:44

SECTION 7 OF TRADITION 1.1.12 TEACHES THE FOLLOWING:

- Following one's forebears and their traditions in place of what God has revealed is contrary to the dictates of the intellect.
- One who fails to use his intellect is doomed, and even a prophet of God cannot help him.
- Our faculties of hearing, speaking, and seeing are tools of the intellect.
- One who fails to use his intellect is worse than cattle.
- One who fails to use his intellect is inevitably cowardly.
- One who fails to use his intellect is inevitably hypocritical.

Section 8

O Hisham! God has also censured the majority. For he has said,[1] *"If you obey the majority of those on earth, they will lead you away from the path of God."*[2]

يَا هِشَامُ، ثُمَّ ذَمَّ اللَّهُ الْكَثْرَةَ فَقَالَ: ﴿وَإِنْ تُطِعْ أَكْثَرَ مَنْ فِي الْأَرْضِ يُضِلُّوكَ عَنْ سَبِيلِ اللَّهِ﴾.

He has also said,[3] *"If you ask them, 'Who created the heavens and the earth?' they will surely say, 'God [did].' Say, 'Praise be to God [that they admitted the truth].'*[4] *However, most of them do not know [that admitting that God is the Creator necessitates that they accept that there is but one god].*

وَقَالَ: ﴿وَلَئِنْ سَأَلْتَهُمْ مَنْ خَلَقَ السَّماواتِ وَالْأَرْضَ لَيَقُولُنَّ: اللَّهُ. قُلِ: الْحَمْدُ لِلَّهِ. بَلْ أَكْثَرُهُمْ لا يَعْلَمُونَ﴾.

He has also said,[5] *"If you ask them, 'Who sends down water from the sky with which he revives the earth after its death?' they will surely say, 'God [does].' Say, 'Praise be to God [that they conceded the truth].'*[6] *However, most of them do not use their intellect [to understand that their admission that God is the sole lord and manager of affairs necessitates that they accept that there is but one god]."*

وَقَالَ: ﴿وَلَئِنْ سَأَلْتَهُمْ مَنْ نَزَّلَ مِنَ السَّماءِ ماءً فَأَحْيا بِهِ الْأَرْضَ مِنْ بَعْدِ مَوْتِها لَيَقُولُنَّ: اللَّهُ. قُلِ: الْحَمْدُ لِلَّهِ بَلْ أَكْثَرُهُمْ لا يَعْقِلُونَ﴾.

---

1. Qurʾān 6:116

2. We must read to the end of this verse to understand its intent properly. It reads, "If you obey the majority of those on earth, they will lead you away from the path of God. They follow nothing but conjecture, and they do nothing but surmise" (Qurʾān 6:116). The end of this verse makes it clear that what is reprehensible about the majority opinion is that it generally relies on mere conjecture and supposition, not solid, unequivocal proof. This is not to say that conjecture and supposition are categorically bad, for in completely mundane matters, there is often no choice but to suppose and guess. For instance, in the course of scientific exploration, one must hypothesize and act according to that hypothesis until it is proven right or wrong. Likewise, in social and cultural matters, there is nothing wrong with following the customs and traditions of a people so long as they do not contradict divine law. There is also nothing wrong with going along with the majority in administrative and governmental issues that do not contradict divine law. However, in matters as critical as deducing one's tenets of faith and discovering divine law, we obviously must not rely on anything but the soundest of evidence. For such issues, relying on the majority opinion is unjustifiable.

It follows that if a time comes when the majority of people do not base their actions and beliefs on such flimsy ground—as will be the case when Imam al-Mahdī returns and establishes his government—then following the majority will no longer be reprehensible.

3. Qurʾān 31:25

4. By admitting that God is the creator of the cosmos, they have unwittingly admitted that he is the sole deity worthy of worship and that their idols are worthless. Let us explain this argument as follows: People only worship what they believe has control over their affairs. The creator of the cosmos, to the exclusion of all others, has inherent authority and power to control and manage its affairs by virtue of being its creator and hence owner. Thus, the only being these people ought to worship, according to their own admission, is God, the Creator and Lord of the cosmos. If only they would use their intellect, they would realize that one belief follows from the other and that they are worshipping the wrong gods.

5. Qurʾān 29:63

6. As in 31:25, by admitting that God is the manager of the affairs of the cosmos, such as controlling rain and the rebirth of spring, the pagans have unwittingly admitted that he is the only one worthy of worship, thereby denouncing their own idols.

SECTION 8 OF TRADITION 1.1.12 TEACHES THE FOLLOWING:

- Following the majority simply because of their numbers is deplorable.
- Polytheists admit that God is the creator of the cosmos.
- The majority, insofar as it is a majority, is the following:
    - ◊ a misguiding force,
    - ◊ lacking in knowledge, since they do not know that admitting that God is the creator of the cosmos necessitates that they admit that he alone deserves worship,
    - ◊ lacking in intellect because they do not realize that admitting that God is the manager of the affairs of the cosmos necessitates that they accept that he alone deserves worship.

Section 9

'O Hishām! He has also praised the minority. For he has said,[1] "*[But] few of my servants are truly thankful.*

يَا هِشَامُ، ثُمَّ مَدَحَ الْقِلَّةَ فَقَالَ: ﴿وَقَلِيلٌ مِنْ عِبادِيَ الشَّكُورُ﴾.

He has also said,[2] "*How few are they [who have faith and do good deeds]!*

وَقَالَ: ﴿وَقَلِيلٌ مَّا هُمْ﴾.

He has also said,[3] "*A man of faith from the house of the Pharaoh who had concealed his faith said, 'Will you kill a man for saying, "My lord is God"?'*"

وَقَالَ: ﴿وَقَالَ رَجُلٌ مُؤْمِنٌ مِنْ آلِ فِرْعَوْنَ يَكْتُمُ إِيمانَهُ: أَتَقْتُلُونَ رَجُلًا أَنْ يَقُولَ رَبِّيَ اللَّهُ؟﴾.

He has also said,[5] "*And [carry in the ark, O Noah, along with a pair of every animal and the faithful from your family,] those who believe. Yet only a few believed along with him.*

وَقَالَ: ﴿وَمَنْ آمَنَ، وَما آمَنَ مَعَهُ إِلَّا قَلِيلٌ﴾.

He has also said,[6] "*However most of them do not know.*"

وَقَالَ: ﴿وَلكِنَّ أَكْثَرَهُمْ لا يَعْلَمُونَ﴾.

And he has said,[8] "*Most of them do not use their intellect.*"

وَقَالَ: ﴿وَأَكْثَرُهُمْ لا يَعْقِلُونَ﴾.

And he has said,[9] "*Most of them do not perceive.*"

وَقَالَ: ﴿وَأَكْثَرُهُمْ لَا يَشْعُرُونَ﴾.

---

1. Qurʾān 34:13

2. Qurʾān 38:24

3. Qurʾān 40:28

4. Imam al-Kāẓim has cited this verse as praise of the minority because this man, known as "The Believer from the House of the Pharaoh," was the sole voice of truth and reason in a family intoxicated by power. He concealed his allegiance to Moses and remained in Pharaoh's court so that he could defend Moses from within the ranks of Pharaoh's staunchest supporters.

5. Qurʾān 11:40

6. Qurʾān 6:37

7. This and the next two sentences ought to have been mentioned in the previous section where he mentioned verses that censure the majority. In fact, that is where they have been placed in *Tuḥaf al-ʿuqūl*'s recension of this same tradition (*Tuḥaf al-ʿuqūl* p.383).

8. Qurʾān 5:103

9. This last sentence is not a verse of the Qurʾān. Most likely, the inclusion of the introductory phrase, "And he has said" is an error attributable to scribes since it does not exist in the aforementioned recension of *Tuḥaf al-ʿuqūl* (p.383).

SECTION 9 OF TRADITION 1.1.12 TEACHES THE FOLLOWING:

- Those who are grateful, those who believe and do good deeds, those who know, those who use their intellect, and those who perceive, are in the minority, just as the man of faith from Pharaoh's household and the faithful from among Noah's people were in the minority.

Section 10

'O Hishām! God has also praised the possessors of intellect with most lavish praise and has adorned them with most exquisite adornment. For he has said,[1] *"He gives wisdom[2] to whomever he wishes. He who is given wisdom is thereby given an abundant good. However, none take heed[3] [of God's verses and thereby prepare the ground for receiving wisdom] but the possessors of intellect."*[4]

يَا هِشَامُ، ثُمَّ ذَكَرَ أُولِي الْأَلْبَابِ بِأَحْسَنِ الذِّكْرِ، وَحَلَّاهُمْ بِأَحْسَنِ الْحِلْيَةِ، فَقَالَ: ﴿يُؤْتِي الْحِكْمَةَ مَنْ يَشاءُ. وَمَنْ يُؤْتَ الْحِكْمَةَ فَقَدْ أُوتِيَ خَيْراً كَثِيراً، وَما يَذَّكَّرُ إِلَّا أُولُوا الْأَلْبَابِ﴾.

He has also said,[5] *"And those steeped in knowledge say, 'We believe in the [entire] book [with its unequivocal and ambiguous verses]; it is all from our Lord.' And none realizes [that both the unequivocal and the ambiguous verses are from God] except [them, for they are] the possessors of intellect."*[6]

وَقَالَ: ﴿وَالرَّاسِخُونَ فِي الْعِلْمِ يَقُولُونَ: آمَنَّا بِهِ، كُلٌّ مِنْ عِنْدِ رَبِّنا. وَما يَذَّكَّرُ إِلَّا أُولُوا الْأَلْبَابِ﴾.

He has also said,[7] *"In the creation of the heavens and the earth and the alternation of night and day are signs for those who possess intellect."*[8]

وَقَالَ: ﴿إِنَّ فِي خَلْقِ السَّماواتِ وَالْأَرْضِ وَاخْتِلافِ اللَّيْلِ وَالنَّهارِ لَآياتٍ لِأُولِي الْأَلْبَابِ﴾.

He has also said,[9] *"Is one who knows that what has been sent down to you from your Lord is truth like one who is blind [in ignorance]? Only those who possess an intellect are aware [that they*

وَقَالَ: ﴿أَفَمَنْ يَعْلَمُ أَنَّما أُنْزِلَ إِلَيْكَ مِنْ رَبِّكَ الْحَقُّ كَمَنْ هُوَ أَعْمى؟ إِنَّما يَتَذَكَّرُ أُولُوا الْأَلْبَابِ﴾.

are not equal].”

He has also said,[10] *“[Is such a staunch unbeliever better] or one who humbly worships at all times of the night, prostrating and standing, in apprehension of the hereafter, yet hopeful of his Lord’s mercy? Say: ‘Are these [humble worshippers] who know equal to those [unbelievers] who do not know?’ Only those who possess intellect realize [that they are vastly different].”*

وَقالَ: ﴿أَمَّنْ هُوَ قانِتٌ آناءَ اللَّيْلِ ساجِداً وَقائِماً يَحْذَرُ الْآخِرَةَ وَيَرْجُوا رَحْمَةَ رَبِّهِ؟ قُلْ: هَلْ يَسْتَوِي الَّذِينَ يَعْلَمُونَ وَالَّذِينَ لا يَعْلَمُونَ؟ إِنَّما يَتَذَكَّرُ أُولُوا الْأَلْبابِ﴾.

He has also said,[11] *“[This is] a blessed book that we have sent down to you so that [all people whether] they [be God-fearing or profligate][12] may contemplate its verses[13] and so that those who possess intellect [among them] may heed [its teachings].”*[14]

وَقالَ: ﴿كِتابٌ أَنْزَلْناهُ إِلَيْكَ مُبارَكٌ لِيَدَّبَّرُوا آياتِهِ وَلِيَتَذَكَّرَ أُولُوا الْأَلْبابِ﴾.

He has also said,[15] *“We gave Moses guidance,*[16] *and we left the book among the Children of Israel [after him], as guidance and admonishment for those who possess intellect.”*[17]

وَقالَ: ﴿وَلَقَدْ آتَيْنا مُوسَى الْهُدى، وَأَوْرَثْنا بَنِي إِسْرائِيلَ الْكِتابَ هُدىً وَذِكْرى لِأُولِي الْأَلْبابِ﴾.

He also said,[18] *“Admonish! For admonishment benefits the believers.”*[19]

وَقالَ: ﴿وَذَكِّرْ، فَإِنَّ الذِّكْرى تَنْفَعُ الْمُؤْمِنِينَ﴾.

1. Qurʾān 2:269

2. Wisdom (*ḥikmah*) denotes knowledge that leads one to righteous acts.

3. The word *tadhakkur* can mean "to take heed of advice or admonishment" or "to realize and be aware of something." It occurs repeatedly in the verses of this section. In each case, we have translated the word according to the meaning that best fits the context.

4. The first sentence of verse 2:269 says, "He gives wisdom to whomever he wishes." It tells us that God bestows wisdom upon whomever he wishes, but it does not tell us what criteria he uses for choosing wisdom's beneficiaries, only that he reserves this choice for himself. The second sentence, "He who is given wisdom is thereby given an abundant good," tells us that there is abundant good in wisdom, so whoever receives wisdom from God has, by the same token, received abundant good. However, the verse still does not tell us how we can qualify to receive God's dispensation of wisdom, which is an abundant good. The third sentence, "However, none take heed [of God's verses and thereby prepare the ground for receiving wisdom] but the possessors of intellect," tells us how we can qualify to receive wisdom and goodness from God.

First, we must be among "the possessors of intellect" who use their intellect for a right purpose ("intellect" is used here in the fourth sense of the word).

Second, we must use our intellect to heed God's teachings (i.e., to take his teachings to heart and act on what we learn). In particular, we must heed God's teachings in the verses preceding 2:269, which explain that we should give charity; refrain from listening to the insinuations of Satan who threatens us with poverty; and trust in God's promise of forgiveness and bounty (see 2:267-8). The teachings of these two verses are examples of wisdom. They are in plain sight, available for anyone to benefit from them, but only those who employ their intellects take them to heart and act on them. Only if we fulfill these two requirements does God allow the wisdom embodied in his verses to flourish within us and blossom into right action. If, on the other hand, we do not employ our intellect to heed God's verses and signs, we will be like those whom he describes in the following verse: "How many a sign there is in the heavens and the earth that they pass by in heedlessness!" (Qur᾿ān 12:105).

Finally, it is important to note that Imam al-Kāẓim has mentioned this verse in this section because it praises the "possessors of intellect" for being the only beneficiaries of wisdom, which is an abundant good.

5. Qur᾿ān 3:7

6. Imam al-Kāẓim has mentioned this verse in this section because it praises the "possessors of intellect" for being the only ones to realize that the entire Qur᾿ān is from God.

7. Qur᾿ān 3:190

8. The verse Imam al-Kāẓim has cited here does not constitute praise for "the possessors of intellect." Most likely, his purpose in citing this verse was to allude to what follows it in 3:191-5 in which God extensively praises "the possessors of intellect" for remembering him at all times, for contemplating his signs, for their well-founded conviction, and for praying with such sincerity that their prayers are answered.

9. Qur᾿ān 13:19

10. Qur᾿ān 39:9

11. Qur᾿ān 38:29

12. We have inferred the words "God-fearing" and "profligate" in this sentence because these two categories of people were mentioned in the verse prior to this one in the Qur᾿ān.

13. Contemplation of Qur᾽ānic verses occurs at different levels. The highest level is to endeavor to discover the meaning of the Qur᾽ān directly from the Arabic text. This level of contemplation is restricted to scholars since it requires skills lacking in non-specialists, least among which is mastery of the Arabic language. Non-specialists, on the other hand, must strive to contemplate the Qur᾽ān with the help of scholars and then apply its teachings to all aspects of their lives. This Qur᾽ānic commandment then is similar to the Prophet's commandment in which he said, "Seeking knowledge is mandatory on every Muslim" (*al-Kāfī* 2.1.1), for there are levels to the pursuit of knowledge. The highest level, to pursue it from primary sources, is the work of scholars. Non-specialists, on the other hand, are required to pursue it by learning from scholars.

14. This verse seems to be saying that contemplating the Qur᾽ān is the duty of all people, while heeding its teachings is only the duty of those with intellect, as though they are two distinct groups. This is clearly not the case. Those with intellect are a subset of all people. There could be nothing better than for *all* people to heed the Qur᾽ān's guidance. However, since only those who employ their intellect do in fact heed its guidance, only they have been mentioned as the goal for which God sent down the Qur᾽ān.

15. Qur᾽ān 40:53-4

16. The word *hudā* or "guidance" here stands for all that God gave Prophet Moses for the guidance of his people among which were the Torah and his many miracles.

17. God sent the Torah to guide all the Children of Israel, not only the possessors of intellect among them. However, since only those endowed with intellect can benefit from divine guidance, only they are mentioned.

18. Qur᾽ān 51:55

19. It may seem puzzling that Imam al-Kāẓim would mention a verse praising "the believers" among verses that purport to praise the possessors of intellect. The secret lies in that the verses quoted prior to this indicated that only the possessors of intellect heed admonishment. The present verse indicates that admonishment benefits the believers. It follows that the true believers are necessarily possessors of intellect, and therein lies their praise.

SECTION 10 OF TRADITION 1.1.12 TEACHES THE FOLLOWING:

- The prerequisite for receiving wisdom is to be heedful of God's verses, and the prerequisite for being heedful is to use one's intellect. Thus, the prerequisite for receiving wisdom is to use one's intellect.
- Those steeped in knowledge accept the Qurʾān's ambiguous verses along with its unequivocal ones.
- One with knowledge has insight, and one lacking in knowledge is blind.
- God's purpose in revealing the Qurʾān was for people to contemplate its verses and heed its teachings.
- Only those with intellect are heedful.
- Believers are possessors of intellect.

Section 11

'O Hishām! God—the Exalted—says in his book,[1] *"There is, in this, admonishment for one who has a heart."* [By "heart"] he means "an intellect."[2] He also said,[3] *"We gave Luqmān[4] wisdom."*

يَا هِشَامُ: إِنَّ اللَّهَ تَعَالَى يَقُولُ فِي كِتَابِهِ: ﴿إِنَّ فِي ذٰلِكَ لَذِكْرَى لِمَنْ كَانَ لَهُ قَلْبٌ﴾، يَعْنِي عَقْلٌ. وَقَالَ: ﴿وَلَقَدْ آتَيْنَا لُقْمَانَ الْحِكْمَةَ﴾،

Al-Kāẓim said [in explaining what God gave Luqmān]:

قَالَ:

'[God gave him] the faculty of understanding, which is intellect.[5]

الْفَهْمَ وَالْعَقْلَ.

---

1. Qur'ān 50:37

2. "Intellect" is used here in the first sense of the word.

3. Qur'ān 31:12

4. Luqmān was not a prophet but a devoted servant of God who loved his Lord and whose Lord loved him, who spent much time in contemplation and accordingly was showered with abundant wisdom.

5. Imam al-Kāẓim uses "intellect" here in the first sense of the word. He apparently wishes to say that God did not give Luqmān wisdom directly, as we might conclude from the verse. Rather, he gave him a strong intellect or faculty of understanding. Luqmān in turn used this faculty to learn the wisdom for which he has become famous.

SECTION 11 OF TRADITION 1.1.12 TEACHES THE FOLLOWING:

- God's admonishment is only meant for those with intellect.
- The "heart" can represent the "intellect."
- Attaining wisdom requires a strong intellect.

Section 12

'O Hishām! Luqmān said to his son, "Submit to truth,[1] and you shall attain the strongest intellect of all people[2]—but the intelligent [who submit] in the face of truth are few. My son, the material world is a fathomless sea in which many people have drowned.[3] So let the fear of God be your ship to traverse it.[4] Let your faith be your ship's ballast. Let reliance [on God] be its sails.[5] Let your intellect be its captain. Let knowledge be its navigator. Let fortitude be its keel."

يَا هِشَامُ، إِنَّ لُقْمَانَ قَالَ لِابْنِهِ: تَوَاضَعْ لِلْحَقِّ، تَكُنْ أَعْقَلَ النَّاسِ - وَإِنَّ الْكَيِّسَ لَدَى الْحَقِّ يَسِيرٌ. يَا بُنَيَّ إِنَّ الدُّنْيَا بَحْرٌ عَمِيقٌ قَدْ غَرِقَ فِيهَا عَالَمٌ كَثِيرٌ. فَلْتَكُنْ سَفِينَتُكَ فِيهَا تَقْوَى اللَّهِ، وَحَشْوُهَا الْإِيمَانَ، وَشِرَاعُهَا التَّوَكُّلَ، وَقَيِّمُهَا الْعَقْلَ، وَدَلِيلُهَا الْعِلْمَ، وَسُكَّانُهَا الصَّبْرَ.

---

1. "Truth" is any statement, belief, or claim that conforms to reality. Luqmān is advising his son, if it becomes clear in the course of an argument, for instance, that his opponent is right, to cede the argument to him.

2. This sentence indicates that submitting to the truth causes one's intellect to become stronger than the intellects of those who do not submit to the truth. We are safe in saying that he has not included the prophets and imams in his comparison, since they submit to truth more wholly than anyone else, and therefore have stronger intellects than anyone else as indicated by Prophet Muḥammad's statement, "God did not send a single prophet or messenger until he perfected his intellect and his intellect became better than the combined intellectual capacities of his people" (*al-Kāfī* 1.1.11).

3. The material world is like a fathomless sea in several ways:

- Both are in a continuous state of transience.
- Just as the sea is a conduit between one place and another but never

a place to take up permanent residence, so the material world is but a means for us to attain our place in the hereafter, not a permanent abode.

- Just as many have drowned in the sea, so too many have lost sight of the true nature of the material world and have consequently been overwhelmed by its glitter. Imam al-Kāẓim has only mentioned the third of these similarities because it is the most ethically compelling of the three.

4. Just as a ship safeguards its passengers and goods from the dangers of the sea, so too the fear of God (*taqwā*) guards us from the dangers of the material world. It is important to note that the word *taqwā* or "the fear of God" is used here in a different sense from what is conventionally used. *Taqwā* in its conventional sense only exists after we have faith (*īmān*) in God, for it only makes sense to fear God once we know him and believe in him. This tradition, on the other hand, supposes that *taqwā* exists *before* faith and that faith protects it as a ship's ballast prevents the ship from toppling and sinking. *Taqwā* in this sense refers to the fear we all feel because of our innate cognizance of God's existence known as *fiṭrah*. Our intellect independently orders us to acknowledge this fear and act in accordance with it. Secondarily, when God reveals himself to us through his prophets, the faith that enters our hearts affirms and protects that innate fear, the way a ship's ballast weighs it down and prevents it from capsizing.

5. Perhaps the reason for comparing reliance (*tawakkul*) on God to the sails of a ship is that, as every sailor knows, whether the wind blows or not, and in which direction, is not in his own hands, but in the hands of God, the mover of the wind. Thus, the sails of a ship are a symbol of reliance on God.

SECTION 12 OF TRADITION 1.1.12 TEACHES THE FOLLOWING:

- Submission to truth increases intellect.
- Submission to the truth is difficult.
- Those who submit to truth are few.

- The standard for "intelligence" is willingness to follow truth, not cleverness.
- Most people do not act intelligently in the face of truth.
- The world in which we live is as perilous as the ocean is for sailors.
- The following qualities are necessary to safely traverse this temporal life: fear of God, faith, reliance on God, intellect, knowledge, and fortitude.

Section 13

'O Hishām! There is a guide for everything [that needs one];[1] the guide for the intellect is contemplation, and the guide for contemplation is silence.[2] And there is a mount [appropriate] for everything [that needs one]; the mount for the intellect is submission [to truth].[3] To perpetrate what you have been forbidden to do is a sufficient indicator of your foolishness.[4]

يَا هِشَامُ، إِنَّ لِكُلِّ شَيْءٍ دَلِيلًا، وَدَلِيلُ الْعَقْلِ التَّفَكُّرُ، وَدَلِيلُ التَّفَكُّرِ الصَّمْتُ. وَلِكُلِّ شَيْءٍ مَطِيَّةً، وَمَطِيَّةُ الْعَقْلِ التَّوَاضُعُ. وَكَفَى بِكَ جَهْلًا أَنْ تَرْكَبَ مَا نُهِيتَ عَنْهُ.

---

1. Some commentators have construed *dalīl* to mean "a sign" or "evidence." We, on the other hand, have translated it as "a guide," for Imam al-Kāẓim paints an image of the intellect as a traveler who needs two things on his journey: a guide to lead him to his destination and a mount to carry him there. Contextually, there is no place for a "sign" in this imagery.

2. The goal of the intellect is to understand reality. The means to reach this goal is to use our intellect to process information and thereby learn about something hitherto unknown. This is known as contemplation (*tafakkur*). It follows that anything that facilitates contemplation will help guide intellect to its destination. Such is silence; for whether it is our own silence or the silence of our surroundings, silence allows us sufficient opportunity to think. For this reason, Imam ʿAlī has said, "Maintain silence, and your thinking will blossom" and "Increase your silence, and your thinking will increase" (*Ghurar al-ḥikam* tradition 10,824 and 10,825).

3. Even if a traveler has a guide, he will not be able to reach his destination if he is without a mount to carry him there. Such is the state of our intellect:

through silent contemplation, our intellect may be able to discern reality, but until we are willing to submit to this reality and accept it, we cannot actually reach it.

It is useful to compare this sentence to Luqmān's admonishment in section twelve, "Submit to truth, and you shall attain the strongest intellect of all people." Both sentences indicate positive consequences of fostering a personality that is humble and submissive to the truth. Section twelve indicates that it increases our intellectual powers. This section indicates that it facilitates our acceptance of the truth.

4. Once Imam al-Kāẓim has established that we need both contemplation and humility before truth in order to reach the truth, he says that a sufficient indicator that a person has not availed himself of one or both of these necessary elements is that he perpetrates a sin despite having been ordered by God to refrain from it. Such a person has either failed to contemplate the necessity of obeying God's commandments or failed to submit himself to these commandments and abide by them. In either case, he is a fool.

SECTION 13 OF TRADITION 1.1.12 TEACHES THE FOLLOWING:

- Contemplation leads the intellect to understand truth.
- Silence leads our contemplation to reach a sound conclusion.
- Submission to truth leads one to accept truth.
- The slightest act that designates one as a fool is sin.

Section 14

يَا هِشَامُ، مَا بَعَثَ اللَّهُ أَنْبِيَاءَهُ وَرُسُلَهُ إِلَى عِبَادِهِ إِلَّا لِيَعْقِلُوا عَنِ اللَّهِ، فَأَحْسَنُهُمُ اسْتِجَابَةً أَحْسَنُهُمْ مَعْرِفَةً، وَأَعْلَمُهُمْ بِأَمْرِ اللَّهِ أَحْسَنُهُمْ عَقْلًا، وَأَكْمَلُهُمْ عَقْلًا أَرْفَعُهُمْ دَرَجَةً فِي الدُّنْيَا وَالْآخِرَةِ.

'O Hishām! God has only sent his prophets and messengers[1] to his servants so that his servants should know him as he has described himself.[2] Thus, those of them who answer [the call of the prophets and messengers] best, know [God and matters related to God] best;[3] and those of them who know about [God and] matters related to God best, employ their intellects best; and those who employ their intellects best are at the highest station in this world and the hereafter.[4]

---

1. For a detailed discussion of the differences between a prophet and messenger, see 4.3.1-4.

2. This sentence states that the sole purpose of the prophetic mission was that people should know God as he has described himself. In the same vein, Imam al-Ḥasan has said, "...God raised among them prophets as bearers of glad tidings and as warners so that those who perish do so despite clear evidence, and those who live do so based on clear evidence and so that his servants may know through their Lord what they knew not, and thus know him as their Lord after having known him not..." (*Biḥār al-anwār* 43.1.17.6).

3. "Matters related to God" is a reference to God's attributes, his books, and his commandments.

4. In summary, this paragraph begins by stating that God's ultimate goal in sending prophets was that people should know God as he has described himself. The rest of the tradition then explains how we can reach this goal and what the consequences of reaching this goal are. In particular, we gain knowledge of God, his attributes, his books, and his law by answering the call of the prophets and accepting their guidance. One of the results of learning these things is an increased ability to employ our intellect. The better we employ our intellect the better will be our understanding of truth and the better equipped we will be to apply divine teachings to our lives. The product of all this is a life of dignity and happiness in this world and in the hereafter.

SECTION 14 OF TRADITION 1.1.12 TEACHES THE FOLLOWING:

- Prophets are sent to guide people, just as messengers are. Thus, the idea that messengers are sent to guide other people while prophets are only meant to guide themselves is incorrect.
- The sole purpose for which God sent prophets was that people should know him correctly.

Section 15

'O Hishām! God has two pieces of evidence against people: [one is] manifest, and [the other is] hidden. That which is manifest is his messengers, prophets, and imams.[1] That which is hidden is the [people's] intellect.[2]

يَا هِشَامُ، إِنَّ لِلَّهِ عَلَى النَّاسِ حُجَّتَيْنِ: حُجَّةً ظَاهِرَةً وَحُجَّةً بَاطِنَةً. فَأَمَّا الظَّاهِرَةُ فَالرُّسُلُ وَالْأَنْبِيَاءُ وَالْأَئِمَّةُ عليهم السلام، وَأَمَّا الْبَاطِنَةُ فَالْعُقُولُ.

---

1. For an explanation of how these divine guides serve as evidence against people refer to our explanation of "divine guides" in section two of 1.1.12.

2. We can divide incriminating evidence (*ḥujjah*) into three categories:

- Sometimes it is brought forth by one person to incriminate another. God uses it in this sense when he tells his Prophet to change the direction of his prayers from Jerusalem to the Kaᶜbah in Mecca (Qurᵓān 2:150). He explains that his reason for issuing this legislation is to ensure that the Prophet's detractors have no evidence with which to argue against the Muslims. In particular, Jews could no longer accuse Muslims of imitating them and praying to "their" holy site. Similarly, the pagans of Mecca could no longer accuse them of having abandoned the Kaᶜbah of Abraham.
- Other times incriminating evidence is brought forth by God against people. God uses it in this sense when he says, "Only God has conclusive *evidence*" (Qurᵓān 6:149) as part of his rebuttal against those who offer flimsy justifications for their polytheistic beliefs.
- Finally, evidence could potentially be brought forth by people against God. It is this sense of the word that God rejects and negates when he says he has sent so many messengers so that people should have no *evidence* left with which to plead ignorance of the divine command (Qurᵓān 4:165).

Interestingly, the intellect acts as evidence (a *ḥujjah*) in all three senses of the word. Tradition 1.1.22 will mention two of these aspects. This sentence in 1.1.12 only mentions one of these three aspects: that God uses the intellect to argue against people.

SECTION 15 OF TRADITION 1.1.12 TEACHES THE FOLLOWING:

- God judges people based on evidence.
- The testimony of God's messengers, prophets, and imams will be admitted on the Day of Judgment.
- The intellect serves as incriminating evidence against those who fail to use it or act against its dictates.

Section 16

يَا هِشَامُ، إِنَّ الْعَاقِلَ الَّـذِي لَا يَشْغَلُ الْحَلَالُ شُكْرَهُ وَلَا يَغْلِبُ الْحَرَامُ صَبْرَهُ.

'O Hishām! He who employs his intellect is never distracted from giving thanks by [an abundance of] things that are [good and] lawful, and his self-restraint is never overwhelmed by [an abundance of] things that are [desirable yet] illicit.[1]

---

1. By using his intellect, this person is able to understand his moral obligation to thank the one who has bestowed on him these innumerable blessings. He then proceeds to act on this understanding and unabatedly thanks him. Likewise, through his intellect he understands the harm that will come of capitulating to temptations, so he proceeds to act on this understanding and restrains himself. On the other hand, one who is distracted by blessings and fails to thank the bestower of those blessings, and likewise one who capitulates to temptation, has failed to use his intellect and can rightfully be called a fool, as though he has no intellect to speak of.

SECTION 16 OF TRADITION 1.1.12 TEACHES THE FOLLOWING:

- One who makes use of one of God's blessings but fails to thank him or sins against him in return has no intellect of which to speak.
- Showing gratitude for a kindness done and abstaining from sin are dictates of the intellect.

Section 17

يَا هِشَامُ، مَنْ سَلَّطَ ثَلَاثاً عَلَى ثَلَاثٍ فَكَأَنَّمَا أَعَانَ عَلَى هَدْمِ عَقْلِهِ. مَنْ أَظْلَمَ نُورَ تَفَكُّرِهِ بِطُولِ أَمَلِهِ، وَمَحَا طَرَائِفَ حِكْمَتِهِ بِفُضُولِ كَلَامِهِ، وَأَطْفَأَ نُورَ عِبْرَتِهِ بِشَهَوَاتِ نَفْسِهِ، فَكَأَنَّمَا أَعَانَ هَوَاهُ عَلَى هَدْمِ عَقْلِهِ، وَمَنْ هَدَمَ عَقْلَهُ أَفْسَدَ عَلَيْهِ دِينَهُ وَدُنْيَاهُ.

'O Hishām! If a man releases three [traits] upon three [others], it is as though he has aided in the destruction of his own intellect.[1] If he obscures the light of contemplation with far-fetched hopes,[2] and expunges wondrous wisdom [from his heart] with excessive talk,[3] and extinguishes his willingness to learn [from life's] lessons with his carnal desires,[4] then it is as though he has aided his carnal soul in destroying his own intellect. And he who destroys his own intellect has ruined his [lot in this] world and the hereafter.

---

1. In the war between intellect and foolish desire, each commander has enlisted soldiers to do his bidding on the battlefield. Foolishness has three soldiers called "far-fetched hopes," "excessive talk," and "carnal desires." Likewise, intellect has enlisted "contemplation," "wisdom," and "a willingness to learn from life's lessons." If we release the soldiers of foolishness upon the soldiers of intellect, we will have conspired with foolishness, thereby increasing its control over our intellect, resulting in the latter's near paralysis. We might as well have destroyed our intellect altogether, for in either case, we render it useless.

2. In traditions, the word "contemplation" (*fikr* and its derivatives) does not connote just any type of thinking. Rather, it refers specifically to contemplation of the transience of the temporal world and its pleasures and the permanence of the hereafter and its pleasures such that one feels indifferent to the former and passionately desirous of the latter. Far-fetched hopes (*ṭūl al-aml*), on the other hand, connote one's expectation, even assurance, that one will live a long life and thereby attain the pleasures of this world in abundance. Far-fetched hopes stem from two qualities: infatuation with the temporal world and ignorance. One who is infatuated with the world sees nothing but the object of his infatuation and strives to serve it and keep it close to him. He is not willing to face the inevitable separation that lies ahead. Likewise, one who is steeped in ignorance does not open his eyes to the reality of death and the transience of this world and assumes that things will always be as they are now. Thus, infatuation and ignorance lead one to entertain unfounded hopes and to shun all thoughts of death and the hereafter, thereby obscuring the luminosity that the latter thoughts inevitably generate.

3. One who speaks excessively leaves himself little opportunity to think and cultivate wisdom in his heart. In addition, one who perpetually speaks to people and wishes to rise in esteem before them must constantly think of things that will amuse them, thus leaving himself little opportunity for the kind of contemplation that leads to wisdom. It is in this vein that Prophet Muḥammad has said, "If you see a believer who maintains silence, stay close to him, for he shall emanate wisdom" (*Biḥār al-anwār* 67.1.58.9).

4. One who lustfully pursues his carnal desires is blinded with respect to all else. Naturally, one who is blind to all that occurs around him cannot learn the lessons that he must.

SECTION 17 OF TRADITION 1.1.12 TEACHES THE FOLLOWING:

- Among the intellect's functions is to contemplate, to learn life's lessons, and to learn and speak wisdom.
- Far-fetched hopes impede fruitful contemplation.
- Our excessive talking deprives us of wisdom.
- Carnal desires prevent us from learning life's lessons.

- Maintaining far-fetched hopes, speaking excessively, and nurturing carnal desires are tantamount to ruining this life and the next.

Section 18

يَا هِشَامُ، كَيْفَ يَزْكُو عِنْدَ اللَّهِ عَمَلُكَ وَأَنْتَ قَدْ شَغَلْتَ قَلْبَكَ عَنْ أَمْرِ رَبِّكَ، وَأَطَعْتَ هَوَاكَ عَلَى غَلَبَةِ عَقْلِكَ؟

'O Hishām! How can [the reward for] your actions increase in God's assessment when you have diverted your heart from [obedience to] the commandments of God[1] and [instead] obeyed your carnal soul [and aided it] in overwhelming your intellect?[2]

---

1. This harsh admonishment is only directed at Hishām rhetorically. It is in reality addressed to those people who defy God's commandments and then expect God to reward them for their few good deeds.

2. God has promised to multiply the reward he gives for good deeds. For instance, he says, "What you pay in charity while seeking God's pleasure [shall be multiplied manifold,] for it is [the likes of] these who will be given a manifold increase" (Qur'ān 30:39). He also says, "Those who spend their money in God's way are like a seed that produces seven ears, each of which contains one hundred seeds. God multiplies [his reward] for whomever he wishes. God is generous and omniscient" (2:261). In these two verses, the phrases "while seeking God's pleasure" and "in God's way" indicate that this multiplied reward depends on certain factors, foremost of which is the actor's intention. If, on the other hand, the actor disregards God's laws and surrenders himself to his carnal desires, God will not double and redouble the reward for the act, even if, on the surface, it is a good act. The beginning of one of the aforementioned verses conveys this message, "What you give in usurious loans so that it may increase [through interest while] in the possession of others, does not increase [in reward] in God's assessment" (Qur'ān 30:39).

SECTION 18 OF TRADITION 1.1.12 TEACHES THE FOLLOWING:

- If we act with close regard for God's commandments, and if we subjugate our carnal souls to our intellects, God will reward us manifold for our deeds.
- There is little reward for a good act done by one with a weak intellect and a distracted heart.
- The goodness of an act does not bring reward without the goodness of the actor.
- The carnal soul is actively engaged in overwhelming the intellect.

Section 19

يَا هِشَامُ، الصَّبْرُ عَلَى الْوَحْدَةِ عَلَامَةُ قُوَّةِ الْعَقْلِ، فَمَنْ عَقَلَ عَنِ اللَّهِ اعْتَزَلَ أَهْلَ الدُّنْيَا وَالرَّاغِبِينَ فِيهَا، وَرَغِبَ فِيمَا عِنْدَ اللَّهِ، وَكَانَ اللَّهُ إِنْسَهُ فِي الْوَحْشَةِ وَصَاحِبَهُ فِي الْوَحْدَةِ وَغِنَاهُ فِي الْعَيْلَةِ وَمُعِزَّهُ مِنْ غَيْرِ عَشِيرَةٍ.

'O Hishām! [The ability] to endure solitude is an indicator of the strength of one's intellect.[1] For, he who knows God [as he has described himself, by using the strength of his intellect] remains aloof of those [immersed] in the material world and those who are desirous of it, and [instead] desires what is with God. God is his comfort in [times of] anxiety, his company in [times of] solitude, his wealth in [times of] poverty, and his honor [in times] when he lacks [the support of his] kin.[2]

---

1. The ability to endure solitude is only one of the indicators of a well-developed intellect, for as we can glean from the end of this tradition, such a person would also be able to endure anxiety, poverty, and degradation. Nonetheless, Imam al-Kāzim only mentions the ability to endure solitude, because solitude is the first consequence of choosing the path of righteousness and is the cause of the other three consequences mentioned.

2. This section praises the fortitude of a person with a well-developed intellect. Such a person, because of his strong intellect, knows God as he has described himself and acknowledges his duty toward him. Consequently, he may be cut off by others. He too must cut himself off from those who are engrossed in the material world if he fears their bad influence or loses all hope of positively influencing them. Thus, he finds himself, many times, alone. Consequently, he suffers from the anxiety of loneliness and from poverty and social scorn. However, because of his strong intellect, he understands that these hardships are minor and short-lived and that the reward for which he is living is eternal, so he endures. In response, God comes to his aid by comforting him, fulfilling his material needs, and guarding his dignity in society. The Qurʾān describes those who are desirous of the material world and those who know God in the story of Korah (Qārūn) where it says, "Those who wanted the material world said, 'We wish that we had the likes of what Korah has been given. He has had great fortune.' Those who were given knowledge said, 'Woe to you! God's reward is better for he who has faith and does good.' However, only the persevering shall receive it" (Qurʾān 28:79-80). Imam ʿAlī also encourages us to endure the hardships entailed in the path of righteousness by saying, "O people! Do not feel anxious while on the path of guidance because of the dearth of those who tread it, for [the majority of] people have gathered around a table at which they will satiate themselves for a while, but after which they will hunger for an eternity" (*Nahj al-balāghah* sermon 201).

SECTION 19 OF TRADITION 1.1.12 TEACHES THE FOLLOWING:

- The ability to endure solitude is an indicator of a well-developed intellect.
- One with a strong intellect cuts himself off from those infatuated with the temporal world.
- Acting on one's strong intellect often brings solitude, anxiety, poverty, and degradation.

Section 20

‘O Hishām! The [religion of] truth[1] has been established so God may be obeyed, and there is no salvation without obedience. Obedience comes from knowledge, and knowledge comes from learning, and [the knowledge gained through] learning is strengthened by understanding. There is no knowledge [to benefit you in this path] except [what comes] from a godly scholar. And one can recognize [beneficial] knowledge with the intellect.[2]

يَا هِشَامُ، نُصِبَ الْحَقُّ لِطَاعَةِ اللَّهِ، وَلَا نَجَاةَ إِلَّا بِالطَّاعَةِ، وَالطَّاعَةُ بِالْعِلْمِ وَالْعِلْمُ بِالتَّعَلُّمِ وَالتَّعَلُّمُ بِالْعَقْلِ يُعْتَقَدُ، وَلَا عِلْمَ إِلَّا مِنْ عَالِمٍ رَبَّانِيٍّ، وَمَعْرِفَةُ الْعِلْمِ بِالْعَقْلِ.

---

1. We have translated *al-ḥaqq* as “the religion of truth.” The basic meaning of the word *ḥaqq* is “reality” or “what *is*.” Islam is called *ḥaqq* because its tenets and commandments are “true” in that they match with “reality.” Its tenets are true because they inform us of what is real like the existence of God, his oneness, the existence of purgatory (*barzakh*) and the hereafter, and the infallibility of the prophets and imams. Its commandments are true because they are based on real standards of benefit and harm and are not arbitrary commandments issued simply to test our obedience.

2. This section tersely outlines the philosophy of religion. God has ordained religion to show people how to obey him, for the only way to attain salvation from misery in this life and the next is through his obedience. Obedience to God’s commandments is only possible if one has knowledge of those commandments, and the only way to attain this knowledge is to learn it. However, it is not sufficient to learn God’s commandments superficially; rather, by contemplating them carefully, this knowledge becomes firmly fixed in one’s heart. Insofar as the knowledge in question is religious knowledge, it can only be found in godly scholars. To discriminate between those scholars who are godly and those who are not, and consequently between knowledge that is beneficial and that which is not, God has given us our intellect. Thus, the intellect performs two functions on the path to salvation: it helps us discriminate between beneficial and useless knowledge, and it helps to strengthen what we learn and make it firm in our hearts. Since these functions are crucial for all the other steps in this series, the goal of which is salvation, we can conclude that there can be no salvation without intellect.

SECTION 20 OF TRADITION 1.1.12 TEACHES THE FOLLOWING:

- The philosophy behind the existence of religion is for us to discern the way to salvation from the harms of this world and the next.
- Salvation cannot be attained except through obedience to God.
- Obedience to God is not possible without knowing which commandments to obey.
- The way to attain knowledge is through learning.
- Knowledge that is learned only becomes firmly fixed in the heart if coupled with contemplation and understanding.
- The only source of divine knowledge is a godly scholar.
- The intellect allows us to discriminate between good and bad knowledge.
- The intellect serves two roles in learning: first, to discriminate between good and bad knowledge; second, to aid in the learning process by allowing understanding.
- Salvation cannot be attained except through the intellect.

Section 21

يَا هِشَامُ، قَلِيلُ الْعَمَلِ مِنَ الْعَالِمِ مَقْبُولٌ مُضَاعَفٌ، وَكَثِيرُ الْعَمَلِ مِنْ أَهْلِ الْهَوَى وَالْجَهْلِ مَرْدُودٌ.

'O Hishām! A few [good] deeds from one with knowledge [and intellect][1] is accepted and [even] multiplied,[2] while many [good] deeds from those who are ignorant and slaves to their desires are rejected.

---

1. The word *ʿālim* literally means "one with knowledge." However, we have translated it here as "one with knowledge *and intellect*." We are justified in translating it thus because this sentence contrasts an *ʿālim* with one who is both ignorant (*ahl al-jahl*) and follows his desires (*ahl al-hawā*), and the opposite of being ignorant and a slave to one's desires is to be knowledgeable and to employ one's intellect. Our translation is further justified by numerous traditions that juxtapose intellect and desire (*hawā*). For instance, Imam ʿAlī says, "Many an intellect is held captive by commandeering desires" (*Nahj al-balāghah* proverb 211). He also says, "Fight your desires with your intellect" (*Nahj al-balāghah* proverb 424). In yet another tradition, he says, "The bane of the intellect is desire" (*Ghurar al-ḥikam* proverb 3925).

2. Such a person's deeds are accepted, and his reward is even multiplied, because of the three traits that are earmarked here. First, his knowledge allows him to know how best to act by fulfilling all requisite conditions and avoiding anything that would detract from his deeds. Second, his intellect allows him to discriminate between what is more and less important, and he always chooses the former over the latter (we discussed this benefit of the intellect in more detail under the phrase "the sleep of one who employs his intellect is better than a fool's vigil..." in 1.1.11). Third, because he does not act according to his whims, his deeds are done purely for God's pleasure.

SECTION 21 OF TRADITION 1.1.12 TEACHES THE FOLLOWING:

- In God's judgment of our deeds, quality is important, not quantity.
- Knowledge and intellect are the standards according to which actions are accepted and rewards are doled out.

Section 22

'O Hishām! One with intellect is pleased with [but] simple pleasures of the material world if he has wisdom. However, he is never pleased with simple wisdom[1] just because he has the [pleasures of the] material world.[2] This is why they have profited [in the bazaar of life].[3]

يَا هِشَامُ، إِنَّ الْعَاقِلَ رَضِيَ بِالدُّونِ مِنَ الدُّنْيَا مَعَ الْحِكْمَةِ، وَلَمْ يَرْضَ بِالدُّونِ مِنَ الْحِكْمَةِ مَعَ الدُّنْيَا، فَلِذَلِكَ رَبِحَتْ تِجَارَتُهُمْ.

---

1. "Simple wisdom" refers to wisdom that all people can comprehend without any great effort or spiritual quest. For instance, even the simplest of people understand the merit of abiding by the behavioral norms of society. Thus, the value of propriety is a simple kind of wisdom. Accordingly, we see many people in society who put great stock in outward politeness because it does not negatively impact their material pleasures at all. Yet these same people never seek to understand the value of complete self-sacrifice for the sake of God or other instances of lofty wisdom because the impact of such wisdom could potentially decimate their material pleasures.

2. This tradition treats the pursuit of material pleasures (*dunyā*) and wisdom (*ḥikmah*) as mutually exclusive because both require one to spend time, and possibly money, and to exert a great amount of energy to attain them. Since these are limited resources, it is possible for circumstances to prevent one from pursuing both. Under such circumstances, one who uses his intellect chooses what is more beneficial to him: wisdom. However, if his resources permit him to attain both, he would and should pursue both. Of course, under all circumstances, he should refrain from excessive exploitation of material pleasures as indicated by the next stanza of this tradition where Imam al-Kāẓim says, "Those with intellect abstain from the excesses of the material world," but there is no contradiction between seeking material pleasures and abstaining from *excessive* material pleasures. In this vein, it has been narrated that "a man told Abū ʿAbd Allāh [al-Ṣādiq], 'We seek material wealth and we love to receive it.' So al-Ṣādiq asked him, 'What do you like to do with it?' He answered, 'I spend it on myself and on my family; I use it to strengthen my ties with my kin; I give it in charity; I perform the hajj and the *ʿumrah.*' Abū ʿAbd Allāh said, 'That is not [called] "seeking material wealth;" that is [called] "seeking the hereafter"' (*Wasāʾil al-shīʿah* 17.1.7.3).

3. Imam al-Hādī has said, "The world is a bazaar in which some have profited and others have lost" (*Tuḥaf al-ʿuqūl* p.483). Those with intellect are concerned with attaining the greatest good in this bazaar called life. They invest their precious, though limited, resources—their time and their energy—in those pursuits that yield the highest profit.

SECTION 22 OF TRADITION 1.1.12 TEACHES THE FOLLOWING:

- One with intellect in the fourth sense of the word concerns himself with attaining lofty levels of wisdom.
- If circumstances dictate that having high levels of wisdom and high levels of worldly wealth are mutually exclusive, one with intellect will choose the former over the latter.
- Intellect naturally draws us toward wisdom, while foolishness naturally draws us toward worldly pleasure.
- Wisdom is of different kinds: some are comprehensible to all, and some are only comprehensible to those with strong intellect.
- Those who have chosen to pursue worldly pleasure to the exclusion of wisdom are fools.
- He who has intellect is wise.

Section 23

'O Hishām! Those with intellect [even] abstain from the excesses of the material world,[1] so how could they not abstain from sin when abstaining from [the excesses of] the material world is [but] a virtue, while abstaining from sin is an obligation?

يَا هِشَامُ، إِنَّ الْعُقَلَاءَ تَرَكُوا فُضُولَ الدُّنْيَا، فَكَيْفَ الذُّنُوبُ، وَتَرْكُ الدُّنْيَا مِنَ الْفَضْلِ وَتَرْكُ الذُّنُوبِ مِنَ الْفَرْضِ؟

---

1. Our intellect dictates that we do only what is beneficial. Since spending our time and energy to attain more than what we need is a waste of time, those who act according to their intellect abstain from such activity. It is important, though, to define what comprises "need" and "excess." Obviously, what one person needs may be excessive for another, and what a person needs in one set of circumstances may be excessive for him in another. Thus, there is no compelling reason to construe their abstinence "from the excesses of the material world" to mean that they only take what they need *to survive* and leave all else, since mere survival may be less than what most people *need* out of life. Rather, they take from it what constitutes their requisite level of comfort and happiness, and leave all else. As always, the golden mean is the ideal path, for God says, "Do not keep your hand chained to your neck [in stinginess], nor open it altogether [in charity], or you will be blameworthy and regretful" (Qur'ān 17:29). He also says, "And [the servants of the All-Merciful are...] those who, when spending, are neither wasteful nor tightfisted, rather [their spending] is moderate, between these [two extremes]" (Qur'ān 25:67).

SECTION 23 OF TRADITION 1.1.12 TEACHES THE FOLLOWING:

- He who uses his intellect does not take more than he needs.
- He who uses his intellect definitely abstains from sin.
- To abstain from the excesses of the material world is not

obligatory, yet he who uses his intellect does so.

- He who uses his intellect seeks virtue and does not content himself with only fulfilling obligatory duties.

Section 24

يَا هِشَامُ، إِنَّ الْعَاقِلَ نَظَرَ إِلَى الدُّنْيَا وَإِلَى أَهْلِهَا فَعَلِمَ أَنَّهَا لَا تُنَالُ إِلَّا بِالْمَشَقَّةِ. وَنَظَرَ إِلَى الْآخِرَةِ فَعَلِمَ أَنَّهَا لَا تُنَالُ إِلَّا بِالْمَشَقَّةِ، فَطَلَبَ بِالْمَشَقَّةِ أَبْقَاهُمَا.

'O Hishām! One with intellect examines the material world and [examines] its devotees and realizes that it cannot be attained without a struggle. He [also] examines the hereafter [and examines its devotees] and realizes that it [too] cannot be attained without a struggle. So through this struggle, [which he must endure in any case], he seeks [to attain] the one that is longer lasting.[1]

---

1. The intellect dictates that we do what promises to give the greatest benefit. It analyzes the material world, its devotees, and the relationship between the two and determines that people must work hard to attain material wealth. Similarly, it analyzes the hereafter, its devotees, and the relationship between the two and determines that people must work hard to attain happiness there too. At this point, the intellect compares the cost of each to the relative benefit of each and sees that the benefit in the hereafter is greater, since it is everlasting, while the benefit of this world is finite.

SECTION 24 OF TRADITION 1.1.12 TEACHES THE FOLLOWING:

- Neither the material world nor the hereafter can be attained except through hard work.
- Anyone who thinks he can attain paradise without hard work is a fool.
- One with intellect contemplates, compares, and draws strong conclusions.
- One with intellect always chooses the most profitable option.

- It is contrary to the dictates of the intellect to prefer to endure hardship to reach finite worldly pleasure over enduring hardship to reach infinite pleasure in paradise.

Section 25

'O Hishām! Those with intellect feel indifferent to the material world and desirous of the hereafter because they know[1] that the material world seeks and is sought after, and that the hereafter [also] seeks and is sought after.[2] Thus, if a person seeks the hereafter, [he will not forgo the material world because] the material world will seek him out until he receives his sustenance from it in full. If, [on the other hand,] he seeks the material world, [he will forgo the material world and the hereafter because] the hereafter will seek him out, and death will come to him, and this world and the hereafter will be ruined for him.[3]

يَا هِشَامُ، إِنَّ الْعُقَلَاءَ زَهِدُوا فِي الدُّنْيَا وَرَغِبُوا فِي الْآخِرَةِ لِأَنَّهُمْ عَلِمُوا أَنَّ الدُّنْيَا طَالِبَةٌ وَ مَطْلُوبَةٌ وَالْآخِرَةَ طَالِبَةٌ وَمَطْلُوبَةٌ. فَمَنْ طَلَبَ الْآخِرَةَ طَلَبَتْهُ الدُّنْيَا حَتَّى يَسْتَوْفِيَ مِنْهَا رِزْقَهُ. وَمَنْ طَلَبَ الدُّنْيَا طَلَبَتْهُ الْآخِرَةُ فَيَأْتِيهِ الْمَوْتُ فَيُفْسِدُ عَلَيْهِ دُنْيَاهُ وَآخِرَتَهُ.

---

1. The word "because" indicates that it is their knowledge of the temporal world and the hereafter that makes them indifferent to the former and desirous of the latter. You might ask: Where do they get this knowledge? Is it knowledge they have been given through divine guidance or knowledge spontaneously produced by their intellects? In reality, both divine guidance and their intellect play an important role in giving them the knowledge to arrive at their conclusions. It is divine guidance that teaches them of the true nature of the temporal world and the hereafter; about God's guarantee to provide sustenance to all things; and about the inevitability of death. However, it is their intellect that compares the advantages and disadvantages of seeking this world and the next. In summary, they synthesize this information as follows: Both the temporal world and the hereafter are worth seeking. However, there is greater advantage in seeking the hereafter, for if I seek the temporal world, I deprive myself of happiness in the hereafter. As Imam ʿAlī says, "He who sells his afterlife for his material life has lost them both" (*Ghurar al-ḥikam* proverb 2489). If, on the other hand, I seek the hereafter, I benefit from both this world and the next. As Imam ʿAlī says, "He who buys his afterlife with his material life profits in both" (*Ghurar al-ḥikam* proverb 2661).

2. The material world can figuratively be said to "seek" because it "seeks" out every person and delivers to him the sustenance apportioned for him as long as he fulfills the prerequisites of sustenance such as expending effort, for God has said, "The responsibility of providing sustenance to every single animal on earth lies solely with God" (Qurʾān 11:6). The hereafter can figuratively be said to "seek" because it "seeks" out every person and delivers his death at the appointed time and transfers him from this realm to the next. Both the material world and the hereafter can be said to be "sought after" because various people desire the best possible station in either the former or the latter.

3. His life in this world will be ruined because death will cut him off from all the pleasures for which he lived. His life in the hereafter will be ruined because he failed to prepare for it in his worldly life.

SECTION 25 OF TRADITION 1.1.12 TEACHES THE FOLLOWING:

- One with intellect knows the true nature of the temporal world and feels indifferent toward it.
- One with intellect knows the true nature of the hereafter and feels desirous of it.
- Our worldly sustenance seeks us out and comes to us.
- To live a life focused on the hereafter does not adversely affect the sustenance guaranteed to us in this world.

- If we seek the pleasures of this world to the exclusion of the hereafter, we lose in this world when we are cut off by death, and we lose in the hereafter when our life of sin and failed obligations comes back to haunt us.

Section 26

يَا هِشَامُ، مَنْ أَرَادَ الْغِنَى بِلَا مَالٍ، وَرَاحَةَ الْقَلْبِ مِنَ الْحَسَدِ، وَالسَّلَامَةَ فِي الدِّينِ، فَلْيَتَضَرَّعْ إِلَى اللَّهِ عَزَّ وَجَلَّ فِي مَسْأَلَتِهِ بِأَنْ يُكَمِّلَ عَقْلَهُ. فَمَنْ عَقَلَ قَنِعَ بِمَا يَكْفِيهِ، وَمَنْ قَنِعَ بِمَا يَكْفِيهِ اسْتَغْنَى، وَمَنْ لَمْ يَقْنَعْ بِمَا يَكْفِيهِ لَمْ يُدْرِكِ الْغِنَى أَبَداً.

'O Hishām! He who wants financial independence without [necessarily increasing his] wealth, and [consequently wants] to free his heart of jealousy and preserve his faith [from the eroding effect of sins that often arise from financial dependence],[1] must humbly beg God—invincible is he and majestic—to perfect his intellect; for he who uses his intellect is content with what suffices him, and he who is content with what suffices him is financially independent. On the other hand, he who is not content with what suffices him will never attain financial independence.[2]

---

1. At first glance, it seems this tradition is speaking of financial independence, freedom from jealousy, and the preservation of faith as three independent goals. However, further examination reveals that there is a hierarchy among these goals and the other elements mentioned. In particular, a strong intellect leads a person to be content with what he has. Being content with what he has leads him to feel independent of what he does not have. This independence in turn relieves him of being jealous of those who have more. When he is not jealous of them, he will refrain from committing sins that are often rooted in jealousy such as stealing, vandalism, and slander. Refraining from such sins preserves his faith. There is further evidence for the existence of this hierarchy in the second half of this section. Imam al-Kāẓim only mentions "financial independence" as the fruit of using one's intellect and does not feel the need to mention "freedom from jealousy" and "the preservation of faith," since these are natural consequences of financial independence, not independent consequences of using one's intellect.

2. This section states that financial independence comes only from contentment and that contentment comes only from a strong intellect and that a strong intellect comes from humble prayer. Other traditions indicate that the path to a stronger intellect lies in such things as abstaining from sin, learning and teaching, discipline, experience, and submission to truth. It is notable that these other factors are not on equal footing with praying humbly for intellect, for we can only successfully engage in the aforementioned activities by the grace and aid of God. Thus, we must first humbly beg God to make us successful in these endeavors before we may strengthen our intellect and reap its benefits.

SECTION 26 OF TRADITION 1.1.12 TEACHES THE FOLLOWING:

- Freedom from jealousy and the preservation of faith follow from financial independence.
- Prayer plays a key role in perfecting the intellect.
- Contentment is the result of a strong intellect.
- Financial independence is the result of contentment.

Section 27

'O Hishām! God has recounted that a righteous people said, when they realized that hearts [can potentially] veer and revert to their [intrinsic] blindness and [consequent] destruction,[1] *"O Lord! Do not make our hearts veer after you have guided us, and bestow your mercy on us, [for] you and you alone are the All-Munificent."*[2] Only he does not fear God who does not know God [as he has described himself]. And he who does not know God [as he has described himself][3] will never bind his heart to any kind of constant knowledge that he can see and whose reality he can palpate in his heart. Only he is [said to know and fear God] like this whose actions confirm his words[4] and whose private [conduct] agrees with his public [conduct]. [We can be sure that this is the case][5] because God—good is his name—has not indicated an inner, hidden aspect of the intellect except through an outer one, that stands for it.

يَا هِشَامُ، إِنَّ اللَّهَ حَكَى عَنْ قَوْمٍ صَالِحِينَ أَنَّهُمْ قَالُوا: ﴿رَبَّنَا لَا تُزِغْ قُلُوبَنَا بَعْدَ إِذْ هَدَيْتَنَا وَهَبْ لَنَا مِنْ لَدُنْكَ رَحْمَةً إِنَّكَ أَنْتَ الْوَهَّابُ﴾، حِينَ عَلِمُوا أَنَّ الْقُلُوبَ تَزِيغُ وَتَعُودُ إِلَى عَمَاهَا وَرَدَاهَا. إِنَّهُ لَمْ يَخَفِ اللَّهَ مَنْ لَمْ يَعْقِلْ عَنِ اللَّهِ. وَمَنْ لَمْ يَعْقِلْ عَنِ اللَّهِ لَمْ يَعْقِدْ قَلْبَهُ عَلَى مَعْرِفَةٍ ثَابِتَةٍ يُبْصِرُهَا وَيَجِدُ حَقِيقَتَهَا فِي قَلْبِهِ. وَلَا يَكُونُ أَحَدٌ كَذَلِكَ إِلَّا مَنْ كَانَ قَوْلُهُ لِفِعْلِهِ مُصَدِّقاً، وَسِرُّهُ لِعَلَانِيَتِهِ مُوَافِقاً، لِأَنَّ اللَّهَ - تَبَارَكَ اسْمُهُ - لَمْ يَدُلَّ عَلَى الْبَاطِنِ الْخَفِيِّ مِنَ الْعَقْلِ إِلَّا بِظَاهِرٍ مِنْهُ وَنَاطِقٍ عَنْهُ.

---

1. The righteous do not assume that their present strength of conviction will always remain. They realize that guidance is a gift from God that he must continuously issue to them and without which they would instantly revert to their intrinsic state of meandering aimlessly through life, not knowing for what purpose they have been created. The Qurʾān even says to Prophet Muḥammad—God's mercy be on him and his family—who was undoubtedly guided by the Divine from the time of his birth, "And [did God not] find you astray and then guide you" (Qurʾān 93:7), thus showing that even he is not guided except by God's good graces. The righteous realize that if guidance is not an intrinsic trait, then it may be lost, and the insight of faith may turn to blindness, and one who had once been guided may find himself in perdition. Thus, they pray earnestly for God's continued guidance.

2. Qurʾān 3:8

3. In the first sentence of this section, Imam al-Kāẓim, describes the venerable fear righteous people feel in their hearts. He then proceeds to identify the cause of this fear; a corollary of this fear; and then mentions an indicator by which we can identify those in whose hearts this fear is present. The cause of their fear is their knowledge of God and his attributes, which they have gained through his description of himself. This causal relationship is indicated by the sentence, "Only he does not fear God who does not know God [as he has described himself]." The more we know God, the more awestruck we become of him and the more fearful we become of earning his displeasure. This causal relationship between knowledge and fear is also mentioned in the verse, "Only those servants of God fear him who have knowledge [of him]" (Qurʾān 35:28).

The corollary he mentions for fear, which exists in tandem with it, is palpable, tangible gnosis of God. This gnosis is the result and the ultimate goal of the more superficial, nonetheless vital, knowledge of God and his attributes. The causal relationship between knowledge of God and deep gnosis of God is indicated by the sentence, "And he who does not know God [as he has described himself] will never bind his heart to any kind of constant knowledge that he can see and whose reality he can palpate in his heart." We have characterized this experiential knowledge of God as a corollary of the fear of God because both are effects of correct knowledge of

God. Accordingly, if a person has correct knowledge of God, the stage is set for him to fear God on one hand and gain experiential knowledge of him on the other.

Finally, the outward indicator he mentions for their fear is the synchrony between what they say and what they do and between what they do in public and what they do in private. This indicator is mentioned in the sentence, "Only he is [said to know and fear God] like this whose actions confirm his words and whose private [conduct] agrees with his public [conduct]."

4. The Arabic of this phrase as it appears in *al-Kāfī* is problematic. It literally reads, "Only he is like this whose *words* confirm his *actions*." Generally, our words are better than our actions. We talk big, but our actions are wanting. What is desirable is that we bring our actions up to par with our words, not that we bring our words down to the level of our actions. Thus, it makes more sense to say that, contrary to most people, the *actions* of a person who truly knows and fears God confirm his *words*, not that his *words* confirm his *actions*, for then there would be nothing to distinguish him from the rest of people. Quite likely, the word order was accidently switched during the transmission or transcription of this tradition. Two pieces of textual evidence, in addition to the line of reasoning we just presented, corroborate this hunch. First, the next clause, his "private conduct agrees with his public conduct," confirms that these people are different from others whose public behavior tends to be better than their private behavior. Thus, the previous clause should also speak of a trait that distinguishes them. Second, another tradition in *al-Kāfī* reads, "If a person's actions agree with his words, then testify for him [that he is saved]" (*al-Kāfī* 2.13.5). Keeping all this in mind, we have translated the phrase in the tradition currently under study as we believe the Imam must have spoken it, not as it now exists in *al-Kāfī*.

5. In other words, "We can be sure that the synchrony between what they say and what they do and between what they do in public and what they do in private is truly an indicator of their knowledge of God because..."

SECTION 27 OF TRADITION 1.1.12 TEACHES THE FOLLOWING:

- One who is guided to the truth may again go astray.
- The righteous do not suffice themselves with their current state of guidance; rather, they beg God to continue to guide them perpetually.
- The righteous have an acute understanding of the nature of the soul.
- A correct understanding of God leads to fear of God and to deeper experiential gnosis of God.
- An indicator that our knowledge of God is sound is that our actions are in synchrony with our words and that our private lives are in synchrony with our public lives.

Section 28

'O Hishām! The Commander of the Faithful [ʿAlī] used to say, "God is not worshipped through any act better than intellection.[1] No person's intellect attains strength until several traits are found in him:[2] unbelief and evil are not feared from him;[3] right guidance and goodness are expected from him;[4] his excess money is given [as alms];[5] his excess words are withheld; his share of the temporal world['s victuals] is bare subsistence;[6] he never fills of knowledge for as long as he lives; [worldly] humiliation is more beloved to him if God is [pleased] with him than [worldly] honor if others are [pleased] with him [but God is displeased with him]; humility is more beloved to him than [flaunting worldly] esteem; he deems the few good deeds of others to be great, and deems his own many good deeds to be naught;[7] he believes in his heart that all people are better than he, and that he is the worst of them.[8] This is the last of the list of traits."

يَا هِشَامُ، كَانَ أَمِيرُ الْمُؤْمِنِينَ عليه السلام يَقُولُ: مَا عُبِدَ اللَّهُ بِشَيْءٍ أَفْضَلَ مِنَ الْعَقْلِ، وَمَا تَمَّ عَقْلُ امْرِئٍ حَتَّى يَكُونَ فِيهِ خِصَالٌ شَتَّى : الْكُفْرُ وَالشَّرُّ مِنْهُ مَأْمُونَانِ، وَالرُّشْدُ وَالْخَيْرُ مِنْهُ مَأْمُولَانِ، وَفَضْلُ مَالِهِ مَبْذُولٌ، وَفَضْلُ قَوْلِهِ مَكْفُوفٌ، وَنَصِيبُهُ مِنَ الدُّنْيَا الْقُوتُ، لَا يَشْبَعُ مِنَ الْعِلْمِ دَهْرَهُ، الذُّلُّ أَحَبُّ إِلَيْهِ مَعَ اللَّهِ مِنَ الْعِزِّ مَعَ غَيْرِهِ، وَالتَّوَاضُعُ أَحَبُّ إِلَيْهِ مِنَ الشَّرَفِ، يَسْتَكْثِرُ قَلِيلَ الْمَعْرُوفِ مِنْ غَيْرِهِ، وَيَسْتَقِلُّ كَثِيرَ الْمَعْرُوفِ مِنْ نَفْسِهِ، وَيَرَى النَّاسَ كُلَّهُمْ خَيْراً مِنْهُ وَأَنَّهُ شَرُّهُمْ فِي نَفْسِهِ، وَهُوَ تَمَامُ الْأَمْرِ.

---

1. We have translated the word *ʿaql* as "intellection" in this context and not "intellect". We have done so because the phrase "God is not worshipped through any act better than x" has appeared in several other traditions. For example, we are told in one tradition, "God is not worshipped through any act better than restraint of the stomach and private parts;" and in another, "than dissimulation (*al-taqiyyah*);" and in another, "than fulfilling one's duty to another believer;" and in yet another "than [the belief in] *badāʾ*, [the contingency of divine decrees]." In each of these traditions, "x" stands for a voluntary human act; thus, *ʿaql* must also be a voluntary act, in this case intellection, and not a God-given human faculty like the intellect.

Here the question arises: Do these five traditions not contradict one another? Is each one not asserting that a particular act is better than all other acts of worship? How can both "intellection" and "restraint of the stomach and private parts" be the best acts of worship? The answer to this quandary lies in a close analysis of these sentences. There is a difference between saying, "x is the best" and saying, "nothing is better than x." "X is the best" leaves no room for "y" to be the best. However, "nothing is better than x" leaves room for nothing to be better than "y" and "z" if "x," "y," and "z" are all on equal footing at the top of their class. Thus, there is no contradiction among these traditions, since their sum message is that these five acts—and any other acts that are mentioned in a similar context—are equal to each other and are better than all other acts of worship. This same solution can be offered for three verses of the Qurʾān that seem to contradict one another. Verse 2:114 asks rhetorically, "Who is more unjust than he who prevents God's name from being invoked in mosques and works to destroy them?" Verse 6:21 asks, "Who is more unjust than he who conjures lies about God?" Verse 18:58 asks, "Who is more unjust than he who is reminded of God's signs, yet turns a blind eye to them?" Their sum message is that these three kinds of people are all equal in being unjust, and they are more unjust than anyone else.

2. We have construed the Arabic word *tamma* to mean "attains strength" rather than "attains perfection." The reason for this interpretive translation is as follows. According to *al-Kāfī* 1.1.11, only the prophets' intellects are perfect and each prophet's intellect is greater than the combined intellects of all his people. Thus, if *tamma* truly meant "attains perfection," this paragraph would only be concerned with extolling the virtues of the prophets, and would have no message for the rest of people. On the contrary, this paragraph is clearly describing traits for which all people are encouraged to strive and through which they can strengthen their intellects in the pursuit of perfection. Thus, *tamma* must be taken in a non-literal sense.

3. "Unbelief" refers to wrong beliefs. "Evil" refers to wrong action.

4. That is, one can reasonably expect that he will be rightly guided in his beliefs and good in his deeds.

5. As we explained earlier under the phrase, "[They] abstain from the excesses of the material world" (1.1.12 section 23), we should not construe "excess money" as all but *bare subsistence*; rather, we should construe it as all but what they *reasonably need*, where "reasonable need" varies from person to person and from circumstance to circumstance.

6. This phrase could be construed to mean, "The share he is given by God is no more than bare subsistence." However, this phrase would then be unrelated to all the other phrases in this section, which describe virtues that we can nurture in ourselves to increase our intellect, for how much or how little God gives a person has only to do with God's apportionment and says nothing about the person's character. Thus, it is only appropriate in the context that we construe "his share" as "the share that he takes of his own volition," not "the share he is given by God." The gist of this phrase is that he chooses, of his own volition, to eat only as much as he reasonably needs from what God has given him.

7. He deems their few deeds to be great because he always assumes the best of people. In particular, he assumes that all their actions are worthy of divine acceptance. However, his humility, his awareness of his own faults of character and weakness of faith, and his recognition of the lofty status of the truly righteous and sincere, make him suspect his own deeds. He assumes the worst about his own acts and feels sure that they will be unacceptable to God unless God accepts them through his grace.

8. When he sees one who is more ignorant than he, he thinks, "He has sinned due to ignorance while I have sinned despite my knowledge, so he shall be exonerated before me." When he sees one with knowledge he thinks, "He knows more than I, so he knows God better and knows how to please him better." When he sees one older than he, he thinks, "He obeyed God before I did, so he is better than I?" When he sees one younger than he, he thinks, "I sinned before he did, so he is better than I?" When he sees an unbeliever, he thinks, "Perhaps he will die a Muslim, and perhaps I shall lose my conviction before I die." Such thoughts make him maintain his humility before all people.

SECTION 28 OF TRADITION 1.1.12 TEACHES THE FOLLOWING:

- Using one's intellect is one of the greatest acts of worship.
- It is possible to strengthen the intellect by developing the virtues stated in this section.
- Belief in truth and right action strengthen the intellect.
- Charity strengthens the intellect.
- To speak only when speaking is beneficial strengthens the intellect.
- To eat sparingly strengthens the intellect.
- To seek knowledge insatiably throughout one's life strengthens the intellect.
- To seek honor before God over honor before men strengthens the intellect.
- Being humble strengthens the intellect.

- To see the best in others and to see the worst in oneself strengthens the intellect.

Section 29

'O Hishām! One with intellect does not lie,[1] even if [attaining] what he desires depends on it.	يَا هِشَامُ، إِنَّ الْعَاقِلَ لَا يَكْذِبُ، وَإِنْ كَانَ فِيهِ هَوَاهُ.

1. There are different opinions among our jurists about what constitutes a truth and a lie. The majority opinion is that a statement is true if its apparent meaning is in accord with reality, and a lie if it is not. Ethically speaking, lying, unlike injustice (*ẓulm*), is not intrinsically deplorable. Accordingly, its ruling depends on the circumstances in which it is spoken. For example, it was permissible for the angel in 1.1.8 to lie—according to one justification—because his education depended on it. In another case, if one must tell a lie to save a person's life, then lying becomes an obligation, since the preservation of human life is more important than telling the truth. In any case, as these are issues of law, each person must refer to his *marji*ʿ *al-taqlīd* (the jurist to whom he refers in legal matters) to understand what constitutes a truth and a lie and to know how to act in various circumstances.

SECTION 29 OF TRADITION 1.1.12 TEACHES THE FOLLOWING:

- A person with intellect understands how deplorable it is to lie simply to get what he wants, so he refrains from it despite the challenge in doing so.

Section 30

يَا هِشَامُ، لَا دِينَ لِمَنْ لَا مُرُوَّةَ لَهُ، وَلَا مُرُوَّةَ لِمَنْ لَا عَقْلَ لَهُ.

وَإِنَّ أَعْظَمَ النَّاسِ قَدْراً الَّذِي لَا يَرَى الدُّنْيَا لِنَفْسِهِ خَطَراً. أَمَا إِنَّ أَبْدَانَكُمْ لَيْسَ لَهَا ثَمَنٌ إِلَّا الْجَنَّةُ، فَلَا تَبِيعُوهَا بِغَيْرِهَا.

'O Hishām! He [virtually] lacks devotion who lacks humanity. He lacks humanity who lacks intellect.[1]

The worthiest of people is he who does not consider [what he has of] the material world to be [an indication of] his worth.[2] Let it be known! Your bodies [and souls] have no [fair] price short of paradise, so do not sell them for less.[3]

---

1. These two sentences speak of humanity (*muruwwah* or *murū'ah*), which is a virtue that comprises all human virtues, for if a person is not humane, it is as though he is not human. The first sentence shows that humanity is such an important virtue that any devotion to religion without it is nearly worthless. Having highlighted the critical role of humanity, Imam al-Kāẓim continues with the second sentence to inform us that the fountainhead of humanity is the intellect. When he says that one who lacks humanity does so because of a *lack* of intellect, he does not intend to criticize the intellectually impaired, for they are not at fault for their condition, and criticizing them bears no fruit. Rather, he refers to those who are endowed with an intellect but fail to use it to develop their humanity, for such people may as well have no intellect.

2. This sentence appears to have no relationship to the previous two. It is a separate exhortation.

3. He mentions the worth of "bodies," but he definitely does not intend to attach a price to the body separate from the soul. Rather, he intends to attach a price to body and soul as one. The following tradition of Imam ʿAlī supports this assertion: "There is no [fair] price for you short of paradise, so do not sell yourselves for less" (*Nahj al-balāghah* proverb 456).

SECTION 30 OF TRADITION 1.1.12 TEACHES THE FOLLOWING:

- If we lack humanity, our devotion to religion and truth are incomplete.
- If we lack humanity, it is because we have failed to act according to the dictates of our intellect.
- Every human being has the potential to go to paradise.
- All who fail to go to paradise have wasted their potential, cheated themselves, and sold themselves short.

Section 31

'O Hishām! The Commander of the Faithful [ʿAlī] used to say, "Among the indicators that a person has [a strong] intellect is that he has the following three traits: he answers [only] when he is asked; he speaks [only] when others are unable to speak [suitably];[1] he advises in the best interest of the recipient of his advice.[2] He in whom not one of these three traits is found is a fool."[3] The Commander of the Faithful [ʿAlī also] said, "Only a man in whom all three of these traits are found—or at least one of them—sits front and center in a gathering.[4] Anyone who has none of these traits and sits [there anyway] is [doubly][5] a fool."

يَا هِشَامُ، إِنَّ أَمِيرَ الْمُؤْمِنِينَ عليه السلام كَانَ يَقُولُ: إِنَّ مِنْ عَلَامَةِ الْعَاقِلِ أَنْ يَكُونَ فِيهِ ثَلَاثُ خِصَالٍ: يُجِيبُ إِذَا سُئِلَ، وَيَنْطِقُ إِذَا عَجَزَ الْقَوْمُ عَنِ الْكَلَامِ ، وَيُشِيرُ بِالرَّأْيِ الَّذِي يَكُونُ فِيهِ صَلَاحُ أَهْلِهِ. فَمَنْ لَمْ يَكُنْ فِيهِ مِنْ هَذِهِ الْخِصَالِ الثَّلَاثِ شَيْءٌ، فَهُوَ أَحْمَقُ. إِنَّ أَمِيرَ الْمُؤْمِنِينَ ع قَالَ: لَا يَجْلِسُ فِي صَدْرِ الْمَجْلِسِ إِلَّا رَجُلٌ فِيهِ هَذِهِ الْخِصَالُ الثَّلَاثُ أَوْ وَاحِدَةٌ مِنْهُنَّ. فَمَنْ لَمْ يَكُنْ فِيهِ شَيْءٌ مِنْهُنَّ فَجَلَسَ، فَهُوَ أَحْمَقُ.

Al-Ḥasan ibn ʿAlī [al-Mujtabā] said, "When you seek what you need,[6] seek it from the right people." It was asked, "O Son of God's Messenger! Who are 'the right people'?" He replied, "[They are] those whom God has mentioned in his book and praised saying, *'Only the possessors of albāb are aware.'*"[7] Then he explained, "They are the possessors of *intellect*."[8]

وَقَالَ الْحَسَنُ بْنُ عَلِيٍّ عليهما السلام: إِذَا طَلَبْتُمُ الْحَوَائِجَ فَاطْلُبُوهَا مِنْ أَهْلِهَا. قِيلَ: يَا ابْنَ رَسُولِ اللَّهِ، وَمَنْ أَهْلُهَا؟ قَالَ: الَّذِينَ قَصَّ اللَّهُ فِي كِتَابِهِ وَذَكَرَهُمْ فَقَالَ: ﴿إِنَّمَا يَتَذَكَّرُ أُولُوا الْأَلْبَابِ﴾ قَالَ: هُمْ أُولُو الْعُقُولِ.

ʿAlī ibn al-Ḥusayn [Zayn al-ʿĀbidīn] has said, "The company of

وَقَالَ عَلِيُّ بْنُ الْحُسَيْنِ عليهما السلام: مُجَالَسَةُ الصَّالِحِينَ دَاعِيَةٌ إِلَى الصَّلَاحِ.

the righteous fosters righteousness.

"[To observe and assimilate] the discipline of scholars increases the intellect.

وَآدَابُ الْعُلَمَاءِ زِيَادَةٌ فِي الْعَقْلِ.

"Obedience to just rulers[9] perfects [human] dignity.[10]

وَطَاعَةُ وُلَاةِ الْعَدْلِ تَمَامُ الْعِزِّ.

"Investing one's wealth perfects one's humanity.[11]

وَاسْتِثْمَارُ الْمَالِ تَمَامُ الْمُرُوءَةِ.

"To guide [in good faith] him who seeks counsel is to fulfill our duty [to God] for having blessed us [with sound judgment].

وَإِرْشَادُ الْمُسْتَشِيرِ قَضَاءٌ لِحَقِّ النِّعْمَةِ.

"To refrain from bothering others stems from strength of intellect;[12] doing so results in one's ease in this world and the hereafter."[13]

وَكَفُّ الْأَذَى مِنْ كَمَالِ الْعَقْلِ وَفِيهِ رَاحَةُ الْبَدَنِ عَاجِلًا وَآجِلًا.

---

1. The first two traits relate to speaking. The first of these relates to speaking in response to questions while the second relates to speaking on one's own initiative. The message of both is that the intellect dictates that we not speak unless speaking is beneficial. Answering an unasked question to an uninquisitive mind yields no benefit. Similarly, there is no benefit in speaking if others have already said what must be said. One with a strong intellect carefully weighs costs against benefits and answers only when asked and speaks only when no one else is able to say what must be said.

2. As it stands, this third trait indicates that such a person would advise a Muslim and non-Muslim alike, and that he would give even a non-Muslim sound advice that would hold him in good stead. This statement must be qualified, since he would certainly have the sense not to advise a non-Muslim to the detriment of a Muslim, since the interests of a Muslim take precedence over the interests of others. Only where his advice to a non-Muslim entails no harm to a Muslim would he dispense it.

3. Indicators are of two types. Some indicators are intrinsically bound to the thing they indicate. Salinity, for example, is an intrinsic indicator of the amount of salt in a solution. Accordingly, if the salinity of a solution increases, it is a certain indicator that the ratio of salt to solvent has increased. Other indicators are just conventional indicators that have no intrinsic connection to the thing they indicate. Wearing a carnelian (*ʿaqīq*) ring, for instance, is a conventional indicator that one is a *Shīʿī*, however there is no intrinsic connection between wearing a ring and being a *Shīʿī*. It follows that one could wear a ring and not be a *Shīʿī* or not wear a ring and be a *Shīʿī*. The indicators mentioned in this tradition are of the first kind. These traits exist in a person to the extent that he has developed his intellect. If some or all are absent, then the person is commensurately a fool. The traditions mention many such traits as indicators of intellect. Some, such as one's cognizance (*maʿrifah*) of God, are extremely important indicators (*Biḥār al-anwār* 1.2.4.1). Others such as not allowing one's beard to grow longer than what can be held in one's fist, are not so important (*Biḥār al-anwār* 1.2.4.2). Those who embody all of these indicators, such as the prophets and imams, have perfectly developed intellects. Others who lack some of these indicators lack intellectual strength to the extent that they lack the indicators. Thus, it is clear that Imam ʿAlī is speaking relatively when he calls one who lacks all three indicators a fool. They do not necessarily lack intellect altogether; rather, they lack that level of intellect of which these three traits are indicative.

4. Apparently, the "front and center" of educational, religious, and consultative gatherings was a place reserved for scholars and wise men. In many traditions, the same term, *ṣadr al-majlis* or "front and center of a gathering," is used for the place of honor extended by a host to his distinguished guests. However, in the context of this tradition, the "front and center of a gathering" is not being *offered* to the scholar; rather, out of a sense of duty, he assumes this position to field questions and offer advice.

5. We have added the word "doubly" since this person was already a fool for not possessing any of these indicators of intellect. When, in addition to this, he sits in a place reserved for the wise, he shows himself to be doubly a fool for being oblivious to his own foolishness.

6. It is significant that Imam al-Ḥasan says, "*When* you seek" and not "*If* you seek." Through his choice of words, he reminds us that it is an inevitable reality of life in this world that we need the help of others. It is reported that the Commander of the Faithful once prayed, "O God! Do not make me dependent on *any* of your creatures." Prophet Muḥammad said, "ʿAlī, do not speak like that. Every single person is in need of [other] people." ʿAlī asked, "How should I pray, Messenger of God?" He said, "Say: 'O God! Do not make me dependent on your *evil* creatures.'" ʿAlī said, "Who are his evil creatures?" He replied, "Those who make you feel obliged when they give you [something], and once they make you feel obliged, they point out your faults [to others]" (*Mustadrak al-wasāʾil* 5.5.55.2).

7. Qurʾān 13:19

8. He quotes this Qur'ānic phrase to show that those with intellect are the only ones aware of that of which they ought to be aware. In particular, they are the only people aware of the importance of preserving a needy person's honor by quickly fulfilling his need so that he need not ask another; by making the help they offer seem ordinary and insignificant so that he does not feel beholden; and by hiding from others the person's need and the help they have offered him. Fools, on the other hand, will trash a needy person's honor and make him feel beholden for having asked a favor. For this reason, Imam ʿAlī said, "A need left unfulfilled is a lighter burden to bear than seeking it from those unworthy" (*Nahj al-balāghah* proverb 66).

9. The phrase *wālī al-ʿadl* or "just ruler" refers specifically to the prophets and imams. There are two reasons for this narrow interpretation: First, the phrase is used so often to refer to them throughout the corpus of traditions that, when left unqualified, it is safe to presume that it refers only to them. Second, the Imam would never praise and encourage absolute obedience to anyone but an infallible ruler; and there is no infallible ruler other than God's prophets and imams.

10. Believers embody dignity (*ʿizzah*) because of their conviction, for God has said, "All dignity is for God and for his Messenger and for the faithful" (Qurʾān 63:8). This dignity is perfected through obedience to a just ruler because, in the words of Imam al-Ṣādiq, "In the authority of the just ruler and his vicegerents lies the revival of rights and justice and the destruction of injustice and corruption. It is for this reason that one who strives to strengthen his dominion and aids him in ruling, strives, in reality, to obey God and to strengthen his religion...[I]n the authority of the unjust ruler lies the effacement of all rights and the revival of all evil, the manifestation of all injustice and corruption, the nullification of the [divine] books, the murder of the prophets and the believers, the razing of mosques, and the adulteration of the customs and laws God has ordained" (*Biḥār al-anwār* 100.1.4.11).

11. By investing our wealth sensibly, we do what we can to increase our wealth and thereby preserve our honor by freeing ourselves from dependence on others and by increasing our ability to extend a helping hand to those in need. Both are essential components of our humanity.

12. Generally, we bother others for one of two reasons: First, due to a weak intellect, we may not correctly discern others' rights upon us or our corresponding responsibilities toward them. Second, we may not observe the rights and responsibilities our intellects have discerned because of our weak resolve. One with a strong intellect, on the other hand, both discerns these rights and responsibilities and acts accordingly, and so does not bother others.

13. We have translated *rāḥat al-badan* as "one's ease" when a literal translation would have read "bodily ease." It is not uncommon in Arabic to refer to a person alternatively as a "body" or as a "soul." We have already encountered an instance of this usage in the phrase, "Your bodies [and souls] have no [fair] price short of paradise," in section thirty of tradition 1.1.12. The Imam has mentioned the body in particular because bodily discomfort is the source of much of a person's overall discomfort. For instance, hunger, pain, and sickness, all of which are causes for a person's discomfort in this world, are related to the body. Similarly, the punishment of hellfire is inflicted primarily on a person's body. Accordingly, Imam al-Kāẓim exhorts us to refrain from bothering others so that they in turn refrain from bothering us and we can live with ease in this world. Similarly, if we refrain from bothering others, God will withhold his punishment in the hereafter, and we can live with ease in that realm also.

SECTION 31 OF TRADITION 1.1.12 TEACHES THE FOLLOWING:

- To speak when no question has been asked, or when another person has already offered a suitable answer, is an indicator of foolishness.
- To fail to advise others with their best interest at heart is an indicator of foolishness.
- One with intellect does not assume a position for which he is not qualified.
- We ought to take our needs to those with strong intellects, not to fools.
- One of the paths to self-improvement is to frequent the company of the righteous.
- Frequenting the company of scholars of Islam leads to a strengthened intellect.
- A person's dignity remains deficient without obedience to

God's infallible guides.

- One way to thank God for giving us a strong intellect is to give good counsel to those who seek it.
- To refrain from bothering others stems from a strong intellect and results in one's well-being in this world and the hereafter.

Section 32

'O Hishām! One with intellect does not address one whose repudiation he fears;[1] he does not ask [anything] of one whose refusal he fears;[2] he does not promise what he cannot do;[3] he does not hope for what he will be chided for hoping;[4] he does not initiate any action that he fears he cannot accomplish.'[5]

يَا هِشَامُ، إِنَّ الْعَاقِلَ لَا يُحَدِّثُ مَنْ يَخَافُ تَكْذِيبَهُ. وَلَا يَسْأَلُ مَنْ يَخَافُ مَنْعَهُ. وَلَا يَعِدُ مَا لَا يَقْدِرُ عَلَيْهِ. وَلَا يَرْجُو مَا يُعَنَّفُ بِرَجَائِهِ. وَلَا يُقْدِمُ عَلَى مَا يَخَافُ فَوْتَهُ بِالْعَجْزِ عَنْهُ.

---

1. At first glance, this statement does not seem to jive with the tenacity with which God expected his prophets to carry out their mission despite their fear of their people's repudiation (*takdhīb*). For instance, when God commanded Moses to go before the Pharaoh and call him to submit to God, Moses said, "My Lord, I fear they will repudiate me." Nevertheless, God goaded Aaron and him saying, "Go to the Pharaoh and say, 'We are envoys of the Lord of all realms'" (Qurʾān 26:12-16). Similarly, Abraham told his people, "If you repudiate me, [I will not cease my efforts, for] many nations before you repudiated [their prophets]" (Qurʾān 29:18). If the prophets, who possessed the greatest intellects of all people, delivered their message despite their people's repudiation, then why does Imam al-Kāzim tell us, "One with intellect does not address one whose repudiation he fears"?

The solution to this apparent contradiction lies in understanding that there are two rational purposes for addressing somebody: to solicit his affirmation for what you are saying; and to give him sufficient notice (referred to in Arabic as *itmām al-ḥujjah*) and thereby leave him no room to say, "I did not know." For the most part, we address people with the first goal in mind. We might offer you advice, for instance, in hopes that you will take our advice on good faith. If however, we feel certain that you will not heed our advice, our intellect dictates that we not waste our time and energy by offering it. When Imam al-Kāẓim says, "One with intellect does not address one whose repudiation he fears," he refers to this sort of situation. The aforementioned prophets, on the other hand, had the second goal in mind, for though they had ample reason to fear that their call would go unheard or unheeded, they persisted in their mission to serve their people sufficient notice so that "he who perishes might perish despite clear knowledge [of the truth]" (Qurʾān 8:42). Thus, taking into account both goals, Imam al-Kāẓim's sentence might have read: "A person with intellect does not address one whose repudiation he fears *unless he wishes to leave that person no room to say, 'I did not know.'*"

2. His intellect dictates that he not do anything unless he can be reasonably sure of attaining his goal. If he is certain that he will be refused by a person, then it makes no sense to ask him.

3. Sometimes we promise to do things without thoroughly considering whether or not we have the time and ability to do them because we feel embarrassed to say "no." Such embarrassment and such empty promises are the products of foolishness.

4. One with intellect only hopes for what is possible. For a farmer to hope for a successful harvest without taking the necessary steps to ensure such a harvest is foolish. That is not to say that setting lofty goals is foolish. What is foolish is to set unattainable goals and to hope for results without working to achieve those results.

5. This final statement seems to contradict Imam ʿAlī's proverb, "If you are apprehensive of a thing, then throw yourself into it, for the severity of your fear is greater than what you fear" (*Nahj al-balāghah* proverb 175). To put these two traditions in perspective, we must look at situations of fear and apprehension from the viewpoint of the intellect, for the intellect is always evaluating benefit and harm. In some situations, the thing we fear we cannot do is of great importance and brings great benefit if we succeed and brings no great harm if we fail. In other situations, simply trying to do what we fear we cannot do—even if it causes some minor harm—fosters courage and self-reliance. Here too the benefit of fostering courage and self-reliance far outweighs any minor harm potentially incurred by the action itself. In both these situations, there is a rational benefit in "throwing yourself into it," so one with intellect would likely choose to spurn his fears and try anyway. It is to these two situations that Imam ʿAlī is referring in proverb 175. On the other hand, if none of these benefits exist in a given situation—in particular, if the benefit of the action is minute or the dangers involved are too great—a rational person will choose not to initiate that action. It is to this situation that Imam al-Kāẓim is referring here.

SECTION 32 OF TRADITION 1.1.12 TEACHES THE FOLLOWING:

- One with intellect does not speak to a person who he knows will repudiate him if his sole goal is to convince that person of his opinion.
- One with intellect does not ask a favor of anyone unless he is reasonably sure that he will comply.
- One with intellect does not promise something out of embarrassment when he knows he cannot fulfill his promise.
- One with intellect refrains from setting unattainable goals and does not hope for results without working to achieve them.
- One with intellect does not initiate an action if he fears he cannot accomplish it unless doing so holds some great benefit.

Tradition 1.1.13

ʿAlī ibn Muḥammad reported from Sahl ibn Ziyād that he reported [without mentioning his source] that the Commander of the Faithful [ʿAlī] said:

عَلِيُّ بْنُ مُحَمَّدٍ عَنْ سَهْلِ بْنِ زِيَادٍ رَفَعَهُ قَالَ: قَالَ أَمِيرُ الْمُؤْمِنِينَ عليه السلام :

"The intellect is a veil concealed [within],[1] and good character is manifest beauty. So hide your bodily imperfections with your good character, and combat your desires [by veiling them] with your intellect.[2] [In so doing,] your love [for others] shall remain unblemished,[3] and [others'] love for you shall become manifest."[4]

الْعَقْلُ غِطَاءٌ سَتِيرٌ، وَالْفَضْلُ جَمَالٌ ظَاهِرٌ، فَاسْتُرْ خَلَلَ خَلْقِكَ بِفَضْلِكَ، وَقَاتِلْ هَوَاكَ بِعَقْلِكَ تَسْلَمْ لَكَ الْمَوَدَّةُ وَتَظْهَرْ لَكَ الْمَحَبَّةُ.

---

1. The basic function of the intellect is comprehension. When, by means of the intellect, we detect in ourselves a deplorable trait, and we understand its negative ramifications, we may, if we choose to obey the counsel of our intellect, decide to rid ourselves of that trait by concealing and suppressing it until it is finally snubbed out altogether. It is to this process that Imam ʿAlī refers when he says, "If you are not forbearing, then act as though you are, for it is rare that one acts like a people without nearly becoming one of them" (*Nahj al-balāghah* proverb 207). Because the intellect plays a pivotal role in this process of self-development through concealing and suppressing, Imam ʿAlī has called it a "veil." And because the intellect is an inner faculty, hidden from view, he has described it as being "concealed within."

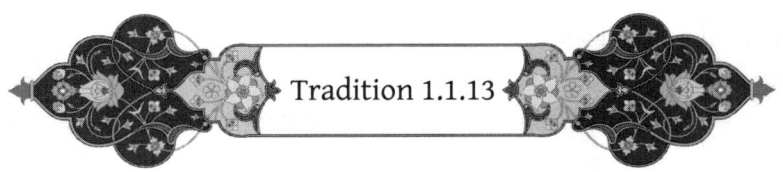

2. Upon deliberation over this tradition, you will notice that each of its three sentences is composed of two independent clauses. In the second sentence, these two clauses are flipped such that the first clause is related to the second clause of the previous sentence as is the second to the first. Likewise, the two clauses in the third sentence are also flipped. Though this flip-flopping of related concepts is good style in Arabic, it proves to be confusing to the English reader. Hence, the tradition may be rearranged for the English reader as follows: "The intellect is a veil concealed within, so fight your whims [by concealing them] with your intellect. [In so doing,] your love [for others] shall remain unblemished. Good character is manifest beauty, so hide your bodily imperfections with your good character. [In so doing, others'] love for you shall become manifest."

3. When we purge ourselves of bad character traits using our intellect, our love for others remains free of selfishness and dishonesty.

4. A similar tradition is found in *Nahj al-balāghah*: "Forbearance is a concealing veil, and intellect is a sharp sword. So conceal your character vices with your forbearance, and fight your base desires with your intellect" (proverb 424).

TRADITION 1.1.13 TEACHES THE FOLLOWING:

- Good character conceals physical ugliness.
- A person's beauty is in his good character.
- One with a strong intellect is sincere in his friendship.
- One who is physically unattractive can gain people's love through his good character.
- One can combat one's whims by contemplating the ramifications of following them.
- A rational person should expend more effort in improving his character than his appearance.

Tradition 1.1.14

A number of our fellow Shīʿah reported from Aḥmad ibn Muḥammad from ʿAlī ibn Ḥadīd from Samāʿah ibn Mihrān that he said, "I was with Abū ʿAbd Allāh [al-Ṣādiq] when a group of his devotees were [also] with him. The topic of intellect and foolishness arose, so Abū ʿAbd Allāh said:

عِدَّةٌ مِنْ أَصْحَابِنَا عَنْ أَحْمَدَ بْنِ مُحَمَّدٍ عَنْ عَلِيِّ بْنِ حَدِيدٍ عَنْ سَمَاعَةَ بْنِ مِهْرَانَ قَالَ: كُنْتُ عِنْدَ أَبِي عَبْدِ اللَّهِ عليه السلام وَعِنْدَهُ جَمَاعَةٌ مِنْ مَوَالِيهِ ، فَجَرَى ذِكْرُ الْعَقْلِ وَالْجَهْلِ فَقَالَ أَبُو عَبْدِ اللَّهِ عليه السلام :

'Know Intellect and its army and Foolishness and its army, and you shall attain guidance.'[1]

اعْرِفُوا الْعَقْلَ وَجُنْدَهُ وَالْجَهْلَ وَجُنْدَهُ تَهْتَدُوا.

I said, 'May I be your ransom![2] We know nothing but what you have taught us.' So Abū ʿAbd Allāh said:

قَالَ سَمَاعَةُ: فَقُلْتُ: جُعِلْتُ فِدَاكَ، لَا نَعْرِفُ إِلَّا مَا عَرَّفْتَنَا. فَقَالَ أَبُو عَبْدِ اللَّهِ عليه السلام :

'God—exalted is he and sublime—created Intellect, the first of the immaterial creatures, out of light, [in a place of honor] on the right side of his throne.[3] He said to it, "Go back," whereupon it went back. Then he said to it, "Come forward," whereupon it came forward. Then God—exalted is

إِنَّ اللَّهَ عَزَّ وَجَلَّ خَلَقَ الْعَقْلَ وَهُوَ أَوَّلُ خَلْقٍ مِنَ الرُّوحَانِيِّينَ عَنْ يَمِينِ الْعَرْشِ مِنْ نُورِهِ، فَقَالَ لَهُ: أَدْبِرْ، فَأَدْبَرَ. ثُمَّ قَالَ لَهُ: أَقْبِلْ، فَأَقْبَلَ. فَقَالَ اللَّهُ تَبَارَكَ وَتَعَالَى: خَلَقْتُكَ خَلْقاً عَظِيماً وَكَرَّمْتُكَ عَلَى

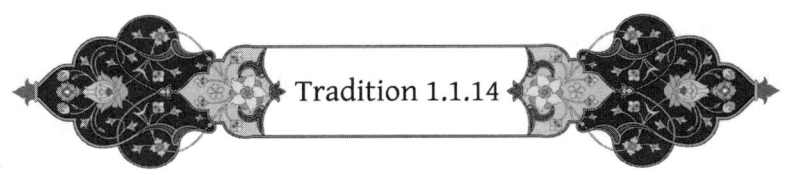

he and good—said, "I have made you great, and I have honored you above all my creatures."

جَمِيعِ خَلْقِي.

Al-Ṣādiq said:

قَالَ:

'Then he created Foolishness out of the dark, acrid sea. He said to it, "Go back," whereupon it went back. Then he said to it, "Come forward," but it did not come forward. So he said to it, "You have acted arrogantly." Then he stripped it of his mercy.[4]

ثُمَّ خَلَقَ الْجَهْلَ مِنَ الْبَحْرِ الْأُجَاجِ ظُلْمَانِيّاً، فَقَالَ لَهُ: أَدْبِرْ، فَأَدْبَرَ. ثُمَّ قَالَ لَهُ: أَقْبِلْ، فَلَمْ يُقْبِلْ. فَقَالَ لَهُ: اسْتَكْبَرْتَ، فَلَعَنَهُ.

Then he created seventy-five units for Intellect.[5] When Foolishness saw what God had given Intellect and how he had thereby honored it, it resolved in its heart to be Intellect's enemy. Foolishness said, "My Lord, this is a creature like me. You have created it, honored it, and strengthened it. I am its rival, yet I have no power [to fight] against it. So grant me an army like the one you have granted it." God said, "Fine, but if you disobey me after this, I shall banish you and your army [completely] from [the sanctuary of] my mercy."[6] Foolishness said, "I am satisfied [with this stipulation]." So God gave it seventy-five units [also].[7]

ثُمَّ جَعَلَ لِلْعَقْلِ خَمْسَةً وَسَبْعِينَ جُنْداً. فَلَمَّا رَأَى الْجَهْلُ مَا أَكْرَمَ اللَّهُ بِهِ الْعَقْلَ وَ مَا أَعْطَاهُ، أَضْمَرَ لَهُ الْعَدَاوَةَ. فَقَالَ الْجَهْلُ: يَا رَبِّ هَذَا خَلْقٌ مِثْلِي. خَلَقْتَهُ وَكَرَّمْتَهُ وَقَوَّيْتَهُ وَأَنَا ضِدُّهُ وَلَا قُوَّةَ لِي بِهِ، فَأَعْطِنِي مِنَ الْجُنْدِ مِثْلَ مَا أَعْطَيْتَهُ. فَقَالَ: نَعَمْ، فَإِنْ عَصَيْتَ بَعْدَ ذَلِكَ أَخْرَجْتُكَ وَجُنْدَكَ مِنْ رَحْمَتِي. قَالَ: قَدْ رَضِيتُ. فَأَعْطَاهُ خَمْسَةً وَسَبْعِينَ جُنْداً.

1. Among the seventy-five units he gave Intellect was Goodness, and it was the vizier of Intellect. He made Evil its rival, and it was the vizier of Foolishness.[8]

فَكَانَ مِمَّا أَعْطَى الْعَقْلَ مِنَ الْخَمْسَةِ وَالسَّبْعِينَ الْجُنْدَ الْخَيْرُ، وَهُوَ وَزِيرُ الْعَقْلِ. وَجَعَلَ ضِدَّهُ الشَّرَّ، وَهُوَ وَزِيرُ الْجَهْلِ.

2. And [among them was] Belief [in God], and its rival was Unbelief [in God];

وَالْإِيمَانُ وَضِدُّهُ الْكُفْرُ،

3. and Attestation [to belief], and its rival was Denial [of belief];[9]

وَالتَّصْدِيقُ وَضِدُّهُ الْجُحُودَ،

4. and Hope [in God's mercy], and its rival was Despair [of God's mercy];

وَالرَّجَاءُ وَضِدُّهُ الْقُنُوطَ،

5. and Justice, and its rival was Iniquity;

وَالْعَدْلُ وَضِدُّهُ الْجَوْرَ،

6. and Satisfaction [with God's decree], and its rival was Ire [at God's decree];

وَالرِّضَا وَضِدُّهُ السُّخْطُ،

7. and Thankfulness, and its rival was Ingratitude;

وَالشُّكْرُ وَضِدُّهُ الْكُفْرَانُ،

8. and Hopelessness [to attain what others possess], and its rival was Covetousness;[10]

وَالطَّمَعُ وَضِدُّهُ الْيَأْسُ،

9. and Reliance [solely on God], and its rival was Greed;[11]

وَالتَّوَكُّلُ وَضِدُّهُ الْحِرْصُ،

وَالرَّأْفَةُ وَضِدُّهَا الْقَسْوَةُ،

10. and Sensitivity, and its rival was Hardness [of heart];

وَالرَّحْمَةُ وَضِدُّهَا الْغَضَبُ،

11. and Mercy, and its rival was Anger;[12]

وَالْعِلْمُ وَضِدُّهُ الْجَهْلُ،

12. and Knowledge, and its rival was Ignorance;

وَالْفَهْمُ وَضِدُّهُ الْحُمْقُ،

13. and Comprehension, and its rival was Idiocy;

وَالْعِفَّةُ وَضِدُّهَا التَّهَتُّكُ،

14. and Restraint, and its rival was Shamelessness;

وَالزُّهْدُ وَضِدُّهُ الرَّغْبَةُ،

15. and Indifference [to the material world] , and its rival was Desire;

وَالرِّفْقُ وَضِدُّهُ الْخُرْقُ،

16. and Kindness, and its rival was Harshness;

وَالرَّهْبَةُ وَضِدُّهُ الْجُرْأَةُ،

17. and Fearfulness [of God], and its rival was Audacity;

وَالتَّوَاضُعُ وَضِدُّهُ الْكِبْرُ،

18. and Humility, and its rival was Arrogance;

وَالتُّؤَدَةُ وَضِدُّهَا التَّسَرُّعُ،

19. and Circumspection, and its rival was Haste;

وَالْحِلْمُ وَضِدُّهَا السَّفَهُ،

20. and Forbearance, and its rival was Impatience;

21. and Silence, and its rival was Garrulousness;

وَالصَّمْتُ وَضِدُّهُ الْهَذَرُ،

22. and Submission [to the truth], and its rival was Contempt [for the truth];

وَالِاسْتِسْلَامُ وَضِدُّهُ الِاسْتِكْبَارُ،

23. and Submission [to the truth], and its rival was Doubt [in what is clearly true];[13]

وَالتَّسْلِيمُ وَضِدُّهُ الشَّكُّ،

24. and Patience [in the face of hardship], and its rival was [uncontrolled] Grief;

وَالصَّبْرُ وَضِدُّهُ الْجَزَعُ،

25. and Magnanimity, and its rival was Vengeance;

وَالصَّفْحُ وَضِدُّهُ الِانْتِقَامُ،

26. and Wealth, and its rival was Poverty;[14]

وَالْغِنَى وَضِدُّهُ الْفَقْرُ،

27. and Awareness, and its rival was Heedlessness;

وَالتَّذَكُّرُ وَضِدُّهُ السَّهْوُ،

28. and Remembrance, and its rival was Forgetfulness;

وَالْحِفْظُ وَضِدُّهُ النِّسْيَانُ،

29. and Building ties, and its rival was Severing ties;

وَالتَّعَطُّفُ وَضِدُّهُ الْقَطِيعَةُ،

30. and Contentment, and its rival was Greed;

وَالْقُنُوعُ وَضِدُّهُ الْحِرْصُ،

31. and Altruism, and its rival was Refusal [to give charity];

وَالْمُؤَاسَاةُ وَضِدُّهَا الْمَنْعُ،

32. and Friendship, and its rival was Enmity;

وَالْمَوَدَّةُ وَضِدُّهَا الْعَدَاوَةُ،

33. and Loyalty, and its rival was Treachery;

وَالْوَفَاءُ وَضِدُّهُ الْغَدْرُ،

34. and Obedience [to whom obedience is due], and its rival was Disobedience [to them] ;

وَالطَّاعَةُ وَضِدُّهَا الْمَعْصِيَةُ،

35. and Humility, and its rival was Arrogance;

وَالْخُضُوعُ وَضِدُّهُ التَّطَاوُلُ،

36. and Well-Being, and its rival was Tribulation;[15]

وَالسَّلَامَةُ وَضِدُّهَا الْبَلَاءُ،

37. and Love [for all that is good], and its rival was Hatred [for all that is good];

وَالْحُبُّ وَضِدُّهُ الْبُغْضُ،

38. and Truthfulness, and its rival was Mendacity;

وَالصِّدْقُ وَضِدُّهُ الْكَذِبُ،

39. and Right, and its rival was Wrong;

وَالْحَقُّ وَضِدُّهُ الْبَاطِلُ،

40. and Trustworthiness, and its rival was Irresponsibility;

وَالْأَمَانَةُ وَضِدُّهَا الْخِيَانَةُ،

41. and Purity [of faith in God's oneness], and its rival was Adulteration [of one's faith with polytheism];[16]

وَالْإِخْلَاصُ وَضِدُّهُ الشَّوْبُ،

42. and Acuity, and its rival was Dullness;

وَالشَّهَامَةُ وَضِدُّهَا الْبَلَادَةُ،

43. and Comprehension, and its rival was Idiocy;

وَالْفَهْمُ وَضِدُّهُ الْغَبَاوَةُ،

44. and Recognition, and its rival was Failure to recognize;[17]

وَالْمَعْرِفَةُ وَضِدُّهَا الْإِنْكَارُ،

45. and Graciousness, and its rival was Hostility;

وَالْمُدَارَاةُ وَضِدُّهَا الْمُكَاشَفَةُ،

46. and Security in absentia,[18] and its rival was Collusion;

وَسَلَامَةُ الْغَيْبِ وَضِدُّهَا الْمُمَاكَرَةُ،

47. and Confidentiality,[19] and its rival was Disclosure [of secrets];

وَالْكِتْمَانُ وَضِدُّهُ الْإِفْشَاءُ،

48. and Prayer, and its rival was Not praying;

وَالصَّلَاةُ وَضِدُّهَا الْإِضَاعَةُ،

49. and Fasting, and its rival was Not fasting;

وَالصَّوْمُ وَضِدُّهُ الْإِفْطَارُ،

50. and Jihad, and its rival was Cowering [in fear of the enemy];

وَالْجِهَادُ وَضِدُّهُ النُّكُولُ،

51. and Hajj, and its rival was Casting God's covenant [into oblivion];[20]

وَالْحَجُّ وَضِدُّهُ نَبْذُ الْمِيثَاقِ،

52. and Guarding one's tongue [against talebearing], and its rival was Talebearing;[21]

وَصَوْنُ الْحَدِيثِ وَضِدُّهُ النَّمِيمَةُ،

53. and Goodness toward one's parents, and its rival was Wickedness [to them];

وَبِرُّ الْوَالِدَيْنِ وَضِدُّهُ الْعُقُوقُ،

54. and Sincerity [in worship], and its rival was Ostentation;[22]

وَالْحَقِيقَةُ وَضِدُّهَا الرِّيَاءُ،

55. and [doing and enjoining] Good, and its rival was [doing and enjoining] Evil;

وَالْمَعْرُوفُ وَضِدُّهُ الْمُنْكَرُ،

56. and Modesty in dress, and its rival was Exhibitionism;

وَالسَّتْرُ وَضِدُّهُ التَّبَرُّجُ،

57. and Dissimulation, and its rival was Announcement;

وَالتَّقِيَّةُ وَضِدُّهَا الْإِذَاعَةُ،

58. and Fairness, and its rival was Partiality;

وَالْإِنْصَافُ وَضِدُّهُ الْحَمِيَّةُ،

59. and Grooming [on the part of men], and its rival was Iniquity [in fulfilling one's duty to one's wife];[23]

وَالتَّهْيِئَةُ وَضِدُّهَا الْبَغْيُ،

60. and Cleanliness, and its rival was

وَالنَّظَافَةُ وَضِدُّهَا الْقَذَرُ،

Filth;

61. and Decency, and its rival was Indecency;

وَالْحَيَاءُ وَضِدُّهَا الْجَلَعُ،

62. and Moderation, and its rival was Excess;

وَالْقَصْدُ وَضِدُّهُ الْعُدْوَانُ،

63. and Restfulness, and its rival was Fatigue;[24]

وَالرَّاحَةُ وَضِدُّهَا التَّعَبُ،

64. and Ease [of an act], and its rival was Difficulty [of an act];[25]

وَالسُّهُولَةُ وَضِدُّهَا الصُّعُوبَةُ،

65. and Increase [in the reward for an act], and its rival was Obliteration [of its reward];[26]

وَالْبَرَكَةُ وَضِدُّهَا الْمَحْقُ،

66. and Well-Being, and its rival was Tribulation;

وَالْعَافِيَةُ وَضِدُّهَا الْبَلَاءُ،

67. and Sustenance [that suffices], and its rival was Hoarding [more than is needed];

وَالْقَوَامُ وَضِدُّهُ الْمُكَاثَرَةُ،

68. and Wisdom, and its rival was Desire;[27]

وَالْحِكْمَةُ وَضِدُّهَا الْهَوَى،

69. and Dignity, and its rival was Flippancy;

وَالْوَقَارُ وَضِدُّهُ الْخِفَّةُ،

70. and Happiness, and its rival was

وَالسَّعَادَةُ وَضِدُّهَا الشَّقَاوَةُ،

Misery;

71. and Repentance, and its rival was Persistence [in sin];

وَالتَّوْبَةُ وَضِدُّهَا الْإِصْرَارُ،

72. and Seeking forgiveness, and its rival was Being deceived [into procrastinating repentance];

وَالِاسْتِغْفَارُ وَضِدُّهُ الِاغْتِرَارُ،

73. and Adherence [to all of God's laws], and its rival was Disdain [of his laws];

وَالْمُحَافَظَةُ وَضِدُّهَا التَّهَاوُنُ،

74. and Supplication, and its rival was Haughtiness;[28]

وَالدُّعَاءُ وَضِدُّهُ الِاسْتِنْكَافُ،

75. and Energy, and its rival was Laziness;

وَالنَّشَاطُ وَضِدُّهُ الْكَسَلُ،

76. and Sadness, and its rival was Exultance;[29]

وَالْفَرَحُ وَضِدُّهُ الْحَزَنُ،

77. and Affability, and its rival was Aloofness;

وَالْأُلْفَةُ وَضِدُّهَا الْفُرْقَةُ،

78. and Generosity, and its rival was Miserliness.

وَالسَّخَاءُ وَضِدُّهُ الْبُخْلُ.

All of these units from the army of Intellect are combined only in a prophet, a successor to a prophet, or a believer whose heart God has

فَلَا تَجْتَمِعُ هَذِهِ الْخِصَالُ كُلُّهَا مِنْ أَجْنَادِ الْعَقْلِ إِلَّا فِي نَبِيٍّ أَوْ وَصِيِّ نَبِيٍّ أَوْ مُؤْمِنٍ قَدِ امْتَحَنَ اللَّهُ قَلْبَهُ لِلْإِيمَانِ. وَأَمَّا سَائِرُ

tested for faith.[30] As for the rest of our devotees, each of them, without exception, possesses some of these units [of Intellect] until he perfects himself and rids himself of the units of Foolishness. At that point he will be at the highest station with the prophets, their successors, [and the believers whose hearts have been tested].[31] This [perfection] can only be attained by knowing Intellect and its army and distancing oneself from Foolishness and its army.[32] May Allah grant you and us success to obey him and please him.'"

ذَلِكَ مِنْ مَوَالِينَا فَإِنَّ أَحَدَهُمْ لَا يَخْلُو مِنْ أَنْ يَكُونَ فِيهِ بَعْضُ هَذِهِ الْجُنُودِ حَتَّى يَسْتَكْمِلَ وَيَنْقَى مِنْ جُنُودِ الْجَهْلِ فَعِنْدَ ذَلِكَ يَكُونُ فِي الدَّرَجَةِ الْعُلْيَا مَعَ الْأَنْبِيَاءِ وَالْأَوْصِيَاءِ. وَإِنَّمَا يُدْرَكُ ذَلِكَ بِمَعْرِفَةِ الْعَقْلِ وَجُنُودِهِ وَبِمُجَانَبَةِ الْجَهْلِ وَجُنُودِهِ. وَفَّقَنَا اللَّهُ وَإِيَّاكُمْ لِطَاعَتِهِ وَمَرْضَاتِهِ.

---

1. Clearly, mere *knowledge* of the armies of intellect and foolishness is not sufficient for reaching guidance; rather, guidance requires *acting* on this knowledge by assimilating the armies of intellect and avoiding the armies of foolishness. However, this sentence structure is often employed in Arabic to show the pivotal role of one thing in causing another. Here, knowledge is so important that it is portrayed as the sole cause of attaining guidance.

2. This phrase, *juʿiltu fidāk*, is commonly used in Arabic as an expression of intense love and devotion, and was used by the *Shīʿah* to open their addresses to the Imam. In paraphrase, this expression means "If it is ordained that anything bad should happen to you, I beg God to afflict me with it instead of you."

3. The following points will clarify the terms used in this sentence:

- "Intellect" is used here in the first sense of the word.
- The intellect is metaphorically said to be made of "light" because it

illuminates things for the one who possesses it.

- God's "throne" (*ʿarsh*) is a metonym for his dominion over all creation. Its "right side" connotes a place of honor.

4. We see that Intellect obeys both of God's commands while Foolishness obeys one and flaunts the other. Many of the commentators of this tradition have suggested various symbolic meanings for "going back" and "coming forward." However, none of these suggested meanings fits the circumstances exactly. Rather, Intellect's unwavering deference to both of God's commands symbolizes its ability to perceive that total subservience to God's command is good. Foolishness, on the other hand, is unable to perceive the virtue of total subservience. Where the divine command accords with human desire, it submits, but where there is conflict between the two, it does not hesitate to flaunt the divine command in favor of base desires.

5. Instead of referring to each trait as one soldier in the army of Intellect, Imam al-Ṣādiq refers to each trait as a *jund* or "unit." He has done this because each trait is actually a set of many different members. For instance, anger comes in an infinite number of degrees of intensity. Thus, anger is a unit comprising many types of anger.

While Imam al-Ṣādiq expressly tells us there are 75 units for Intellect, according to this tradition, he actually enumerates 78. A scrutinizing look at these 78 reveals that the following three units have been mentioned twice: "humility" is referred to by the synomyms *khuḍuʿ* and *tawāḍuʿ*, and its opposite, "arrogance," is referred to by the synomyms *taṭāwul* and *kibr*; "idiocy" is referred to as *ghabāwah* and *ḥumq*, and for this reason, the rival of both is *fahm* or "comprehension;" likewise "well-being" is referred to as *salāmah* and *ʿāfiyah*, and for this reason, the rival of both is *balāʾ* or "tribulation." Quite likely, some of the transmitters of this tradition narrated these passages using their synonyms, and with the passage of time, the synonyms came to be considered part of the original text. Thus, without these three repeats the number of soldiers remains at 75.

6. It might seem strange that God would threaten Foolishness with excommunication from divine mercy when he had already stripped it of his mercy earlier. The solution to this dilemma lies in viewing the circumstances under which Foolishness disobeyed God in each instance. In the first instance, Foolishness was alone, weak, and without vizier or army. Accordingly, its disobedience was not so grave in God's eyes, so it was stripped of God's mercy only partially. However, after it is given 75 units and its strength is increased through divine endowment, its disobedience would be intolerable and would lead to complete and irrevocable damnation.

7. There is much debate among the commentators surrounding this tradition, 1.1.1, 1.1.26, and 1.1.31, which all speak of the creation of intellect and God's conversation with it. Some suggest the story is an allegory while others insist that it narrates historical events that took place on some other plane of existence. The following pieces of evidence corroborate the claim that it is an allegory.

- Foolishness is a non-entity: it does not actually exist. It is, in reality, the absence of intellect. Accordingly, it is farfetched to say that foolishness *was created*, and any reference to its creation is likely metaphorical.
- Intellect is, in reality, the sum total of these 75 units; it does not exist separately from them. Likewise, foolishness does not "exist" separately from its 75 units. Thus, it is far-fetched to say that intellect and foolishness were created at some point in time and were then given an army except as an allegory of those traits essential to their very existence.
- It is far-fetched to say that the intellect and foolishness were actually commanded to "go back" and "come forward," since neither of them is a sentient being that can obey or disobey and then be held responsible for its actions. Rather, these commands and their obedience and refusal are expressions of their essential nature: intellect has the ability to perceive that total subservience to God's command is good; foolishness does not.
- Intellect is mentioned in three distinct sections of this tradition. First,

Samāʿah mentions it in his introduction to the tradition where he says, "The topic of intellect and foolishness arose." Then Imam al-Ṣādiq mentions it in his description of "Intellect and its army and Foolishness and its army." Lastly, after completing the list of 75 units, Imam al-Ṣādiq exhorts his followers to acquire as many elements of intellect as possible when he says, "All of these units from the army of Intellect are combined only in a prophet, a successor to a prophet, or a believer whose heart God has tested for faith..."

Obviously, the intellect mentioned in the first and third instances is intellect in the first sense of the word: the faculty of discernment that lies within each person. Accordingly, it is most appropriate to construe the Imam's usage of intellect in the second instance in the same meaning, not as some independent creature created on some other plane of existence. (Granted, the intellect that exists in you and us was not the first of God's immaterial creatures, rather it was created when we were created. Thus, the word "first" in the phrase "the first of the immaterial creatures" must be construed to mean "the best of creatures." While this does not jive with the literal wording of the tradition, it is not unusual in Arabic to use "first" to mean "best.")

Despite all this, it is possible to construe the entire tradition literally as some commentators have done. In the final estimation, whether we construe this tradition allegorically or literally has little bearing on the important lesson it means to impart: to encourage us to know the intellect, foolishness, and their characteristics and to push us to assimilate the characteristics of one with intellect and avoid the characteristics of a fool.

8. Goodness was made the vizier of Intellect because it is a quality so broad that it includes all the other units of Intellect's army. Similarly, Evil includes all the other units of Foolishness's army, and so it qualifies to be its vizier.

9. The difference between "attesting to belief" and "belief" itself is that "attesting to belief" entails an outward display or declaration that one believes while "belief" itself is a matter of the mind and heart.

10. In the Arabic, "covetousness" or *ṭamaʿ* is mentioned first and "hopelessness" or *yaʾs* comes second. *Ṭamaʿ*, however, is usually used pejoratively to indicate a desire for material possessions. For instance, in one tradition, Imam al-Kāẓim tells Hishām ibn al-Ḥakam, "Beware of covetousness (*ṭamaʿ*) and foster within yourself hopelessness (*yaʾs*) to attain what others possess" (*Mustadrak al-wasāʾil* 12.1.67.5). Based on this, "hopelessness" ought to be mentioned first, among the armies of Intellect, and "covetousness" ought to be mentioned second, among the armies of Foolishness. Quite likely, the copyists mistakenly switched the word order because *yaʾs* or "hopelessness" is sometimes used to indicate "despair in God's mercy," which is among the greatest of sins. Accordingly, we have returned the word order in the translation to what we believe was its original form.

It is, however, possible to make sense of the word order as it has been transmitted. Occasionally, the word *ṭamaʿ* is used in a positive sense to indicate an intense desire for God's forgiveness or for the pleasures of paradise. For instance, the Prophet Abraham describes God as he "whom I desire (*aṭmaʿu*) to absolve me of my failings on the Day of Judgment" (Qurʾān 26:82). However, since *ṭamaʿ* is more commonly used pejoratively, we believe our first explanation to be stronger.

11. Greed or *ḥirṣ* is mentioned twice among the ranks of Foolishness's army, once as the rival of Reliance or *tawakkul*, and once as the rival of Contentment or *qunūʿ*. At first glance we might consign this repetition to another mistake perpetrated by the transmitters of the tradition. However, if we carefully analyze greed, we find that it is closely intertwined with two distinct vices: deluded self-reliance and an insatiable desire for amassing material possessions. One who is self-reliant is ignorant of God's oneness, power, knowledge, and wisdom. He does not know—or does not act on the knowledge—that God is the only one upon whom one ought to rely.

He believes he can only succeed by ruthlessly looking out for himself. He believes he must greedily hoard and stingily retain if he is to have enough for himself. In this sense, greed is similar to self-reliance, and its rival is *tawakkul* or reliance on God. One who is greedy also has an insatiable desire to amass things. In this sense, its rival is contentment or *qunūʿ*.

12. While anger is mentioned here in the army of Foolishness, it can also be a positive trait as in Imam ʿAlī's laudatory statement to Abū Dharr al-Ghifārī, "You anger for God's sake" (*Nahj al-balāghah* sermon 130). Similarly, mercy can sometimes be a fault. For instance, the faithful are bid not to be overcome by feelings of mercy during the flogging that must be meted out to the adulterer and adulteress (Qurʾān 24:2). Thus, in reality, certain instances of anger and mercy belong in each of the armies of Foolishness and Intellect. Nonetheless, this tradition only considers the positive sort of mercy and the negative sort of anger and categorizes them accordingly.

13. Both *istislām* and *taslīm* mean "submission." However, the former has been mentioned as the rival of "contempt," and the latter as the rival of "doubt." This is because submitting to the truth entails two corollaries: one is the urge to follow the truth to which one has submitted; the other is the peace of mind that comes with following the truth. If we consider the first corollary of submission, its opposite is *istikbār* or "contempt," for one with contempt for truth recognizes it for what it is but refuses to submit to it and follow it. If we consider its second corollary, the opposite of submission is *shakk* or "doubt." Doubt itself is of two kinds. In some instances a person willfully places himself in doubt by refusing to seek the answers to his questions or by stubbornly refusing to accept the answers he is given. In this vain, Imam ʿAlī has said, "Do not reduce your knowledge to ignorance or your certainty to doubt. When you know [something], act [on it], and when you are certain [of something], proceed [with it]" (*Nahj al-balāghah* proverb 274). Such self-inflicted doubt is obviously part of Foolishness's army. In other instances, a person doubts because of no shortcoming of his own, but because he has not yet gathered enough information to achieve certainty. In this case too, doubt is among Foolishness's army because, if left unattended, it opens the door for Satan's machinations much the same way poverty does. In either sense, one with doubt remains in a state of agitation and does not have peace of mind.

14. At first glance it seems that qualities such as poverty, forgetfulness, and heedlessness should not be in the ranks of Foolishness's army because they are outside the bounds of human volition. In particular a person's poverty is not necessarily an indication that he is foolish, since God is the one who "gives sustenance to whom he wishes and withholds [it from whom he wishes]" (Qurʾān 13:26). Similarly, forgetfulness and heedlessness are states that afflict a person, often due to no failing on his part. Nevertheless, these qualities are part of Foolishness's army, not because the person possesses them for any shortcoming on his part, but because they facilitate Satan's exploitation of the person. For instance, a poor person may be pressed by hunger and feel a need to resort to illicit means to provide for himself and his family.

15. Well-being and tribulation are like wealth and poverty in that they are outside the bounds of human volition. Accordingly, they are counted among the armies of Intellect and Foolishness because they pave the way for each to act. In a state of well-being, a person can easily make use of God's blessings to further the cause of the intellect. Likewise, tribulation strips him of those blessings thereby increasing his temptation to act foolishly.

16. The term *ikhlāṣ* can either mean purity of faith so that one believes in no deity except God *or* purity of action such that one acts for no purpose other than God's pleasure. However, the intended meaning here is the former since purity of action is mentioned independently in line 54 of this tradition, albeit under the guise of a synonym, "sincerity."

17. The word *maʿrifah* (recognition) is sometimes conflated with *ʿilm* (knowledge). In fact, "recognition" is a specific type of "knowledge" in which a person relates some general and conceptual knowledge to a specific individual. The story of Joseph provides an illustrative example of "recognition." We are told that when Joseph's brothers entered Egypt for the first time, Joseph recognized who they were (*ʿarafahum*), but they failed after all those years to recognize him (*hum lahū munkirūn*; see Qurʾān 12:58). Certainly, they *knew* who their brother was, but they failed to *recognize* that the man who stood before them was the very brother they had thrown down the well so many years before. Generally speaking, "recognition" is among the ranks of Intellect's army because it is a necessary link between knowing and doing. For instance, one may *know* about the prophethood and the need for divine guidance. However, without *recognizing* who the prophet is, one cannot practically become his follower, learn from him, and act righteously.

18. By "security" he means that others should feel secure while in absence from his company and not feel that he will collude with others to harm them.

19. It is a virtue to be able to keep certain kinds of information in confidence and secrecy. For instance, we must keep in confidence the secrets entrusted to us by others. We must conceal our awareness of the hidden faults of others. We must even conceal the truth at times if revealing it would elicit unnecessary harm.

20. This phrase alludes to one of the purposes of hajj: to renew the covenant with God that is mentioned in the Qurʾān in 7:172-3. Many traditions mention that God has consigned this covenant to the charge of the Black Stone located in the Kaʿbah. For instance, it has been narrated that a person asked Imam al-Ṣādiq, "Why has it been ordained that we touch the stone?" He replied, "When Allah—almighty and sublime is he—made a covenant with the children of Adam [to perform the rites of hajj], he called the [Black] Stone from paradise and commanded it [to swallow the covenant for safe-keeping], so it did. Thus, it shall testify on behalf of those who enter its presence [and touch it] that they entered its presence [and held true to their covenant]'" (*al-Kāfī* 15.1.2).

21. We have translated *namīmah* as "talebearing." It is the practice of maliciously communicating to a person what another person has said about him with the intent of sowing seeds of enmity between the two.

22. The word *ḥaqīqah*, in the many instances where it is used, can often only be understood by looking at its opposite. Here, since it is juxtaposed with *riyāʾ* or "ostentation," we can deduce that it means "sincerity." If we refrain from worshipping God ostentatiously, to make a show of it for others, we will succeed in worshipping only for God's pleasure. Only then, will we realize the true purpose of worship or *ḥaqīqat al-ʿibādah*.

23. We have translated the word *tahyiʾah*, which literally means "to make ready" or "to improve," as "grooming" because it fits in the context, and because several other traditions use this same word to extol the merit of grooming oneself for one's spouse. For instance, Imam al-Riḍā has said, "One of the things that increases the chastity of women is for their husbands to groom themselves. Women have abandoned chastity because their husbands have abandoned grooming themselves" (*al-Kāfi* 18.176.50). Imam al-Riḍā also said, "Women love to see you groomed just as you love to see them groomed. Some women have abandoned chastity for sin. The only thing that made them do this was that their husbands did not groom themselves enough" (*Biḥār al-anwār* 73.2.8.9). The rival of "grooming" is "iniquity" because a husband who does not groom himself sufficiently has trampled the rights of his wife, and has thus been iniquitous with her.

24. Fatigue, in and of itself, is an unfavorable state because it opens a pathway for satanic insinuations. For instance, when we become excessively tired, we may shirk responsibilities to God and our families, feeling justified by our tiredness. In fact, it is dangerous even to tire ourselves excessively in worship, for we may begin to begrudge worship and leave it off completely. It is for this reason that Islam cautions us to be moderate, even in good deeds.

25. Clearly, the attributes "easy" and "difficult" are attributes of human acts and not of the human being himself. However, since the difficulty of an act, such as jihad or enjoining good and forbidding evil, can place a seemingly insurmountable barrier to doing it, it is counted among the ranks of Foolishness's army.

26. *Barakah*, which is the increased reward and blessing that comes of an act of goodness, is an incentive offered by God to encourage people to do good. It is counted among the ranks of Intellect, since it helps us to act according to the good influence of our intellect.

27. To understand the rivalry between Desire and Wisdom, we must look back to section ten of *al-Kāfī* 1.1.12. In that section, Imam al-Kāẓim mentioned verse 2:269 from the Qurʾān to show that while God can give wisdom to whomever he wishes, he only gives it to those who use their intellect to contemplate and heed the guidance embodied in the Qurʾān's verses. In contrast, those who fail to use their intellects—or use them, but choose to act according to their desires rather than their intellects—are denied that gift of wisdom.

28. This is an allusion to the verse, "Your Lord said, 'Call on me and I shall answer you. Those who are too haughty to worship me shall enter hell in utter humiliation" (Qurʾān 40:60).

29. In the Arabic text, Exultance is mentioned first, as though it is part of the army of Intellect, and Sadness is mentioned second, as though it is part of the army of Foolishness. We believe the order of these two units has been reversed just as the order of the eighth pair of units was reversed. *Faraḥ*, which we have translated as "exultance," is usually used pejoratively to indicate a frolicking sense of abandon in carnal delights. For this reason, God says, "Do not exult, for God does not love the exultant" (Qurʾān 28:76). *Ḥazan*, which we have translated as "sadness," on the other hand, is frequently mentioned as a desirable emotional state in which a person feels sad for the existence of sin, oppression, and unbelief in the world and for his own inability to be as good as he ought to be in front of his perfect Lord. In this vein, Imam Zayn al-ʿĀbidīn has said, "God loves a sad heart" (*Al-Kāfī* 5.48.30). Similarly, Imam ʿAlī extols the God-fearing saying, "Their hearts are sad" (*Nahj al-balāghah* sermon 193).

It is, however, possible to construe *faraḥ* as a positive trait if one "rejoices" in the grace and mercy of God as the Qurʾān says, "In God's grace and mercy let them rejoice" (10:58). Similarly, we could construe *ḥazan* pejoratively if a person feels sad because of some worldly loss he has incurred. In this vein Imam ʿAlī says, "He who is satisfied with his sustenance will not feel sad for what passes him up (*Wasāʾil al-shīʿah* 15.2.36.20544). However, we believe the first possibility to be the stronger of the two because of the predominant usage of these two terms in Islamic sources.

30. This third category of believers whose faith has been tested are people who were created with perfect intellects but were neither prophets nor their successors. They were people like Fāṭimah al-Zahrāʾ; Mary, Jesus' mother; and Luqmān, the Wise. The following tradition supports this view: "[Imam] Abū Jaʿfar [al-Jawād] said [to one of his cousins], 'When you go to the grave of your grandmother, Fāṭimah, say [to her], "O you who have been tested; whom God, your Creator, tested before creating you; [whom] he then found patient in the face of his test"'" (*Tahdhīb al-aḥkām* 6.1.3.12).

31. From the context, we can be sure he intended to include this third category, which we have mentioned in brackets. Perhaps he did not mention them here since he had just mentioned them two sentences prior and he expected us to continue the list.

32. Certainly, we cannot attain perfection simply by "knowing Intellect and its army." Rather, in addition to knowing, we must take steps to assimilate those traits into our being. Only then can we reasonably hope to attain perfection. Imam al-Ṣādiq left off mention of this vital step to show the pivotal role of knowledge in the process—as though knowledge alone leads to perfection.

TRADITION 1.1.14 TEACHES THE FOLLOWING:

- According to one interpretation, the first of God's immaterial creatures was intellect.
- The intellect is like a divine light.
- The intellect perceives that total submission before God is good.
- The intellect is great, honored above all of God's creatures.
- Foolishness is like darkness.
- Foolishness is the root of sin.
- Foolishness is the root of arrogance and thus makes its possessor accursed in God's eyes.
- The intellect gains strength through the assimilation of 75 attributes.
- Foolishness gains strength through the assimilation of 75 attributes.
- Foolishness is the rival of intellect.
- The entire army of Intellect joins forces in God's prophets, their successors, and the believers whose hearts God has tested.
- Some of the units of Intellect's army are found in the *Shīʿah*, while they must endeavor to acquire all the other units.
- It is possible for the *Shīʿah* to perfect their intellects to the level of the prophets, their successors, and the believers whose hearts God has tested.
- We can perfect our intellect by learning about the armies of intellect and foolishness and by assimilating the former and ridding ourselves of the latter.

Tradition 1.1.15

A group of our fellow Shīʿah reported from Aḥmad ibn Muḥammad ibn ʿĪsā from al-Ḥasan ibn ʿAlī ibn Faḍḍāl from one of our fellow Shīʿah that Abū ʿAbd Allāh [al-Ṣādiq] said:

جَمَاعَةٌ مِنْ أَصْحَابِنَا عَنْ أَحْمَدَ بْنِ مُحَمَّدِ بْنِ عِيسَى عَنِ الْحَسَنِ بْنِ عَلِيِّ بْنِ فَضَّالٍ عَنْ بَعْضِ أَصْحَابِنَا عَنْ أَبِي عَبْدِ اللَّهِ عليه السلام قَالَ:

"The Messenger of God never spoke to people[1] using the highest levels of his intellect."[2]

مَا كَلَّمَ رَسُولُ اللَّهِ ﷺ الْعِبَادَ بِكُنْهِ عَقْلِهِ قَطُّ.

And [then] he said,[3]

وَ قَالَ:

"The Messenger of God said, 'We the legions of prophets have been commanded to speak to people according to their intellectual capacities.'"[4]

قَالَ رَسُولُ اللَّهِ ﷺ : إِنَّا مَعَاشِرَ الْأَنْبِيَاءِ أُمِرْنَا أَنْ نُكَلِّمَ النَّاسَ عَلَى قَدْرِ عُقُولِهِمْ.

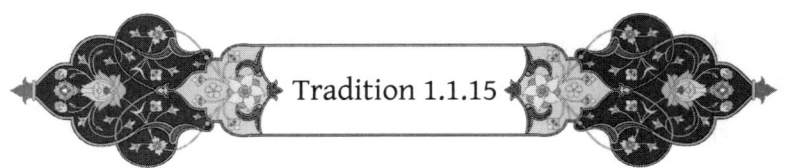

1. We have translated *ʿibād* as "people" rather than "servants." In many instances, the word *ʿabd* refers to one who is obedient to God as a faithful servant is obedient to his master. However, it is not uncommon for *ʿabd* to refer, not to one who chooses to obey God, but to any creature of God inasmuch as it is—whether or not it wants to be—God's servant: dependent on him for its every need, subservient to his every decree. *ʿAbd* is used in the Qurʾān in the latter sense in the following verse: "Everyone in the heavens and on earth shall come to the All-Merciful as a servant" (Qurʾān 19:93). Even those who chose not to serve God in their life will have no choice on the Day of Judgment but to come to him as a servant.

2. Without a doubt, this statement does not include Imam ʿAlī, though he deemed himself to be but "a servant among the many servants of Muḥammad" (*al-Kāfī* 3.6.5). The Prophet, being an outstanding teacher, considered the aptitude of every pupil and spoke to him at his own level. If he refrained from speaking to people at large using his full intellectual capacity, it was not because he sought to deprive them of something of benefit, but because they did not have the requisite ability to comprehend. However, in ʿAlī he found a disciple so brilliant that he would come to call him "The Gateway to the City of Knowledge." In their private sessions, the Prophet could speak without restriction, and in so doing, he acted according to his own teaching where he said, "Do not share wisdom with the unworthy lest you wrong *it*, and do not withhold wisdom from the worthy lest you wrong *them*" (*Biḥār al-anwār* 2.1.13.69).

3. Apparently, Imam al-Ṣādiq spoke both these sentences in the course of a single conversation. The close relationship between the two statements makes it clear that he sought to corroborate his own claim by citing this famous prophetic tradition.

4. The mandate of the prophets was to explain the tenets of faith and the law to each person in a manner best suited to that person: simply for the average person and more rigorously for those of higher aptitude. In addition, they would teach the intellectually elite things incomprehensible to those endowed with less intellect. You might wonder why, if the prophet spoke to the level of his audience, must our scholars deliberate so laboriously over the meaning of these traditions—especially those of a legal and practical nature—before being able to issue a legal opinion? For that matter, why do we need *ijtihād*, the process of deriving laws from primary sources, if the teachings of the Prophet and, by extension, the imams, are simple and clear? The answer lies, not in any obscurity in their teachings themselves, but in myriad external factors that have obscured their teachings over time. For instance, some teachings were spoken in a state of dissimulation (*taqiyyah*); transmitters paraphrased many traditions before recording them; and both transmitters and scribes inevitably made mistakes in passing these traditions down to us. These and other factors, foreign to the actual teachings of the Prophet and imams, have made it very difficult for anyone but trained experts to accurately uncover the precise intent of the original speaker.

It might seem that Imam al-Ṣādiq's assertion in this tradition is at odds with what has been transmitted in *al-Kāfī* 4.102.1-5 where he contends that "the traditions of the family of Muḥammad are difficult." There is no contradiction between these traditions, since the message of those traditions is that their traditions are difficult to *accept*, not that they are difficult to *comprehend*.

TRADITION 1.1.15 TEACHES THE FOLLOWING:

- A teacher must consider the intellectual aptitude of his students.
- The Prophet had a perfect intellect, the highest levels of which no one can comprehend.

Tradition 1.1.16

ᶜAlī ibn Muḥammad reported from Sahl ibn Ziyād from al-Nawfalī from al-Sakūnī from Jaᶜfar [al-Ṣādiq] from his father [al-Bāqir] that he said:

عَلِيُّ بْنُ مُحَمَّدٍ عَنْ سَهْلِ بْنِ زِيَادٍ عَنِ النَّوْفَلِيِّ عَنِ السَّكُونِيِّ عَنْ جَعْفَرٍ عَنْ أَبِيهِ عليهما السلام قَالَ:

"The Commander of the Faithful [ᶜAlī] said, 'The hearts of the foolish[1] are carried away by [unfettered] desires, held as collateral by far-fetched hopes, and ensnared by guiles.'"[2]

قَالَ أَمِيرُ الْمُؤْمِنِينَ عليه السلام : إِنَّ قُلُوبَ الْجُهَّالِ تَسْتَفِزُّهَا الْأَطْمَاعُ وَ تَرْتَهِنُهَا الْمُنَى وَ تَسْتَعْلِقُهَا الْخَدَائِعُ.

---

1. The "heart" is mentioned in this tradition to refer to the intellect. The "foolish" are those who do not use their intellect or do not follow its guidance.

2. This tradition describes the weakness of the foolish by conjuring three images. First, because they have not strengthened their intellects, they are not grounded in anything solid. Whichever way their desires lead them, they follow without engaging their intellects to determine what is in their best interest. Second, their far-fetched hopes, like a usurious money-lender, hold their hearts as collateral and do not release them to pursue rational, realistic goals that will lead them to God's proximity. Third, they are easily deceived by Satan and his nefarious cohorts who are constantly setting traps for them. Because they lack intellectual strength, they cannot escape these traps.

TRADITION 1.1.16 TEACHES THE FOLLOWING:

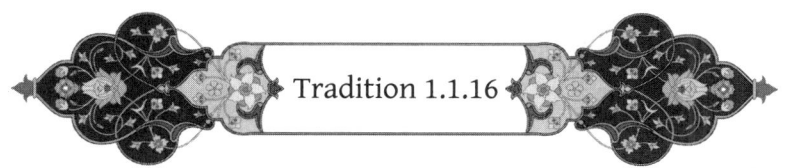

- The intellect of the fool is heavily under the influence of his desires and far-fetched hopes from within and the tricks of others from without.

- The hearts of those with strong intellects are firm, not affected by unfettered desires, far-fetched hopes, or trickery.

Tradition 1.1.17

ʿAlī ibn Ibrāhīm reported from his father from Jaʿfar ibn Muḥammad al-Ashʿarī from ʿUbayd Allāh al-Dihqān from Durust from Ibrāhīm ibn ʿAbd al-Ḥamīd that he said, "Abū ʿAbd Allāh [al-Ṣādiq] said:

عَلِيُّ بْنُ إِبْرَاهِيمَ عَنْ أَبِيهِ عَنْ جَعْفَرِ بْنِ مُحَمَّدٍ الْأَشْعَرِيِّ عَنْ عُبَيْدِ اللَّهِ الدِّهْقَانِ عَنْ دُرُسْتَ عَنْ إِبْرَاهِيمَ بْنِ عَبْدِ الْحَمِيدِ قَالَ: قَالَ أَبُو عَبْدِ اللَّهِ عليه السلام :

'The people with the strongest intellect[1] are the best in character.'"[2]

أَكْمَلُ النَّاسِ عَقْلاً أَحْسَنُهُمْ خُلُقاً.

---

1. We have translated *akmal* as "strongest" even though its literal translation would be "most perfect" because perfection is not a gradated concept: one is either perfect or imperfect, not more or less perfect.

2. This tradition indicates that intellectual strength causes good character, not that good character is always an indicator of a strong intellect, for in many instances, we find people who have good character despite their weak intellects. In such cases, their character is the result of environmental factors such as a good upbringing or a moral—albeit secular—education. On the other hand, those with strong intellects comprehend the virtue of good character and its positive ramifications, and so their character always reflects their intellectual strength. Thus, the only surefire way to strengthen our character is to strengthen our intellect.

TRADITION 1.1.17 TEACHES THE FOLLOWING:

- Intellectual strength leads to good character—though this does not imply that good character is necessarily an indication of a strong intellect.

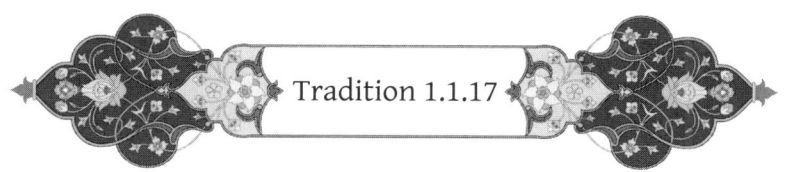

- Prophet Muḥammad embodied the best possible character as indicated by the verse, "Indeed, you have outstanding character" (Qurʾān 68:4); the reason for his outstanding character was that he had the strongest possible intellect.
- If we want to improve our character, we must use our intellect to contemplate the ramifications of virtue and vice.

Tradition 1.1.18

ʿAlī reported from Abū Hāshim al-Jaʿfarī[1] that he said, "We were with [Imam] al-Riḍā, and we mentioned intellect and discipline, so he said:

عَلِيٌّ عَنْ أَبِيهِ عَنْ أَبِي هَاشِمٍ الْجَعْفَرِيِّ قَالَ: كُنَّا عِنْدَ الرِّضَا عليه السلام فَتَذَاكَرْنَا الْعَقْلَ وَ الْأَدَبَ فَقَالَ:

'O Abū Hāshim! Intellect is a gift from God while discipline can be attained through human endeavor. Thus, whoever endeavors to attain discipline is able to attain it,[2] but whoever endeavors to attain intellect increases, through his efforts, only in foolishness.'"[3]

يَا أَبَا هَاشِمٍ، الْعَقْلُ حِبَاءٌ مِنَ اللَّهِ وَ الْأَدَبُ كُلْفَةٌ، فَمَنْ تَكَلَّفَ الْأَدَبَ قَدَرَ عَلَيْهِ وَ مَنْ تَكَلَّفَ الْعَقْلَ لَمْ يَزْدَدْ بِذَلِكَ إِلَّا جَهْلاً.

---

1. In some recensions of *al-Kāfī*, this chain reads, "ʿAlī reported from his father from Abū Hāshim al-Jaʿfarī." For a full discussion of the chain, see Dār al-Ḥadīth's edition (vol. 1, p. 53).

2. Discipline (*adab*) in this context refers to propriety in speech and behavior. One who acts and speaks appropriately in various societal interactions is said to possess good discipline or etiquette.

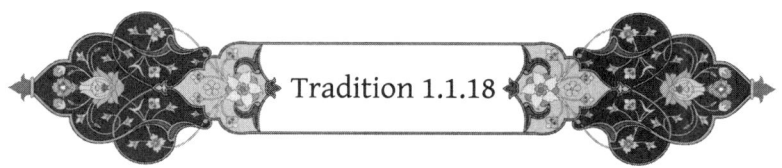

3. We are able to achieve many results by simply availing ourselves of the means that God has placed at our disposal. For instance, if we exercise or lift weights, we will unfailingly achieve a level of fitness commensurate with our effort. Similarly, if we study a particular subject, we will unfailingly gain a level of proficiency commensurate with our diligence in studying, assuming we have the aptitude to do so. God has placed the means for these and most other things at our disposal such that whoever avails himself of those means unfailingly attains the desired result. Notably, achieving these results does not require that we take any additional help from God or even that we believe in him.

According to this tradition, discipline and good character can similarly be attained through natural means that have been placed at our disposal. If we want to become generous, we can force ourselves to give charity and to make sacrifices until such acts become habit. If we want to become punctual, we can plan ahead and force ourselves to abide by a strict schedule until punctuality becomes custom. In this vein, Imam ʿAlī has said, "If you are not forbearing, then act as though you are, for it is rare that one acts like a people without becoming one of them" (*Nahj al-balāghah* proverb 207).

This tradition explains that intellect differs from discipline and other such things in that it is a gift from God that cannot be attained through simple human endeavor. We cannot simply study something or practice something and expect that our intellect will automatically increase. Rather, God has reserved the bestowal of intellect for himself.

You might think this is odd, since other traditions tell us that we can strengthen our intellect by using what intellect God has already given us, by abstaining from sin, by learning and teaching, through discipline, through experience, and by submitting to truth, among other things. The truth is that these acts are not natural causes for increased intellect, but prerequisites we must fulfill to prepare the grounds for God to dispense his gift. These acts are to intellect what the study of religious sciences is to true gnosis and experiential knowledge of God. In particular, religious sciences such as Arabic grammar, commentary of the Qurʾān, theology, and jurisprudence are like any secular field of study in that anyone who has a strong aptitude and studies hard can achieve proficiency. However, true experiential knowledge of God is a gift from God to those who have not only achieved proficiency in the aforementioned fields of study, but have earned God's special favor and, as a result, have been bestowed with his special gift. This is the meaning of the tradition of Imam al-Kāẓim, "And he who does not know God [as he has described himself] will never bind his heart to any kind of constant knowledge that he can see and whose reality he can palpate in his heart" (*al-Kāfī* 1.1.12 section 27).

Since intellect cannot be attained through human endeavor, one who endeavors to attain it without seeking God's favor is striving in vain. Since his efforts have no benefit, he ironically increases his foolishness through the very act he thought would increase his intellect.

TRADITION 1.1.18 TEACHES THE FOLLOWING:

- Intellect is a gift that God gives to whomever he wishes.
- We can attain discipline through our own endeavor; however, we cannot strengthen our intellect no matter how much we endeavor, unless we earn God's favor.
- To endeavor to attain something that we cannot attain is to endeavor in vain, and to endeavor in vain is an act of foolishness.

Tradition 1.1.19

ʿAlī ibn Ibrāhīm reported from his father from Yaḥyā ibn al-Mubārak from ʿAbd Allāh ibn Jabalah from Isḥāq ibn ʿAmmār from [the time of] Abū ʿAbd Allāh [al-Ṣādiq] that Isḥāq said, "I told him (i.e., al-Ṣādiq), 'May I be your ransom! I have a neighbor who prays much, gives much in charity, performs the hajj often,[1] [and] harms no one.' So he asked [me]:

عَلِيُّ بْنُ إِبْرَاهِيمَ عَنْ أَبِيهِ عَنْ يَحْيَى بْنِ الْمُبَارَكِ عَنْ عَبْدِ اللَّهِ بْنِ جَبَلَةَ عَنْ إِسْحَاقَ بْنِ عَمَّارٍ عَنْ أَبِي عَبْدِ اللَّهِ عليه السلام قَالَ: قُلْتُ لَهُ: جُعِلْتُ فِدَاكَ، إِنَّ لِي جَاراً كَثِيرَ الصَّلَاةِ كَثِيرَ الصَّدَقَةِ كَثِيرَ الْحَجِّ لَا بَأْسَ بِهِ. قَالَ: فَقَالَ:

'Isḥāq, how is his intellect?'

يَا إِسْحَاقُ، كَيْفَ عَقْلُهُ؟

I replied, 'May I be your ransom! He has no intellect [to speak of].'[2] So he said:

قَالَ: قُلْتُ لَهُ: جُعِلْتُ فِدَاكَ، لَيْسَ لَهُ عَقْلٌ . قَالَ: فَقَالَ:

'Nothing [of the deeds you have mentioned] shall ascend from him because of this [weakness of intellect].'"[3]

لَا يَرْتَفِعُ بِذَلِكَ مِنْهُ.

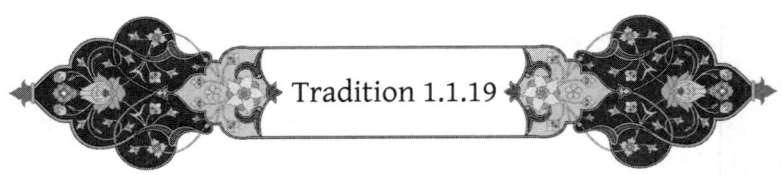

1. Isḥāq praises his neighbor for praying much, giving much in charity, and performing hajj often. In all three instances, he is referring to the neighbor's many supererogatory, and not obligatory, acts of devotion. With regard to prayers, it would not make sense to say that someone offers his obligatory prayers much, since the obligatory prayers are limited in number. A person either offers *all* his obligatory prayers and deserves praise or fails to offer *all* his obligatory prayers and deserves censure. Supererogatory prayers, on the other hand, are practically unlimited, so it makes sense to praise someone for choosing to offer them much. Likewise, the many times his neighbor has performed hajj must be supererogatory pilgrimages, since only one is obligatory. Since charity is mentioned in the same context, it must also be optional charity, known as *ṣadaqah*, which a person gives of his own initiative, not *khums* and *zakāh*, which are obligatory forms of charity that must be given in limited instances under specific circumstances.

2. Isḥāq does not mean that his neighbor is devoid of intellect altogether, for that would mean he is insane, and the insane do not "pray much, give much charity, and perform the hajj often." Rather, he means that he does not have powers of intellect strong enough to distinguish right from wrong in all walks of life. He is like one of the pupils Imam ʿAlī complains about in his famous soliloquy to Kumayl ibn Ziyād: "[Occasionally, I find] one who yields to the bearers of truth while no insight is to be found in any part of his being. At the first hint of a problem, uncertainty flares up in his heart" (*Nahj al-balāghah* proverb 147).

3. Imam al-Ṣādiq apparently means to say that his reward, when compared to the apparent volume of his acts of devotion, is so little that it is as though his deeds do not ascend and are not accepted. Thus, Isḥāq's neighbor is similar to the Jewish man of *al-Kāfī* 1.1.8 who will be rewarded meagerly, "in proportion to his intellect."

TRADITION 1.1.19 TEACHES THE FOLLOWING:

- Intellect, and not the sheer volume of one's deeds, is the standard for reward.
- One who is pious but lacking in intellect does not deserve praise.

Tradition 1.1.20

Al-Ḥusayn ibn Muḥammad reported from Aḥmad ibn Muḥammad al-Sayyārī from Abū Yaʿqūb al-Baghdādī that he said, "Ibn al-Sikkīt asked Abū al-Ḥasan [al-Hādī], 'Why did God send Moses, the son of ʿImrān, with his staff and white hand[1] and the means to [counter] magic? And [why] did he send Jesus with the means to [practice] medicine? And [why] did he send Muḥammad—may God shower him and his family and all the prophets with mercy—with [eloquent] speech and oratory?' Abū al-Ḥasan replied:

الْحُسَيْنُ بْنُ مُحَمَّدٍ عَنْ أَحْمَدَ بْنِ مُحَمَّدٍ السَّيَّارِيِّ عَنْ أَبِي يَعْقُوبَ الْبَغْدَادِيِّ قَالَ: قَالَ ابْنُ السِّكِّيتِ لِأَبِي الْحَسَنِ عليه السلام: لِمَاذَا بَعَثَ اللَّهُ مُوسَى بْنَ عِمْرَانَ عليه السلام بِالْعَصَا وَ يَدِهِ الْبَيْضَاءِ وَ آلَةِ السِّحْرِ؟ وَ بَعَثَ عِيسَى بِآلَةِ الطِّبِّ؟ وَ بَعَثَ مُحَمَّداً—صَلَّى اللَّهُ عَلَيْهِ وَ آلِهِ وَ عَلَى جَمِيعِ الْأَنْبِيَاءِ—بِالْكَلَامِ وَ الْخُطَبِ؟ فَقَالَ أَبُو الْحَسَنِ عليه السلام:

'When God sent Moses, magic ruled supreme over the people of that age. Accordingly, he brought for them, on God's behalf, [the miracle of his staff], the likes of which they lacked the power [to conjure] and with which he debunked [their claim to infinite power nested in] their magic, and [thereby] sealed his case against them.[2]

إِنَّ اللَّهَ لَمَّا بَعَثَ مُوسَى عليه السلام كَانَ الْغَالِبُ عَلَى أَهْلِ عَصْرِهِ السِّحْرَ، فَأَتَاهُمْ مِنْ عِنْدِ اللَّهِ بِمَا لَمْ يَكُنْ فِي وُسْعِهِمْ مِثْلُهُ وَ مَا أَبْطَلَ بِهِ سِحْرَهُمْ وَ أَثْبَتَ بِهِ الْحُجَّةَ عَلَيْهِمْ.

'[Likewise,] God sent Jesus in a time

وَ إِنَّ اللَّهَ بَعَثَ عِيسَى عليه السلام فِي وَقْتٍ قَدْ

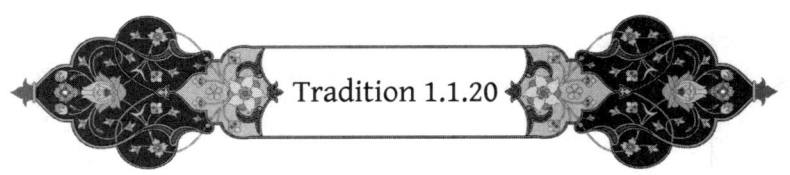

when diseases were epidemic and people needed medical treatment. Accordingly, Jesus brought for them, on God's behalf, [a panacea] the likes of which they did not have and by which he raised for them the dead, cured—by God's leave—the congenitally blind and the leprous,[3] and sealed his case against them.

ظَهَرَتْ فِيهِ الزَّمَانَاتُ وَ احْتَاجَ النَّاسُ إِلَى الطِّبِّ، فَأَتَاهُمْ مِنْ عِنْدِ اللَّهِ بِمَا لَمْ يَكُنْ عِنْدَهُمْ مِثْلُهُ وَ بِمَا أَحْيَا لَهُمُ الْمَوْتَى وَ أَبْرَأَ الْأَكْمَهَ وَ الْأَبْرَصَ بِإِذْنِ اللَّهِ وَ أَثْبَتَ بِهِ الْحُجَّةَ عَلَيْهِمْ.

'[Likewise,] God sent Muḥammad—may God shower him and his family with mercy—in a time when [eloquent] speech and oratory (and I believe he said 'poetry')[4] ruled supreme over the people of that time. Accordingly, he brought for them, on God's behalf, [a book of] admonishment and wisdom by which he refuted their allegations[5] and sealed his case against them.'

وَ إِنَّ اللَّهَ بَعَثَ مُحَمَّداً ﷺ فِي وَقْتٍ كَانَ الْغَالِبُ عَلَى أَهْلِ عَصْرِهِ الْخُطَبَ وَ الْكَلَامَ - وَ أَظُنُّهُ قَالَ: الشِّعْرَ - فَأَتَاهُمْ مِنْ عِنْدِ اللَّهِ مِنْ مَوَاعِظِهِ وَ حِكَمِهِ مَا أَبْطَلَ بِهِ قَوْلَهُمْ وَ أَثْبَتَ بِهِ الْحُجَّةَ عَلَيْهِمْ.

Ibn al-Sikkīt said, 'By God, I have never seen the likes of you! [However, if it was through his prophets' miracles that God sealed his case against his enemies in the past] then what seals God's case against his creatures today?'[6] Abū al-Ḥasan replied:

قَالَ: فَقَالَ ابْنُ السِّكِّيتِ: تَاللَّهِ مَا رَأَيْتُ مِثْلَكَ قَطُّ. فَمَا الْحُجَّةُ عَلَى الْخَلْقِ الْيَوْمَ؟ قَالَ: فَقَالَ عليه السلام:

'The intellect. Through it one can know who speaks truthfully about

الْعَقْلُ. يُعْرَفُ بِهِ الصَّادِقُ عَلَى اللَّهِ فَيُصَدِّقُهُ وَ الْكَاذِبُ عَلَى اللَّهِ فَيُكَذِّبُهُ.

God and can thus confirm his claim, and [one can know] who speaks lies about God and can thus repudiate him.'[7]

قَالَ فَقَالَ ابْنُ السِّكِّيتِ: هٰذَا وَ اللَّهِ هُوَ الْجَوَابُ.

Ibn al-Sikkīt said, 'This, by God, is the answer.'"

---

1. This is an allusion to Qurʾān 28:31-32.

2. Moses, by God's leave, could turn his staff into a serpent, and thereby achieve two goals. First, he showed that the source of his power was not mere sorcery, a fact to which even the greatest Egyptian magicians attested. Second, he effectively corroborated his claims as a prophet of God and silenced the Pharaoh's claims to divinity thereby leaving no excuse for the Pharaoh, his magicians, or his people to persist in their false ways.

This sentence contains an allusion to Qurʾān 10:81. The phrase *ibṭāl al-siḥr* in both the verse and this tradition literally means "to invalidate magic." However, when Moses threw his staff, he did not *invalidate* the magic of the Pharaoh's sorcerers, for their snakes continued to slither even as they were swallowed by Moses' serpent. Rather, he debunked their claims to infinite power, which their magic was meant to bolster. Accordingly, we have translated the phrase as follows: "he debunked [their claim to infinite power nested in] their magic," rather than, "he invalidated their magic."

3. This is an allusion to Qurʾān 3:49.

4. The interjection was either spoken by Ibn al-Sikkīt or Abū Yaʿqūb.

5. Imam al-Ḥādī is referring to the allegations with which the pagans of Mecca charged the Prophet. For they were astounded that God would send them a mere mortal as a warner, and they called him "a sorcerer and a liar" (see Qur'ān 38:4). The Qur'ān effectively refuted these allegations and established the truth of the matter in two ways particularly suited to Arabs who were masters of the art of words. First, its linguistic beauty and style of expression were, and remain, unparalleled. Second, unlike the hollow poetry of pre-Islamic Arabs, the Qur'ān is filled with meaningful, life-altering admonishment and wisdom. Thus, it was glaringly obvious to them that no man could write such a book, and the levelheaded among them conceded that he who brought it was indeed the Prophet of God.

6. Ibn al-Sikkīt realized the pivotal role that miracles played historically in corroborating the truth of each prophet's claim and realized that after the revelation of the Qur'ān, there had been no such public miracles to confirm the claims of the imams. So he asked Imam al-Hādī what currently served this role, which had previously been served by miracles.

7 . In the olden days, miracles had been the means for prophets to prove their legitimacy. When a prophet claimed to have been sent by God, and then performed a miracle that was not humanly possible, people knew without a doubt that he was truthful in his claim. In reality, it was their intellect that drew this conclusion, for it understood that anyone who could do what only God could do must be from God. This is how things continued up through the time of Prophet Muḥammad who brought a book so eloquent, so full of wisdom, and so perfect, that it made even the staunchest of his enemies admit that it, and by association, he, was from God.

Accordingly, Ibn al-Sikkīt asks about a new miracle that would prove to all Muslims the legitimacy of the Prophet's vicegerents, the imams. Imam al-Ḥādī responds saying that human intellect needs no new miracle to determine who among the claimants to the Prophet's vicegerency is truthful and who is lying. It must simply compare the claimants' qualities to the Qur'ān, which is the Prophet's extant miracle, and the Prophet's *sunnah*, his exemplary life, significant aspects of which can be known with certainty from the countless historical reports that have reached us. For he who is truthful in his claim would know the Qur'ān and uphold its teachings better than anybody and would emulate the example of the Prophet more completely than anybody. Conversely, the false claimant would abandon both the Qur'ān and *sunnah* through his words and actions. Thus, the intellect alone, through this process of comparison, plays the same role in the current age that the intellect and miracles together played in the past.

TRADITION 1.1.20 TEACHES THE FOLLOWING:

- The miracles of the prophets were appropriate for the age in which they were performed.
- The purpose of miracles is to identify whose claims to having been sent by God are true and whose are false.
- Miracles must comprise a feat that people are unable to match.
- Man always needs his intellect to determine who is truthful in his claim to having been sent by God and who is lying. He must either use his intellect to evaluate the miracles brought by the claimant or use his intellect to make a comparison between the claimant and the prophet he claims to be representing.
- The right way to discover the prophet's legitimate successor is to compare the claimants to the teachings of the Qur'ān and to known aspects of the Prophet's example. He who is truthful in his claim knows the Qur'ān and upholds its teachings better than anybody and emulates the example of the Prophet more completely than anybody. Conversely, the false claimant abandons both the Qur'ān and *sunnah* through his words and actions.

Tradition 1.1.21

Al-Ḥusayn ibn Muḥammad reported from Muʿallā ibn Muḥammad from al-Washshāʾ from al-Muthannā al-Ḥannāṭ from al-Qutaybah al-Aʿshā from Ibn Abī Yaʿfūr from an ally of Banū Shaybān[1] that Abū Jaʿfar [al-Bāqir] said:

الْحُسَيْنُ بْنُ مُحَمَّدٍ عَنْ مُعَلَّى بْنِ مُحَمَّدٍ عَنِ الْوَشَّاءِ عَنِ الْمُثَنَّى الْحَنَّاطِ عَنْ قُتَيْبَةَ الْأَعْشَى عَنِ ابْنِ أَبِي يَعْفُورٍ عَنْ مَوْلًى لِبَنِي شَيْبَانَ عَنْ أَبِي جَعْفَرٍ عليه السلام قَالَ:

"When the *Qāʾim*[2] establishes his government, God will place his hand upon the heads of the people.[3] Through his hand, God will unify their intellects,[4] and through him, intellects will attain perfection."

إِذَا قَامَ قَائِمُنَا وَضَعَ اللَّهُ يَدَهُ عَلَى رُؤُوسِ الْعِبَادِ فَجَمَعَ بِهَا عُقُولَهُمْ وَ كَمَلَتْ بِهِ أَحْلَامُهُمْ.

---

1. We have translated the term *mawlā* as "ally." To be an ally of a tribe is to have made a covenant with them without having any blood relation to them.

2. *Al-Qāʾim* is a title of the twelfth imam, Imam al-Mahdī—may God hasten his return. He is called *al-Qāʾim* because he will, on his return, establish and take charge of God's government on earth (*yaqūmu bi ʾamr allāh*). The imams have advised us to stand when we hear this title as a mark of respect and as a sign of our readiness to rise up with him when he gives the call (*Muntakhab al-athar* vol. 3, p. 226, tradition 1244).

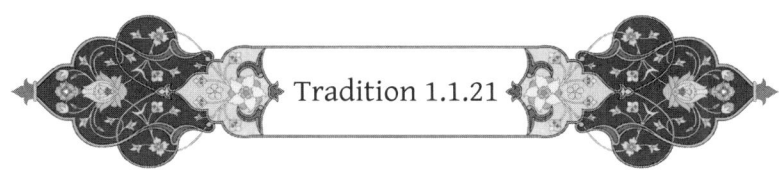

3. The "hand" referred to here is the metaphorical hand of Imam al-Mahdī, not the metaphorical hand of God, for this tradition is extolling the Imam and the tremendous role he will play in the intellectual development of humankind. This view is corroborated by Shaykh al-Ṣadūq's narration of this tradition which reads, "When the *Qāʾim* establishes his government, he will place his hand upon the heads of the people" (*Kamāl al-dīn* 2.58.31). The placement of his hand on people's heads is a metonym for his power and sovereignty over them, not his compassion for them as some commentators have suggested, for unifying people's minds requires the exercise of power and skilled leadership first and foremost. Of course, he will have compassion for people, but this tradition does not speak of that aspect.

4. Through the strong leadership of Imam al-Mahdī, God will unify all people's intellects so that they know and accept the truth.

TRADITION 1.1.21 TEACHES THE FOLLOWING:

- Imam al-Mahdī will play a major role in unifying people under the banner of true faith.
- Imam al-Mahdī will play a major role in the development and perfection of people's intellects.
- A healthy, harmonious society founded on the precepts of Islam is influential in the positive development of people's intellects.

Tradition 1.1.22

ᶜAlī ibn Muḥammad reported from Sahl ibn Ziyād from Muḥammad ibn Sulaymān from ᶜAlī ibn Ibrāhīm from ᶜAbd Allāh ibn Sinān that Abū ᶜAbd Allāh [al-Ṣādiq] said:

عَلِيُّ بْنُ مُحَمَّدٍ عَنْ سَهْلِ بْنِ زِيَادٍ عَنْ مُحَمَّدِ بْنِ سُلَيْمَانَ عَنْ عَلِيِّ بْنِ إِبْرَاهِيمَ عَنْ عَبْدِ اللَّهِ بْنِ سِنَانٍ عَنْ أَبِي عَبْدِ اللَّهِ عليه السلام قَالَ:

"The prophets are God's evidence against people, and the intellect is God's evidence against people and people's evidence against God."[1]

حُجَّةُ اللَّهِ عَلَى الْعِبَادِ النَّبِيُّ وَ الْحُجَّةُ فِيمَا بَيْنَ الْعِبَادِ وَ بَيْنَ اللَّهِ الْعَقْلُ.

---

1. Two valuable pieces of evidence will be brought forth on the Day of Judgment: the prophets and the intellect. This tradition explains a major difference between these two pieces of evidence. The prophets are God's evidence against man as we explained in section two of 1.1.12. The intellect, on the other hand, serves a dual purpose. It serves, in one sense, to incriminate man if, despite being endowed with it, he fails to know God or, having known him, fails to obey him; for the intellect is the sole tool to know God, and the intellect deems his obedience obligatory. In another sense, it serves to exonerate man for those duties that he is incapable of fulfilling and for which he does not know he is responsible (also refer to section fifteen of 1.1.12).

TRADITION 1.1.22 TEACHES THE FOLLOWING:

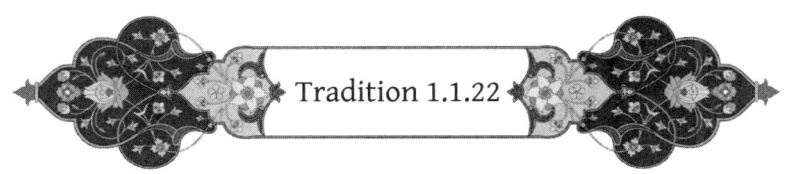

- This tradition reinforces the lessons of section two and section fifteen of 1.1.12, and in addition, teaches that the intellect exonerates man for those duties that he is incapable of fulfilling and for which he does not know he is responsible.

Tradition 1.1.23

A group of our fellow Shīʿah reported from Aḥmad ibn Muḥammad that he said [without mentioning his source] that Abū ʿAbd Allāh [al-Ṣādiq] said:

عِدَّةٌ مِنْ أَصْحَابِنَا عَنْ أَحْمَدَ بْنِ مُحَمَّدٍ مُرْسِلًا قَالَ: قَالَ أَبُو عَبْدِ اللَّهِ عليه السلام :

"The backbone of man is his intellect,[1] [for] from his intellect do keenness, comprehension, memory, and knowledge issue,[2] and by his intellect does he become complete.[3] It is his guide, his [exonerating] evidence,[4] and the key to his affairs. Subsequently, if his intellect is bolstered with the light [of divine guidance],[5] he will know, remember, be aware, and have keenness and comprehension,[6] and consequently, because of that [enlightenment], will know how, why, and where.[7] He will know who wishes him well and who wishes to defraud him.[8] Then, when he knows that, he will know his path and to what he must cling and from what he must keep his distance;[9] and he will attribute singularity only to God and consent to obey none but him.[10] Then, when he has done that, he will have atoned for what eluded

دِعَامَةُ الْإِنْسَانِ الْعَقْلُ. وَ الْعَقْلُ مِنْهُ الْفِطْنَةُ وَ الْفَهْمُ وَ الْحِفْظُ وَ الْعِلْمُ، وَ بِالْعَقْلِ يَكْمُلُ وَ هُوَ دَلِيلُهُ وَ مَبْصَرُهُ وَ مِفْتَاحُ أَمْرِهِ. فَإِذَا كَانَ تَأْيِيدُ عَقْلِهِ مِنَ النُّورِ كَانَ عَالِماً حَافِظاً ذَاكِراً فَطِناً فَهِماً، فَعَلِمَ بِذَلِكَ كَيْفَ وَ لِمَ وَ حَيْثُ، وَ عَرَفَ مَنْ نَصَحَهُ وَ مَنْ غَشَّهُ. فَإِذَا عَرَفَ ذَلِكَ عَرَفَ مَجْرَاهُ وَ مَوْصُولَهُ وَ مَفْصُولَهُ وَ أَخْلَصَ الْوَحْدَانِيَّةَ لِلَّهِ وَ الْإِقْرَارَ بِالطَّاعَةِ. فَإِذَا فَعَلَ ذَلِكَ كَانَ مُسْتَدْرِكاً لِمَا فَاتَ وَ وَارِداً عَلَى مَا هُوَ آتٍ يَعْرِفُ مَا هُوَ فِيهِ وَ لِأَيِّ شَيْءٍ هُوَ هَاهُنَا وَ مِنْ أَيْنَ يَأْتِيهِ وَ إِلَى مَا هُوَ صَائِرٌ وَ ذَلِكَ كُلُّهُ مِنْ تَأْيِيدِ الْعَقْلِ.

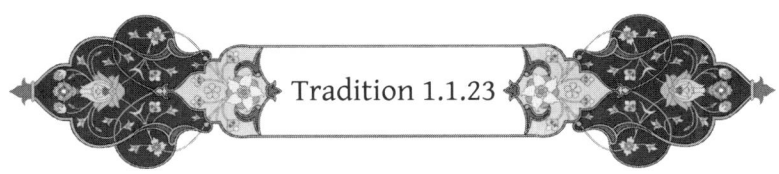

him,[11] and he will meet what [reward] he has coming.[12] He will know what [a transitory realm] he lives in, for what purpose he is here,[13] how he can fulfill that purpose, and where he is heading.[14] All that is caused by the bolstering of the intellect."

---

1. We have translated *diʿāmah* as "backbone" even though it literally means "pillar." The intellect of a human being is compared to a structural support such as a pillar without which a house cannot stand. Similarly, a human being cannot stand as a human being without his intellect, for it is the source of all traits of perfection—such as keenness, comprehension, memory, and knowledge—that set humans apart from God's other creatures. Nonetheless, we have chosen "backbone" over "pillar" simply because it communicates the idea of support better in this context in the English language.

2. It is important to note that "intellect" is used here in a different sense than it has been used in other traditions thus far, for here it refers to the faculty in humankind to analyze, learn, and memorize without considering whether or not they use that faculty to differentiate between truth and falsehood. Thus, in this sense, even the likes of Muʿāwiyah possessed a strong intellect while the "intellect" that Imam al-Ṣādiq said Muʿāwiyah lacked in 1.1.3 was the enlightened intellect, which will be mentioned shortly in this tradition.

Apparently, Imam al-Ṣādiq has singled out these four traits—along with a fifth one, "awareness," which he mentions a bit later—because the basic function of the intellect is comprehension, and all five of these traits are closely tied to comprehension. All other good traits from the Army of Intellect are in fact secondary and tertiary products of comprehension.

3. A person without the critical level of intellectual capacity is not complete and does not differ much from an animal.

4. We have translated this word as "evidence" assuming that the Arabic is *mabṣar* because 1.1.22 taught us that one of the roles of the intellect is to exonerate man of those things of which he is ignorant. The same word could alternatively be read as *mubaṣṣir* meaning "a thing that gives one insight." This translation is also appropriate in the context, for the intellect's guidance is hardly useful if the person's heart cannot see. Thus, the intellect gives him the sight he needs to benefit from its guidance.

5. "Light" is used here as a symbol for the guidance God has offered man in the form of the Qurʾān and the example of the Prophet and imams. Thus, one who avails himself of this guidance has bolstered his intellect with light.

6. This conditional sentence does not imply that if his intellect is not bolstered with the light of divine guidance, he will not know, remember, be aware, and have keenness and comprehension, for Imam al-Ṣādiq has already established that the intellect, by itself, is the source of these laudable traits, whether or not the person knows and accepts divine guidance. Rather, the message here is that one whose intellect is enlightened by divine guidance *truly benefits* from these traits in this world and the next. On the other hand, one whose intellect is not enlightened benefits only superficially in the temporal world at most.

7. He will know "how" and "why" he was created and "where" he stands in relation to God.

8. At the head of these well-wishers are the prophets and imams. The Prophet Hūd for instance says, "I am a trustworthy well-wisher for you" (Qurʾān 7:68). Likewise, at the head of those who wish to defraud him are false prophets, self-appointed imams, and of course, Satan.

9. He will know the people, acts, and ethics to which he must cling and those from which he must keep clear.

10. There is no contradiction between obeying only God on the one hand and obeying his Prophet and imams on the other, for God himself has commanded us to obey them when he said, "O you who believe! Obey God and obey his Messenger and those vested with authority among you" (Qurʾān 4:59). Thus, obeying the Prophet and the imams is tantamount to obeying God himself. It is in this vein that God has said, "He has obeyed God who obeys the Messenger" (Qurʾān 4:80).

11. We have translated *kāna mustadrikan* in the future perfect tense based on one meaning of *istidrāk*, which is "atonement." A person who undergoes such a powerful transformation in which he comes to believe in, and obey, no one but God has proven himself worthy of divine grace, and accordingly, God shall forgive him for all the sins he committed prior to his transformation even if he does not repent for each sin specifically. Thus, this sentence corresponds to the following verses of the Qurʾān: "Good deeds expiate bad deeds (11:114);" "If you avoid the major sins that you are forbidden, we shall absolve you of your [minor] misdeeds" (4:31). This is not to say that he does not have to make up for missed prayers and fasts, for instance, or that he does not have to fulfill any obligations, monetary or otherwise, to people whom he has wronged, for these obligations are separate from the original command that he disobeyed.

The phrase *kāna mustadrikan* can also be translated as follows based on another meaning of *istidrāk*: "He will endeavor to obtain what eluded him," for a person who acknowledges God as his sole deity and realizes that no one must be obeyed except him owns to his personal shortcomings, turns to God, and endeavors to make up for his past sins where possible and seeks forgiveness where he cannot.

12. The clause, "he will meet what he has coming" can be interpreted in two ways depending on which of the two meanings for *istidrāk* we prefer in the previous sentence. If we prefer the first meaning of *istidrāk*, then both these sentences extol this person for having undergone a transformation in belief and action. Accordingly, the phrase, "what he has coming" refers to the great reward of everlasting paradise that God has in store for him. For this reason, we have inferred the word "reward" in the translation.

On the other hand, according to the second meaning of *istidrāk*, these two clauses are not extolling him so much as describing his newfound resolve to atone for the past and to meet his future with proactive assertiveness because of his newly acquired awareness of the nature of the world in which he lives and the purpose for which he was created. Accordingly, this clause should be translated as follows: "He shall meet [with assertiveness] all [events] that face him."

13. God states this purpose in the Qurʾān: "I only created jinn and man that they should worship me" (51:56).

14. He will know that he, inasmuch as he is human, is heading toward death, purgatory, resurrection, judgment, and finally, either heaven or hell.

TRADITION 1.1.23 TEACHES THE FOLLOWING:

- Man is only complete with intellect; without it, he is like a house without a support or an animal without a backbone.
- Keenness, comprehension, memory, knowledge, and awareness are products of the intellect.
- The intellect guides man in worldly and spiritual affairs.
- The intellect is evidence in man's favor that absolves him of some duties, or it gives man insight (based on whether we read the word *mabṣar* or *mubaṣṣir*).
- The intellect is like a key that opens doors that seem otherwise to be locked.
- Only through his enlightened intellect can man truly know himself, know why he was created, and know his station before God.

- An intellect that is not enlightened through religious guidance is murky and blind to many realities.
- Only through his enlightened intellect can man know what tenets he must believe in, what laws he must abide by, and what ethics he must assimilate.
- Knowledge in general, and knowledge of God's oneness and his unique right to be obeyed in particular, are the result of the enlightened intellect.
- Belief in God's oneness expiates one's past sins or allows one to face the future with assertiveness (based on the two meanings of this phrase).
- Through his enlightened intellect, man knows the temporal world, the purpose for his creation, how to fulfill that purpose, and what can potentially lead him to heaven or hell.

Tradition 1.1.24

ʿAlī ibn Muḥammad reported from Sahl ibn Ziyād from Ismāʿīl ibn Mihrān from one of his teachers that Abū ʿAbd Allāh [al-Ṣādiq] said:

عَلِيُّ بْنُ مُحَمَّدٍ عَنْ سَهْلِ بْنِ زِيَادٍ عَنْ إِسْمَاعِيلَ بْنِ مِهْرَانَ عَنْ بَعْضِ رِجَالِهِ عَنْ أَبِي عَبْدِ اللَّهِ عليه السلام قَالَ:

"The intellect is the believer's guide."[1]

الْعَقْلُ دَلِيلُ الْمُؤْمِنِ.

---

1. In 1.1.23, Imam al-Ṣādiq said that the intellect is *man's* guide, and here he says it is the *believer's* guide. There is a lesson to be learned from the juxtaposition of these two sentences. Intellect guides all human beings toward Islam. However, this is not its only purpose. Once a person becomes a Muslim, he is in no less need of his intellect. Rather, he needs it to maintain and grow in his faith. He must also use it to choose a path through life that is most attuned to the principles of Islam by setting his priorities based on Islamic standards and by appropriately applying divine law to his life. Thus, the intellect is similar to the Qurʾān, which describes itself at once as "a guide for people" (3:4) and "a guide for those who fear [God]" (2:2).

TRADITION 1.1.24 TEACHES THE FOLLOWING:

- Just as a person needs his intellect to attain faith, so does he need it to maintain his faith and live in the best manner as a believer.
- A believer should never cease to use his intellect in worldly and spiritual matters.

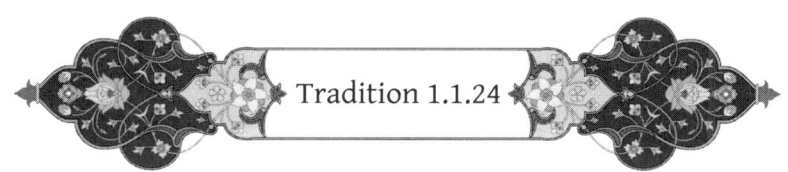

Tradition 1.1.25

Al-Ḥusayn ibn Muḥammad reported from Muʿallā ibn Muḥammad from al-Washshāʾ from Ḥammād ibn ʿUthmān from al-Sarī ibn Khālid that Abū ʿAbd Allāh [al-Ṣādiq] said:

الْحُسَيْنُ بْنُ مُحَمَّدٍ عَنْ مُعَلَّى بْنِ مُحَمَّدٍ عَنِ الْوَشَّاءِ عَنْ حَمَّادِ بْنِ عُثْمَانَ عَنِ السَّرِيِّ بْنِ خَالِدٍ عَنْ أَبِي عَبْدِ اللَّهِ عليه السلام قَالَ:

"The Messenger of God—may God shower him and his family with mercy—said, 'O ʿAlī! There is no poverty more severe than foolishness, and no capital more profitable than intellect.'"[1]

قَالَ رَسُولُ اللَّهِ صلى الله عليه وآله : يَا عَلِيُّ، لَا فَقْرَ أَشَدُّ مِنَ الْجَهْلِ وَ لَا مَالَ أَعْوَدُ مِنَ الْعَقْلِ.

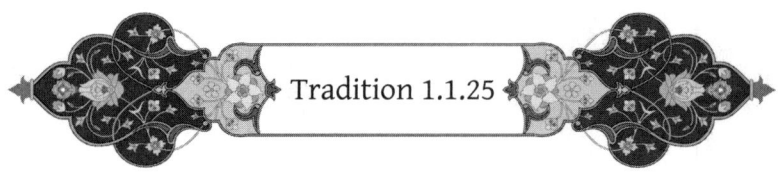

1. To understand this tradition, we must first realize that "foolishness" and "poverty" each has two different meanings. Based on each meaning, this sentence teaches a different lesson. Let us first construe "foolishness" to be the opposite of *ʿaql* in the third sense of the word (i.e., to put one's intellect to use). Accordingly, "foolishness" is the failure to use the intellect God has given us. Similarly, some people are poor because they fail to use the human capital God has given them. They may be lazy and disinclined to work, or they may be spendthrift and thereby squander what resources they have. This kind of poverty—which one tradition refers to as "a source of disgrace in this world and the next" (*Biḥār al-anwār* 69.1.94.26)—is a vice that any sensible person would seek to eradicate from himself. However, the Prophet says here that there is a deficiency even more severe than poverty: foolishness. Thus, you should expend more effort to eradicate your foolishness by using your intellect than you do to eradicate poverty by laboring hard and spending wisely.

Let us now construe "foolishness" and "poverty" in a different way and see how the meaning of this sentence changes. Let us construe "foolishness" to be the opposite of *ʿaql* in the second sense of the word (i.e., to simply have an intellectual capacity). Accordingly, "foolishness" is to lack intellect altogether like those who are mentally handicapped or insane. In this sense of the word, to be a fool is not reprehensible, for it is the result of God's apportionment, not of one's own shortcoming. Similarly, some people are poor, not because they are lazy or spendthrift, but because God has ordained them to be poor to test them. If we construe "foolishness" and "poverty" like this, the Prophet's message changes accordingly. He is at once comforting the poor and giving them hope for the future. Though they may be economically poor, they should realize that there is a worse form of poverty: the intellectual poverty of mental retardation and insanity. They, on the other hand, being possessed of sound intellect, own a resource with incredible potential, which if used correctly, will prove to be more profitable than any amount of material capital.

To further understand how foolishness can be more severe than poverty and how intellect can be more profitable than other types of capital, we must look at the ramifications of foolishness and intellect mentioned in other traditions and compare them to what we know of the ramifications of poverty and wealth. The traditions tell us the fool always goes to extremes (*Mīzān al-ḥikmah* tradition 2831), is a slave to his lusts (*ibid.* 2833), rejects his well-wisher (*ibid.* 2817), reminds you of his favors to you (*ibid.* 2850), acts without consultation (*Nahj al-balāghah* proverb 161), pokes his nose where it does not belong (*ibid.* 2849), and passes judgment without knowing the facts (*ibid.* 2848). Clearly, one possessed of such traits is far more deficient than one who lacks only money.

Similarly, one endowed with intellect possesses a resource from which he can profit just as a wealthy businessman profits from his monetary capital. However, the capital of the former is more profitable than that of the latter because, according to the traditions, one endowed with intellect interacts with people with grace (*Biḥār al-anwār* 75.1.19.6), puts stock in his accomplishments and not in his aspirations (*Mīzān al-ḥikmah* tradition 13422), works hard (*ibid.* 13423), makes fun of no one (*ibid.* 13426), heeds advice (*ibid.* 13433), is forbearing in his interactions with people (*ibid.* 13438), and is never bitten from the same hole twice (*ibid.* 13442). Clearly, one possessed of such traits reaps greater profits than one endowed with only monetary wealth.

TRADITION 1.1.25 TEACHES THE FOLLOWING:

- The harm incurred through foolishness is worse than the harm incurred through poverty.
- Monetary wealth cannot alleviate the poverty of the foolish.
- We should strive harder to alleviate our foolishness than we do to alleviate our poverty.
- The benefits of intellect are far greater than the benefits of money.
- We should strive to increase our intellect more than we strive to increase our monetary wealth.

Tradition 1.1.26

مُحَمَّدُ بْنُ الْحَسَنِ عَنْ سَهْلِ بْنِ زِيَادٍ عَنِ ابْنِ أَبِي نَجْرَانَ عَنِ الْعَلَاءِ بْنِ رَزِينٍ عَنْ مُحَمَّدِ بْنِ مُسْلِمٍ عَنْ أَبِي جَعْفَرٍ عليه السلام قَالَ:

Muḥammad ibn al-Ḥusayn reported from Sahl ibn Ziyād from Ibn Abī Najrān from al-ʿAlāʾ ibn Razīn from Muḥammad ibn Muslim that Abū Jaʿfar [al-Bāqir] said:

لَمَّا خَلَقَ اللَّهُ الْعَقْلَ قَالَ لَهُ: أَقْبِلْ، فَأَقْبَلَ. ثُمَّ قَالَ لَهُ: أَدْبِرْ، فَأَدْبَرَ. فَقَالَ: وَ عِزَّتِي وَ جَلَالِي، مَا خَلَقْتُ خَلْقاً أَحْسَنَ مِنْكَ. إِيَّاكَ آمُرُ وَ إِيَّاكَ أَنْهَى وَ إِيَّاكَ أُثِيبُ وَ إِيَّاكَ أُعَاقِبُ.

"When God created intellect, he said to it, 'Come forward,' whereupon it came forward. Then he said to it, 'Go back,' whereupon it went back. Then he said, 'By my might and my majesty, I have not created a creature better than you. You alone do I command, and you alone do I forbid. [According] to you alone do I confer reward, and [according to] you alone do I punish.'"[1]

---

1. This tradition is nearly identical to 1.1.1. The minor variance between them is understandable considering that their chains of transmission diverge after al-ʿAlāʾ ibn Razīn. Most likely, Shaykh al-Kulaynī repeated this tradition through different chains of transmission to increase our certainty that the Imam actually spoke these words. Each tradition strengthens the other where they overlap, and each one provides new information where they differ.

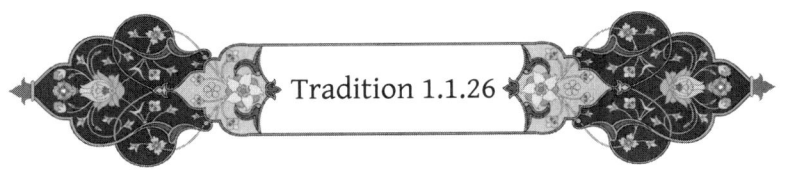

Tradition 1.1.27

A number of our fellow Shīʿah reported from Aḥmad ibn Muḥammad from al-Haytham ibn Abī Masrūq al-Nahdī from al-Ḥusayn ibn Khālid that Isḥāq ibn ʿAmmār said, “I told Abū ʿAbd Allāh [al-Ṣādiq], ‘[Among people] there is one [kind of] person whom I approach and to whom I speak [only] a portion of what I have to say, whereupon he comprehends it all. And among them, there is another [kind of person] whom I approach and to whom I speak what I have to say, whereupon he imbibes all that I have to say; then [if I were to ask him to repeat what I have said,] he would regurgitate it for me just as I spoke it. And among them, there is a third [kind of person] whom I approach and to whom I speak [what I have to say], whereupon he says, “Repeat [that] for me.”’[1] Imam al-Ṣādiq asked:

عِدَّةٌ مِنْ أَصْحَابِنَا عَنْ أَحْمَدَ بْنِ مُحَمَّدٍ عَنِ الْهَيْثَمِ بْنِ أَبِي مَسْرُوقٍ النَّهْدِيِّ عَنِ الْحُسَيْنِ بْنِ خَالِدٍ عَنْ إِسْحَاقَ بْنِ عَمَّارٍ قَالَ: قُلْتُ لِأَبِي عَبْدِ اللَّهِ عليه السلام: الرَّجُلُ آتِيهِ وَ أُكَلِّمُهُ بِبَعْضِ كَلَامِي فَيَعْرِفُهُ كُلَّهُ. وَ مِنْهُمْ مَنْ آتِيهِ فَأُكَلِّمُهُ بِالْكَلَامِ فَيَسْتَوْفِي كَلَامِي كُلَّهُ ثُمَّ يَرُدُّهُ عَلَيَّ كَمَا كَلَّمْتُهُ. وَ مِنْهُمْ مَنْ آتِيهِ فَأُكَلِّمُهُ. فَيَقُولُ: أَعِدْ عَلَيَّ. فَقَالَ:

‘O Isḥāq! And you do not know why it is so?’

يَا إِسْحَاقُ، وَ مَا تَدْرِي لِمَ هَذَا؟

I replied, ‘No.’ So he said:

قُلْتُ: لَا.

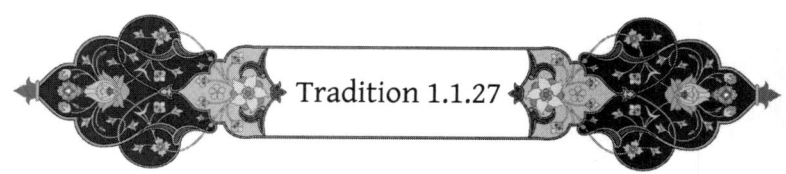

'[With regard to] the one to whom you speak [but] a portion of what you have to say whereupon he comprehends it all: The sperm of which he was born fused with his intellect [before conception]. And with regard to the one to whom you speak, who imbibes all that you have to say, and then answers you [if you were to ask him what you said, based] on what you have said: He is one whose intellect was combined within him while he was in his mother's womb. And with regard to the one to whom you speak what you have to say whereupon he says, "Repeat [that] for me": He is one whose intellect was combined within him after he grew bigger [in the womb and was born]; thus, he tells you "Repeat [that] for me."'"[2]

قَالَ: الَّذِي تُكَلِّمُهُ بِبَعْضِ كَلَامِكَ فَيَعْرِفُهُ كُلَّهُ فَذَاكَ مَنْ عُجِنَتْ نُطْفَتُهُ بِعَقْلِهِ. وَ أَمَّا الَّذِي تُكَلِّمُهُ فَيَسْتَوْفِي كَلَامَكَ ثُمَّ يُجِيبُكَ عَلَى كَلَامِكَ فَذَاكَ الَّذِي رُكِّبَ عَقْلُهُ فِيهِ فِي بَطْنِ أُمِّهِ. وَ أَمَّا الَّذِي تُكَلِّمُهُ بِالْكَلَامِ فَيَقُولُ أَعِدْ عَلَيَّ فَذَاكَ الَّذِي رُكِّبَ عَقْلُهُ فِيهِ بَعْدَ مَا كَبِرَ، فَهُوَ يَقُولُ لَكَ أَعِدْ عَلَيَّ.

---

1. Isḥāq describes these three kinds of people to find out why they differ in the rapidity with which they comprehend what they hear. Accordingly, Imam al-Ṣādiq tells him the reason.

2. This tradition clearly indicates that the intellect is given to a person at a particular time during his development and that his intellectual capacity differs depending on when it is given. The intellect of the brightest of these three "fused" with the sperm of his father before his conception, indicating the intensity of the connection, as though his intellect and his father's sperm became as one. The intellect of each of the other two, on the other hand, is simply "combined within him" as though he is a mere container for his intellect without it infusing his very being.

We may not understand the process that Imam al-Ṣādiq is describing here, but there is no reason to deny his explanation, for it is neither logically impossible nor empirically refutable. However, it is important to note that the first and second categories of people are in no way better than the third. Rather, the better of the three is the one who better uses whatever level of intellect God has given him.

TRADITION 1.1.27 TEACHES THE FOLLOWING:

- The stage in human development at which our intellect is given to us differs from person to person.
- Our intellectual strength depends on the developmental stage in which intellect was given to us.
- In *some* cases, those who learn slowly do so of no fault of their own; thus they cannot be blamed for this.

Tradition 1.1.28

عِدَّةٌ مِنْ أَصْحَابِنَا عَنْ أَحْمَدَ بْنِ مُحَمَّدٍ عَنْ بَعْضِ مَنْ رَفَعَهُ عَنْ أَبِي عَبْدِ اللَّهِ عليه السلام قَالَ:

A number of our fellow Shīʿah reported from Aḥmad ibn Muḥammad from someone who reported [without mentioning his source] that Abū ʿAbd Allāh [al-Ṣādiq] said:

قَالَ رَسُولُ اللَّهِ صلى الله عليه وآله: إِذَا رَأَيْتُمُ الرَّجُلَ كَثِيرَ الصَّلَاةِ كَثِيرَ الصِّيَامِ فَلَا تُبَاهُوا بِهِ حَتَّى تَنْظُرُوا كَيْفَ عَقْلُهُ.

"The Messenger of God—may God shower him and his family with mercy—said, 'When you see a man who prays much and fasts much, do not boast about him[1] until you consider the extent of his intellect.'"[2]

---

1. A person only boasts about himself or about those who are in some way related to him. Thus, we must infer here that there is some sort of kinship or other connection between the person being admonished and the apparently pious man of whom he boasts.

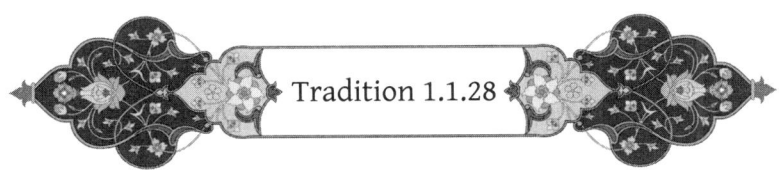

2. This conditional statement seems to imply that it is perfectly all right to boast once we examine his intellect and determine that he is well-endowed. However, the Qurʾān and traditions denounce self-praise and boastfulness (see for example Qurʾān 53:32 and 31:18). Thus, the Prophet could not have meant for us to go around boasting about such a person. Rather, he wanted to show us that our standards for evaluating people are skewed, for we boast about what is not important and ignore what is important. It is as though he is saying, "If you must boast about something, at least boast about something worth boasting about." Imam ʿAlī uses a similar expression to praise strong moral character when he says, "If you must vaunt something, then vaunt your noble character and good deeds" (*Nahj al-balāghah* sermon 192). Clearly, he does not want us to vaunt *anything*; rather, he wants to show that one who brags about his financial accomplishments or his racial superiority, for instance, is bragging about something that is worthless. If he must vaunt something, at least he should vaunt what has value.

Tradition 1.1.28 teaches the following:

- We must not judge someone on his outer appearance.
- One's intellectual strength is the source of his worth, not his outer appearance.

Tradition 1.1.29

بَعْضُ أَصْحَابِنَا رَفَعَهُ عَنْ مُفَضَّلِ بْنِ عُمَرَ عَنْ أَبِي عَبْدِ اللَّهِ عليه السلام قَالَ:

One of our fellow Shīʿah recounted [without mentioning his source] from Mufaḍḍal ibn ʿUmar that Abū ʿAbd Allāh [al-Ṣādiq] said:

يَا مُفَضَّلُ، لَا يُفْلِحُ مَنْ لَا يَعْقِلُ، وَ لَا يَعْقِلُ مَنْ لَا يَعْلَمُ.

"O Mufaḍḍal! He shall not attain felicity [in paradise] who does not use his intellect, and he shall not use his intellect who does not have knowledge.[1]

وَ سَوْفَ يَنْجُبُ مَنْ يَفْهَمُ.

He shall be distinguished who comprehends.[2]

وَ يَظْفَرُ مَنْ يَحْلُمُ.

He shall triumph who is forbearing.[3]

وَ الْعِلْمُ جُنَّةٌ.

Knowledge is a shield.[4]

وَ الصِّدْقُ عِزٌّ.

Veracity brings dignity.

وَ الْجَهْلُ ذُلٌّ.

Ignorance brings disgrace.[5]

وَ الْفَهْمُ مَجْدٌ.

Comprehension brings excellence.

وَ الْجُودُ نُجْحٌ.

Generosity [to others] fulfills [one's] needs.[6]

وَ حُسْنُ الْخُلُقِ مَجْلَبَةٌ لِلْمَوَدَّةِ.

Good character draws affection.

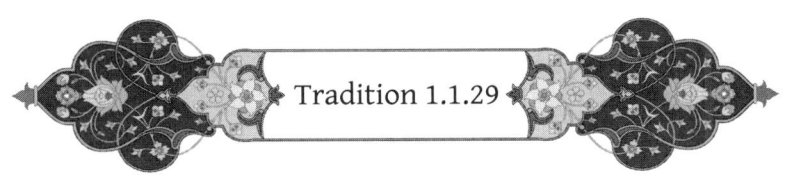

Perplexities do not assault one who is aware of his times.[7]

وَ الْعَالِمُ بِزَمَانِهِ لَا تَهْجُمُ عَلَيْهِ اللَّوَابِسُ.

Prudence calls for cynicism.[8]

وَ الْحَزْمُ مَسَاءَةُ الظَّنِّ.

The blessing of a scholar['s presence is all that] lies between a man [eager to learn] and wisdom; while one who is ignorant [and does not seek knowledge] remains wretched compared to both [the scholar and the student].[9]

وَ بَيْنَ الْمَرْءِ وَ الْحِكْمَةِ نِعْمَةُ الْعَالِمِ وَ الْجَاهِلُ شَقِيٌّ بَيْنَهُمَا.

God is the ally of one who knows him and the enemy of one who feigns to know him.[10]

وَ اللَّهُ وَلِيٌّ مَنْ عَرَفَهُ وَ عَدُوٌّ مَنْ تَكَلَّفَهُ.

One who uses his intellect [for good] is forgiving.

وَ الْعَاقِلُ غَفُورٌ.

One who uses his intellect for evil is fraudulent.[11]

وَ الْجَاهِلُ خَتُورٌ.

If you wish to be esteemed, be gentle, and if you wish to be disparaged, be harsh.[12]

وَ إِنْ شِئْتَ أَنْ تُكْرَمَ فَلِنْ وَ إِنْ شِئْتَ أَنْ تُهَانَ فَاخْشُنْ.

If one's stock is noble, one's heart will be gentle, and if one's stock is harsh, one's heart will be crude.[13]

وَ مَنْ كَرُمَ أَصْلُهُ لَانَ قَلْبُهُ وَ مَنْ خَشُنَ عُنْصُرُهُ غَلُظَ كَبِدُهُ.

He who fails [in his obligations] shall

وَ مَنْ فَرَّطَ تَوَرَّطَ.

be consumed [by the fire].

He who fears a [bad] end ponders over, and restrains himself from, setting foot in what he does not know. He who rushes into a thing without knowledge shall publicly humiliate himself.[14]

وَ مَنْ خَافَ الْعَاقِبَةَ تَثَبَّتَ عَنِ التَّوَغُّلِ فِيمَا لَا يَعْلَمُ، وَ مَنْ هَجَمَ عَلَى أَمْرٍ بِغَيْرِ عِلْمٍ جَدَعَ أَنْفَ نَفْسِهِ.

He who does not know [what he must about his religion],[15] cannot comprehend [his religious beliefs and duties]; and he who cannot comprehend [his religious beliefs and duties], is not safe [from deviant beliefs and actions]; and he who is not safe [from deviant beliefs and actions], has no self-worth; and he who has no self-worth, is easily bent and broken [by nefarious influences];[16] and he who is easily bent and broken [by nefarious influences], is most deserving of censure; and he who is like that, ought to lament."

وَ مَنْ لَمْ يَعْلَمْ لَمْ يَفْهَمْ، وَ مَنْ لَمْ يَفْهَمْ لَمْ يَسْلَمْ، وَ مَنْ لَمْ يَسْلَمْ لَمْ يَكْرُمْ، وَ مَنْ لَمْ يَكْرُمْ يُهْضَمْ، وَ مَنْ يُهْضَمْ كَانَ أَلْوَمَ، وَ مَنْ كَانَ كَذَلِكَ كَانَ أَحْرَى أَنْ يَنْدَمَ.

---

1. Like traditions 1.1.3, 1.1.6, and 1.1.23, this sentence teaches that the intellect is necessary for reaching paradise, but not sufficient. Rather, the intellect only leads one to salvation if one uses it to acquire, and act on, the knowledge embodied in divine guidance.

2. Like tradition 1.1.23, this sentence teaches that comprehension (*fahm*), in and of itself, is a positive trait that leads to distinction in the temporal world. However, it only leads to worldly *and* spiritual distinction when enlightened by divine guidance, as indicated by 1.1.23.

3. It is tempting to think that the way to triumph in day-to-day squabbles is to hold one's ground and enforce one's opinion. To back down is to admit defeat. In reality, the opposite is true, for by turning a blind eye to people's harmless offenses and surrendering the insignificant battles, one always triumphs in the greater cause. For this reason, the Qurʾān admonishes us to "repel ill [conduct] with your best character" (23:96).

4. Knowledge is a shield that guards us against the ill consequences of ignorance, foremost of which is doubt in the tenets of faith.

5. This sentence could also read, "Foolishness brings disgrace."

6. Those with whom we are generous today will repay our generosity in our time of need. And God will shower us with mercy when we need it most for the kindness we have shown others when they have needed it most.

7. One who is aware of the times knows his enemies, their tricks, and their innovative methods for making evil seem enticing and falsehood seem like truth. Since "knowledge is a shield," this awareness shields him from the perplexities that confuse the ignorant and unaware, rendering their assault ineffectual.

8. Imam al-Ṣādiq encourages us to be cynical of people until we know their true mettle, just as Imam al-Ḥasan said, "Prudence is to protect oneself from people through cynicism" (*Biḥār al-anwār* 78.115.10). It may seem that this advice contradicts the Qurʾānic injunction against cynicism and suspicion (49:12) and its encouragement to give people the benefit of the doubt (24:12). In reality, there is no contradiction, for there are times for giving the benefit of the doubt, and there are times for cynicism. We should assume the best under two circumstances: when Islamic law dictates it, such as when buying meat from a Muslim grocer or restaurant; or when no great harm will result if our assumption turns out to be incorrect. On the other hand, we should be cynical and assume the worst wherever an incorrect assumption could lead to moral, financial, or personal harm, such as when evaluating a suitor for marriage, entering a business partnership, or vesting someone with legal or political authority on our behalf.

9. One who is eager to learn needs only a good teacher to lead him to his desired goal. On the other hand, one who is ignorant and content with his ignorance is neither enlightened by knowledge like the scholar nor in the process of enlightening himself like a student. In another tradition, Imam ʿAlī has described these three groups as follows: "People are of three kinds: the godly scholar, the student on the path to salvation, and [veritable] gnats, senseless masses, followers of every shepherd; they sway with every breeze; neither have they been enlightened with the light of knowledge [like the scholar], nor have they leaned on a sturdy column [like the student]" (*Nahj al-balāghah* proverb 147).

10. Those who pretend to be gnostics (*ʿurafāʾ*) deserve God's enmity more than those who are ignorant and heedless of God, for the former claim to have something they know they lack, whereas the latter make no such false claims. God manifests his enmity toward them by denying them his mercy and grace and by punishing them.

11. We have translated *jāhil* as "one who uses his intellect for evil" because neither an ignoramus nor a fool—the other two meanings for this word—has the wits to defraud others. Rather, *jāhil* here refers to people like Muʿāwiyah and ʿAmr ibn al-ʿĀṣ who are well-endowed with powers of intellect, but use them for evil.

12. This sentence clearly indicates that gentleness brings esteem and harshness brings disparagement. But it does not say that it is always incumbent to seek the former and avoid the latter. In fact, in some cases, Islamic law calls for harshness, which, in light of the truth stated here, necessarily reduces one's esteem in the eyes of society; however, we must fulfill our duty and not fear the consequences. For example, we are commanded to enjoin good and forbid evil, and in some cases this may entail verbal or even physical harshness. It is for this reason that Imam al-Bāqir has said to enjoin good and forbid evil, and "for God's sake, do not fear people's censure" (*al-Kāfī* 16.28.1).

13. We have translated the words *qalb* and *kabid* as "heart" while only the former literally means "heart" while the latter means "liver." Both terms refer to the human soul, not the anatomical organs, but usually *qalb* refers to the seat of knowledge and good qualities, while *kabid* refers to the seat of base qualities like anger. However, since in English the "liver" is not symbolic of the soul, we have not translated *kabid* as such.

The apparent message of this sentence is that the stock of which one is born, one's nature, as opposed to nurture, determines whether one will be gentle or hard-hearted. Besides screaming of determinism, this message contradicts the previous sentence, which implied that one can choose whether to be gentle or harsh. It also contradicts what we know to be one of the goals of religion: to improve one's character and purify one's soul. God himself has stated, "He has attained salvation who purifies [his soul]" (Qurʾān 91:9), thereby encouraging all people to build character and improve themselves. Even tradition 1.1.18 acknowledged that we can attain discipline through hard work. Then why is this sentence saying that the stuff of which we are made makes us gentle or harsh?

This tradition, and many others like it, shows that nature has a role to play in our character; but we must not consider it to be a determining role. In fact, neither nature nor nurture measure up to the influence of one's own will. Thus, the message to take away from the juxtaposition of these two apparently—but not actually—contradictory statements is that the choice to be gentle or harsh is in one's hands; however, other circumstances are also at play. Some people are harsher by nature, so becoming gentle will be a greater challenge for them than those who are naturally gentle. Since their struggle is greater, God's justice dictates that their reward also be greater. Imam al-Ṣādiq summed it up when he said, "[Good] character is of two kinds: one built on intention and the other built on natural disposition...The one built on intention [is greater] because the one who is naturally disposed to goodness cannot [easily] do otherwise, while the one with intention strives to do good, so that is better" (*Biḥār al-anwār* 75.1.23 p.257 among the proverbs of Imam al-Ṣādiq).

14. This phrase literally reads, "He who rushes into a thing...shall chop off his own nose." This is an idiomatic expression in Arabic for humiliating oneself in public, for a severed nose is a hideous thing that cannot normally be concealed.

15. We have restricted the term "knowledge" to knowledge of religion, and in particular Islam, because of the consequences Imam al-Kāẓim enumerates for *not* having this knowledge. It is a lack of knowledge about Islam, not mundane things, that leads to a lack of safety and self-worth and eventually earns us censure and makes us lament.

16. If we have a strong sense of self-worth rooted in well-reasoned conviction and morality, we feel confident in who we are and what we stand for. We cannot then be easily swayed by nefarious influences, whether from within or without. In an aforementioned tradition, Imam ʿAlī described those who lack self-worth and are swayed by nefarious influences as "[veritable] gnats, senseless masses, followers of every shepherd; they sway with every breeze" (*Nahj al-balāghah* proverb 147).

TRADITION 1.1.29 TEACHES THE FOLLOWING:

- We cannot attain salvation without using our intellect.
- To use our intellect we must have knowledge.
- A Muslim should keep abreast of the world around him.

- In circumstances where prudence is appropriate, a Muslim must be cynical of people so that he is not harmed in his naiveté.
- The scholar is a necessary link between a person and knowledge.
- The presence of a scholar is a blessing.
- One who is ignorant is deprived of the virtues of the scholar and the student.
- Gentleness in speech and action brings esteem while harshness in speech and action brings disparagement.
- The stock of which one is born influences one's character.
- To comprehend Islam, one must have knowledge of Islam.
- To safeguard one's religion from deviant beliefs and actions, one must comprehend its teachings.
- One with self-worth cannot easily be swayed by nefarious influences.
- One without sufficient knowledge of Islam is deserving of censure and ought to lament over his ignorance.

Tradition 1.1.30

Muḥammad ibn Yaḥyā recounted [without mentioning his source] that the Commander of the Faithful [ʿAlī] said:

مُحَمَّدُ بْنُ يَحْيَى رَفَعَهُ قَالَ: قَالَ أَمِيرُ الْمُؤْمِنِينَ عليه السلام:

"If I am assured that [at least] one trait of goodness is deeply rooted in a person, I will tolerate him because of that trait, and I will turn a blind eye to his lack of any other. However, I do not turn a blind eye to a lack of intellect or [a lack of] devotion [in him],[1] for to lack devotion is to lack inner peace,[2] and one cannot savor life with fear [and uncertainty].[3] And to lack intellect is to lack life [itself],[4] and such a person can be compared to none but the dead."[5]

مَنِ اسْتَحْكَمَتْ لِي فِيهِ خَصْلَةٌ مِنْ خِصَالِ الْخَيْرِ احْتَمَلْتُهُ عَلَيْهَا وَ اغْتَفَرْتُ فَقْدَ مَا سِوَاهَا، وَ لَا أَغْتَفِرُ فَقْدَ عَقْلٍ وَ لَا دِينٍ لِأَنَّ مُفَارَقَةَ الدِّينِ مُفَارَقَةُ الْأَمْنِ فَلَا يُتَهَنَّأُ بِحَيَاةٍ مَعَ مَخَافَةٍ، وَ فَقْدَ الْعَقْلِ فَقْدُ الْحَيَاةِ وَ لَا يُقَاسُ إِلَّا بِالْأَمْوَاتِ.

---

1. In summary, Imam ʿAlī says he is willing to tolerate a person, however devoid of goodness he may be, if he has three things: one deeply rooted trait of goodness; an intellect; and devotion to the true religion.

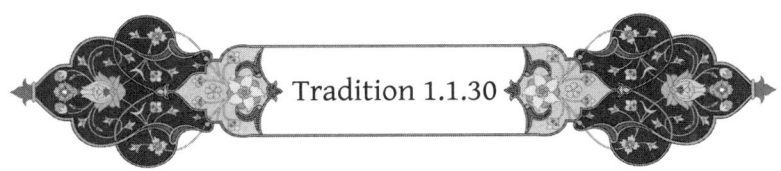

2. We have translated *amn* as "*inner* peace." God says, "Let it be known! Hearts find peace in God's remembrance" (Qurʾān 13:28). One who devotes himself to Islam knows that God only does what is in his servants' best interest, that he wrongs no one, and that every religious obligation and hardship is a test for which he rewards the perseverant. Such knowledge and devotion brings inner peace, and those who find this peace savor the life of this world and the next. God says, "Whoever does good, whether male or female, should he be faithful—we shall give him a good life, and we shall pay them their reward according to the best of what they used to do" (Qurʾān 16:97).

3. Just as he who remembers God finds inner peace and savors life, so "he who shuns my remembrance shall have a wretched life" (Qurʾān 20:124). However, it is vital to note that not all fear makes life wretched. For our conception of God's greatness and our feeling of our own relative insignificance instills a fear that brings felicity in this world and unending reward in the next. In fact, God commands us to fear him by saying, "Fear me if you be believers!" (Qurʾān 3:175); and he praises those who fear him by saying, "They call out to their Lord in fear [of his punishment] and desire [for his reward]" (Qurʾān 32:16).

4. "To lack intellect" in this instance means to lack powers of intellect strong enough to distinguish right from wrong in all walks of life, just as we mentioned in 1.1.19.

5. Just as a dead man fails to benefit from the blessing of life, so too does a fool.

TRADITION 1.1.30 TEACHES THE FOLLOWING:

- A good trait is worthless unless it is coupled with intellect and devotion to Islam.
- A good trait is worthless unless it becomes second nature.
- Life without Islam is unsavory.
- One who does not use his intellect is as good as dead.
- Even a single good trait, if coupled with intellect and devotion to Islam, is sufficient to qualify a person to be trained by a righteous teacher.

Tradition 1.1.31

ᶜAlī ibn Ibrāhīm ibn Hāshim reported from Mūsā ibn Ibrāhīm al-Muḥāribī from al-Ḥasan ibn Mūsā from Mūsā ibn ᶜAbd Allāh from Maymūn ibn ᶜAlī that Abū ᶜAbd Allāh [al-Ṣādiq] said:

عَلِيُّ بْنُ إِبْرَاهِيمَ بْنِ هَاشِمٍ عَنْ مُوسَى بْنِ إِبْرَاهِيمَ الْمُحَارِبِيِّ عَنِ الْحَسَنِ بْنِ مُوسَى عَنْ مُوسَى بْنِ عَبْدِ اللَّهِ عَنْ مَيْمُونِ بْنِ عَلِيٍّ عَنْ أَبِي عَبْدِ اللَّهِ عليه السلام قَالَ:

"The Commander of the Faithful [ᶜAlī] said, 'Conceit is a sign of weak intellect.'"[1]

قَالَ أَمِيرُ الْمُؤْمِنِينَ عليه السلام : إِعْجَابُ الْمَرْءِ بِنَفْسِهِ دَلِيلٌ عَلَى ضَعْفِ عَقْلِهِ.

---

1. Conceit (*ᶜujb*) is a deplorable trait. Anyone who employs his intellect realizes this. However, it often happens that a person understands that something is wrong but does it anyway. This is not because he fails to understand that it is deplorable, but because he lacks the resolve to act according to his understanding. Thus, conceit is not a sign that a person lacks intellect or has failed to employ his intellect, but that he lacks the resolve to act according to the dictates of his intellect. Imam ᶜAlī figuratively calls this lack of resolve a "weak intellect."

TRADITION 1.1.31 TEACHES THE FOLLOWING:

- A strong resolve to act on one's intellect prevents conceit.
- All who are conceited have weak resolve.
- One of the roles of the intellect is to understand which traits are deplorable.
- Humility, the opposite of conceit, is an indicator of a strong intellect.

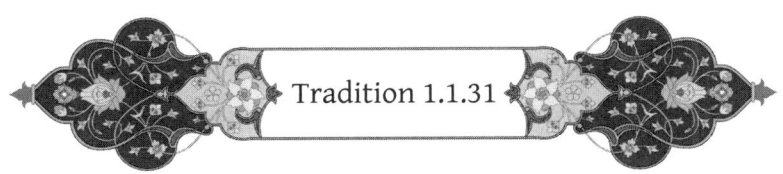

Tradition 1.1.32

أَبُو عَبْدِ اللَّهِ الْعَاصِمِيُّ عَنْ عَلِيِّ بْنِ الْحَسَنِ عَنْ عَلِيِّ بْنِ أَسْبَاطٍ عَنِ الْحَسَنِ بْنِ الْجَهْمِ عَنْ أَبِي الْحَسَنِ الرِّضَا عليه السلام قَالَ: ذُكِرَ عِنْدَهُ أَصْحَابُنَا وَ ذُكِرَ الْعَقْلُ، قَالَ: فَقَالَ عليه السلام:

Abū ʿAbd Allāh al-ʿĀṣimī reported from ʿAlī ibn al-Ḥasan from ʿAlī ibn Asbāṭ from al-Ḥasan ibn al-Jahm from [the time of] Abū al-Ḥasan [al-Riḍā] that al-Ḥasan said,[1] "[The state of] our [Shīʿah] brethren and [the various levels of their] intellect were mentioned before him (i.e., al-Riḍā). So he said:

لَا يُعْبَأُ بِأَهْلِ الدِّينِ مِمَّنْ لَا عَقْلَ لَهُ.

'No heed should be paid to followers of the faith who have no intellect.'[2]

قُلْتُ: جُعِلْتُ فِدَاكَ، إِنَّ مِمَّنْ يَصِفُ هَذَا الْأَمْرَ قَوْماً لَا بَأْسَ بِهِمْ عِنْدَنَا وَ لَيْسَتْ لَهُمْ تِلْكَ الْعُقُولُ. فَقَالَ:

I said, 'May I be your ransom! Among the Shīʿah[3] are some in whom we see no harm,[4] but they do not have those [great] intellectual capacities [that you speak of. Should we pay no heed to the likes of these?]' So Imam al-Riḍā said:

لَيْسَ هَؤُلَاءِ مِمَّنْ خَاطَبَ اللَّهُ. إِنَّ اللَّهَ خَلَقَ الْعَقْلَ فَقَالَ لَهُ: أَقْبِلْ، فَأَقْبَلَ. وَ قَالَ لَهُ: أَدْبِرْ، فَأَدْبَرَ. فَقَالَ: وَ عِزَّتِي وَ جَلَالِي، مَا خَلَقْتُ شَيْئاً أَحْسَنَ مِنْكَ أَوْ أَحَبَّ إِلَيَّ

'[Precisely, for] they are not among those whom God has addressed, [for] God created intellect and said to it,[5] "Come forward," whereupon it came forward. And he said to it, "Go back," whereupon it went back. Then he said, "By my might and my majesty,

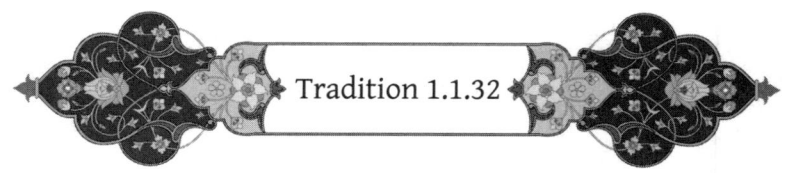

I have not created anything better than you (or [he said] more beloved to me than you).[6] According to you alone do I punish, and according to you alone do I give [reward].'"

مِنْكَ، بِكَ آخُذُ وَ بِكَ أُعْطِي.

---

1. This tradition is similar in content to 1.1.5 with notable differences in the chain of transmission and wording.

2. This is a reference to those with weak powers of intellect as we mentioned in 1.1.5. If he had intended those with no intellect at all (i.e., the insane) he would not have called them "followers of the faith," for the insane have no faith, nor is faith expected of them.

3. The phrase, "Those who ascribe to this matter" is an expression commonly used in the traditions to refer discreetly to the *Shīʿah*.

4. They neither sin against God nor do they cause anyone harm.

5. Imam al-Riḍā refers to this allegory to show that when God addresses us, it is the intellect within us that he is addressing. Inasmuch as the people in question have weak intellects, God does not address them, and they are accordingly not held accountable for what they do.

6. The parentheses belong to the transmitter, not to the Imam.

TRADITION 1.1.32 TEACHES THE FOLLOWING:

- There is no merit in a Muslim if he has no intellect.
- Allah only addresses those with intellect.
- To merely be called a *Shīʿah* does not make one worthy of being addressed by God if one has no intellect.

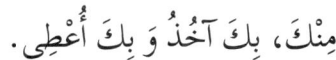

Tradition 1.1.33

عَلِيُّ بْنُ مُحَمَّدٍ عَنْ أَحْمَدَ بْنِ مُحَمَّدِ بْنِ خَالِدٍ عَنْ أَبِيهِ عَنْ بَعْضِ أَصْحَابِنَا عَنْ أَبِي عَبْدِ اللَّهِ عليه السلام قَالَ:

ʿAlī ibn Muḥammad reported from Aḥmad ibn Muḥammad ibn Khālid from his father from one of our fellow Shīʿah that Abū ʿAbd Allāh [al-Ṣādiq] said:

لَيْسَ بَيْنَ الْإِيمَانِ وَ الْكُفْرِ إِلَّا قِلَّةُ الْعَقْلِ.

"Nothing separates weak faith from conviction but a dearth of intellect."[1]

قِيلَ: وَ كَيْفَ ذَاكَ، يَا ابْنَ رَسُولِ اللَّهِ؟ قَالَ:

It was asked, "And how can that be, O son of God's Messenger?" He replied:

إِنَّ الْعَبْدَ يَرْفَعُ رَغْبَتَهُ إِلَى مَخْلُوقٍ. فَلَوْ أَخْلَصَ نِيَّتَهُ لِلَّهِ لَأَتَاهُ الَّذِي يُرِيدُ فِي أَسْرَعَ مِنْ ذَلِكَ.

"[I'll give you an example of someone who has weak faith due to a weak intellect.[2] Consider] a person who takes his need to a [fellow] creature,[3] [when] if only he would sincerely ask God, God would give him what he wants more quickly than that [creature would]."[4]

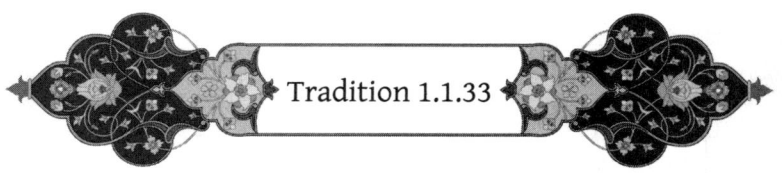

1. In the Arabic text of this tradition, the Imam uses the words *īmān* or "belief" and *kufr* or "unbelief;" however, it is obvious that he does not intend the usual sense of these words. Rather, *īmān* here refers to strong conviction, while *kufr* refers to weaker levels of belief. We are justified in saying this because the hypothetical person in the Imam's example is guilty, not of *worshipping* someone other than God, which would actually make him an unbeliever (*kāfir*), but of *relying on* someone other than God. While this is a moral vice, it is indicative only of weak faith, not a total absence thereof. Thus, the Imam's usage of *kufr* here is similar to the Qurʾān's usage of *shirk* (polytheism) in verse 12:106 where it says that most believers are guilty of "polytheism," not because they actually worship other gods, but because they often act in a way that contradicts strict monotheism, if only in subtle ways. For instance, they may rely on, fear, or rest their hopes on, someone other than God.

2. A strong intellect allows us to attain strong conviction. One of the effects of strong conviction is that we rely solely upon God. This tradition teaches us that if we rely solely upon God to fulfill our needs, he will fulfill them faster than if we rely on others. If, on the other hand, we do rely upon others, this shows that our faith in God is weak. Our weak faith, in turn, is caused by our weak intellect. In short, as the Imam stated at the beginning of this tradition, what separates weak faith and a lack of reliance on God from conviction and total reliance on God is a weak intellect.

3. This man has made the mistake of relying on someone besides God to fulfill his need. His doing so was only deplorable because he ignored God completely. However, if he had seen his fellow creature as simply the means by which God fulfills his need, the Imam would have praised him for having relied solely on God, as the Prophet Joseph did when he asked his cellmate, who was about to be released from prison, to mention him before his master (Qurʾān 12:42). He saw his cellmate, not as an independent alternative to God's help, but as a means through which God could help him. In short, to rely on God is to make use of the means at one's disposal insofar as they have been placed at one's disposal by God. And to fail to rely on God is to make use of the means at one's disposal without recognizing that they have been placed at one's disposal by God.

4. God would fulfill his needs assuming all the conditions were ripe for his prayers to be answered. However, if the conditions were not ripe, God would not fulfill his need. Imam ʿAlī has mentioned some of the reasons why prayers are not answered in his admonishment to Imam al-Ḥasan. For instance, it may not be in the person's best interest; God may want him to prolong his beseeching so that he can receive more reward; or he may give him what is better than that for which he asked in this world or the next (see *Nahj al-balāghah* letter 31).

TRADITION 1.1.33 TEACHES THE FOLLOWING:

- A weakness in intellect prevents one from attaining strong conviction.
- One of the effects of strong conviction is that we rely solely upon God.
- If we rely solely upon God to fulfill our needs, he will fulfill them faster than if we rely on others.
- If we rely upon someone other than God, this shows that our faith in God is weak. Our weak faith, in turn, is caused by our weak intellect.

Tradition 1.1.34

عِدَّةٌ مِنْ أَصْحَابِنَا عَنْ سَهْلِ بْنِ زِيَادٍ عَنْ عُبَيْدِ اللَّهِ الدِّهْقَانِ عَنْ أَحْمَدَ بْنِ عُمَرَ الْحَلَبِيِّ عَنْ يَحْيَى بْنِ عِمْرَانَ عَنْ أَبِي عَبْدِ اللَّهِ عليه السلام قَالَ:

A group of our fellow Shīʿah reported from Sahl ibn Ziyād from ʿUbayd Allāh al-Dihqān from Aḥmad ibn ʿUmar al-Ḥalabī from Yaḥyā ibn ʿImrān that Abū ʿAbd Allāh [al-Ṣādiq] said:

كَانَ أَمِيرُ الْمُؤْمِنِينَ عليه السلام يَقُولُ: بِالْعَقْلِ اسْتُخْرِجَ غَوْرُ الْحِكْمَةِ وَ بِالْحِكْمَةِ اسْتُخْرِجَ غَوْرُ الْعَقْلِ.

"The Commander of the Faithful, [ʿAlī] used to say, 'Through the intellect can the depths of wisdom be extracted, and through wisdom can the depths of the intellect be extracted.[1]

وَ بِحُسْنِ السِّيَاسَةِ يَكُونُ الْأَدَبُ الصَّالِحُ.

Good discipline is only through good management.'"[2]

قَالَ:

al-Ṣādiq said:

وَ كَانَ يَقُولُ: التَّفَكُّرُ حَيَاةُ قَلْبِ الْبَصِيرِ كَمَا يَمْشِي الْمَاشِي فِي الظُّلُمَاتِ بِالنُّورِ بِحُسْنِ التَّخَلُّصِ وَ قِلَّةِ التَّرَبُّصِ.

"The Commander of the Faithful, [ʿAlī] also used to say, 'Contemplation[3] gives life to the heart of those with insight; [They are] like a man walking in the darkness with a light, adroitly avoiding the pitfalls, taking no longer than he must.'"[4]

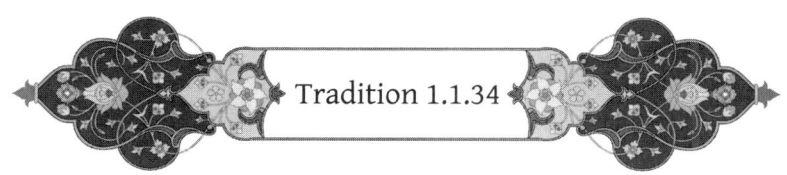

1. Imam ʿAlī has likened wisdom and intellect to veins of silver and gold extending deep into the earth. To extract some shards of wisdom from this mine, one must use a tool called intellect. In turn, to access the deeper recesses of the intellect, one must use those same shards of wisdom. In this way, every deeper level of wisdom leads to greater development of the intellect, and a stronger intellect allows one to understand more profound wisdom.

2. Discipline (*adab*) refers to virtuous character and righteous action. It can only be attained through a well-managed training program. This statement holds true for a person who wishes to empower himself with discipline, for a teacher or parent who wishes to instill the principle of discipline in a child, and for a leader who wishes to instill discipline in the people he leads.

3. Contemplation (*tafakkur*) in the language of the traditions indicates the act of pondering over and taking lessons from the ephemeral nature of the material world and its pleasures such that one looks upon it with indifference and sets one's sights on the hereafter with its everlasting felicity.

4. In this parable, the man with a light represents a man with insight. The pitfalls in the path that he so adroitly avoids because of his light are the incessant doubts and ordeals that plague those who have no insight and who do not contemplate the reality of the material world. This man's keen avoidance of the pitfalls and his quick passage along the path to his destination represents the ease and surefootedness with which one with insight avoids these doubts and ordeals.

TRADITION 1.1.34 TEACHES THE FOLLOWING:

- It is not possible to reach the acme of wisdom except by the intellect.
- It is not possible to reach the acme of the intellect except by means of wisdom.

- Strong management is the only way to teach discipline to ourselves or to others.
- It is possible to improve our character.
- Contemplation gives life to the heart.
- Contemplation saves us from the perils of life.
- Contemplation helps us reach our destination faster.

Tradition 1.1.35

A group of our fellow Shīʿah reported from ʿAbd Allāh al-Bazzāz from Muḥammad ibn ʿAbd al-Raḥmān ibn Ḥammād from al-Ḥasan ibn ʿAmmār that Abū ʿAbd Allāh [al-Ṣādiq] said as part of a lengthy tradition:[1]

عِدَّةٌ مِنْ أَصْحَابِنَا عَنْ عَبْدِ اللَّهِ الْبَزَّازِ عَنْ مُحَمَّدِ بْنِ عَبْدِ الرَّحْمَنِ بْنِ حَمَّادٍ عَنِ الْحَسَنِ بْنِ عَمَّارٍ عَنْ أَبِي عَبْدِ اللَّهِ عليه السلام فِي حَدِيثٍ طَوِيلٍ:

"The precursor to all things [essential to a person's humanity], their source, their essence, and what nurtures them, without which a person cannot benefit from any of those things [essential to his humanity], is the intellect, which God has made to adorn humankind and as a light for them.[2] For it is through their intellects that people [can] know their creator and [know] that they are [his] creatures; that it is he who is the manager [of their affairs] and that it is they who are subject to his management; and that it is he who is the everlasting and that it is they who shall perish.[3] They [also] reason with their intellects [based] on what [characteristics] they see in his creation—in his sky, his earth,

إِنَّ أَوَّلَ الْأُمُورِ وَ مَبْدَأَهَا وَ قُوَّتَهَا وَ عِمَارَتَهَا الَّتِي لَا يَنْتَفِعُ شَيْءٌ إِلَّا بِهِ الْعَقْلُ الَّذِي جَعَلَهُ اللَّهُ زِينَةً لِخَلْقِهِ وَ نُوراً لَهُمْ. فَبِالْعَقْلِ عَرَفَ الْعِبَادُ خَالِقَهُمْ وَ أَنَّهُمْ مَخْلُوقُونَ، وَ أَنَّهُ الْمُدَبِّرُ لَهُمْ وَ أَنَّهُمُ الْمُدَبَّرُونَ، وَ أَنَّهُ الْبَاقِي وَ هُمُ الْفَانُونَ. وَ اسْتَدَلُّوا بِعُقُولِهِمْ عَلَى مَا رَأَوْا مِنْ خَلْقِهِ مِنْ سَمَائِهِ وَ أَرْضِهِ وَ شَمْسِهِ وَ قَمَرِهِ وَ لَيْلِهِ وَ نَهَارِهِ وَ بِأَنَّ لَهُ وَ لَهُمْ خَالِقاً وَ مُدَبِّراً لَمْ يَزَلْ وَ لَا يَزُولُ. وَ عَرَفُوا بِهِ الْحَسَنَ مِنَ الْقَبِيحِ وَ أَنَّ الظُّلْمَةَ فِي الْجَهْلِ وَ أَنَّ النُّورَ فِي الْعِلْمِ. فَهَذَا مَا دَلَّهُمْ عَلَيْهِ الْعَقْلُ.

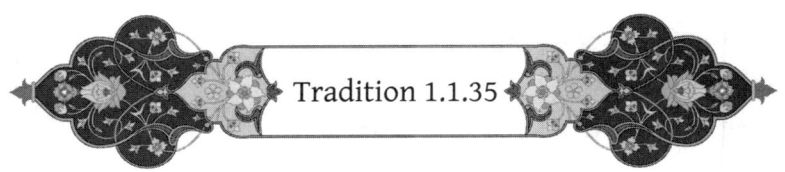

his sun, his moon, his night, and his day—[that these creatures and they have been created] and that these creatures and they [therefore] have a creator and a manager who has always been and will always be.[4] [It is also] through their intellects that they [can] know what is good [and distinguish] it from what is evil[5] and [know, for instance] that evil lies in ignorance [of God] and goodness lies in knowledge [of him]. To these [three types of knowledge] do their intellects guide them."

It was asked of him, "[Since the intellect perceives so much,] can people suffice themselves with their intellect to the exclusion of all else?" He replied:

قِيلَ لَهُ: فَهَلْ يَكْتَفِي الْعِبَادُ بِالْعَقْلِ دُونَ غَيْرِهِ؟ قَالَ:

"One with intellect knows—by virtue of his intellect, which God has made his essence,[6] his adornment, and his guide—that God is the Everlasting and that he alone is his Lord;[7] and he knows that his creator has likes, and that he has dislikes,[8] and that he has commandments that can be obeyed and disobeyed.[9] However, he does not find his intellect guiding him to [any of] that. Rather, he knows

إِنَّ الْعَاقِلَ لِدَلَالَةِ عَقْلِهِ الَّذِي جَعَلَهُ اللَّهُ قِوَامَهُ وَ زِينَتَهُ وَ هِدَايَتَهُ عَلِمَ أَنَّ اللَّهَ هُوَ الْحَقُّ وَ أَنَّهُ هُوَ رَبُّهُ وَ عَلِمَ أَنَّ لِخَالِقِهِ مَحَبَّةً وَ أَنَّ لَهُ كَرَاهِيَةً وَ أَنَّ لَهُ طَاعَةً وَ أَنَّ لَهُ مَعْصِيَةً، فَلَمْ يَجِدْ عَقْلَهُ يَدُلُّهُ عَلَى ذَلِكَ وَ عَلِمَ أَنَّهُ لَا يُوصَلُ إِلَيْهِ إِلَّا بِالْعِلْمِ وَ طَلَبِهِ وَ أَنَّهُ لَا يَنْتَفِعُ بِعَقْلِهِ إِنْ لَمْ يُصِبْ ذَلِكَ

that these things cannot be reached except through the pursuit of knowledge, and [he knows] that he cannot benefit from his intellect if he does not attain this [knowledge] through it[s pursuit. Having known all this with his intellect] it becomes incumbent upon this [man, insofar as he is a] possessor of intellect, to seek knowledge—particularly knowledge of ethics—without which he cannot exist [as a human].

بِعِلْمِهِ. فَوَجَبَ عَلَى الْعَاقِلِ طَلَبُ الْعِلْمِ وَ الْأَدَبِ الَّذِي لَا قِوَامَ لَهُ إِلَّا بِهِ.

---

1. The phrase, "as part of a lengthy tradition," indicates that what is quoted here is only a part of a lengthier tradition. Sadly, the rest of this lengthy tradition may have been lost to time, or its relation to this tradition is no longer known. In fact, even this portion of the tradition was nearly lost. Traditions 1.1.35 and 1.1.36 are not included in any but one of the extant manuscripts of *al-Kāfī*. None of the 17th Century commentators included them in their commentaries. We have included them because they were included in Dār al-Ḥadīth's recension.

2. According to this sentence, the intellect plays the following roles vis-à-vis human beliefs, actions, and morality:

- It is more important than they are;
- It is the source from which they issue;
- It is their essence;
- It nurtures them so they increase and improve;
- It adorns humans;
- It is a guiding light for humans.

3. Imam al-Ṣādiq begins this tradition with a claim that the intellect is the most important human faculty because of its pivotal role vis-à-vis human beliefs, actions, and morality, which are what make humans human. In the next three sentences, he corroborates his claim by telling us that the intellect is the sole means for us to attain three vital kinds of knowledge:

- The first is direct, innate knowledge of God as our everlasting creator and the manager of our affairs. This type of knowledge is usually referred to as *fiṭrah*, which is literally "the *way* God has *created* humankind," but has come to refer to the innate knowledge of God present in all human beings.
- The second is conceptual, theoretical knowledge, which we attain through rational means. It is knowledge of the existence of *an* everlasting creator and *a* manager of our affairs, without identifying for us who he is.
- The third is rational knowledge of good and evil and some examples of each. For instance, our intellect independently comprehends that knowledge is good and ignorance is bad.

The first two kinds of knowledge are necessary for us to know and believe in God while the latter is necessary for our systems of law and ethics. And all are only possible by means of the intellect.

4. An example of a rational argument for the existence of a creator (*khāliq*) is the cosmological argument (*burhān al-imkān wa al-wujūb*). In this argument, we begin with our knowledge that contingent beings, such as those mentioned in the tradition exist, and we reason that they could only exist if there were a necessary being to cause them, who, in turn, must have always existed.

An example of a rational argument for the existence of a manager (*mudabbir*) is the teleological argument (*burhān al-naẓm*). In this argument, we begin with our knowledge that the creatures around us, such as those mentioned in the tradition, display a high level of functional order and reason that this functional order could only exist if there were an "orderer" to confer this order upon them.

5. Good and evil (or bad) are used in three different meanings depending on the context in which they occur:

- We sometimes say, "Learning and knowledge are good" and "Not learning and ignorance are bad." In this context, we mean that learning and knowledge perfect us and add something to our existence while not learning and ignorance render us lacking in something. In this sense, we might say, "Knowing is better than not knowing," without any consideration for the type of knowledge in question. Thus, in this sense, there is no ethical value attached to "good" or "bad."
- We sometimes say, "Sleep is good for the weary," "Food is good for the hungry," "Sleeping on a full stomach is bad," and "This food is bad." In this context, we mean that these actions or these things are agreeable to our sensibilities or abhorrent to them. In this sense also, there is no ethical value attached to "good" or "bad."
- We sometimes say, "Being kind to one's parents is good" and "Being unkind to an orphan is bad." In this context, we mean kindness to one's parents is an act deserving of praise and reward, which should be done, while unkindness to an orphan is an act deserving of censure and punishment, which should be avoided.

Out of these three meanings for "good" and "evil," only the third is appropriate in this tradition, for only knowledge of "good" and "evil" in this sense leads us to what is moral and praiseworthy, chief among which is knowledge of God and our duty to him. Knowing what is "good" and "evil" in the first sense, on the other hand, has no moral, and hence religious, benefit. Finally, knowing "good" and "evil" in the second sense has nothing to do with intellect, rather it is a factor of pleasure and pain.

6. Earlier in this tradition, Imam al-Ṣādiq said that the intellect is the essence of a human being's most essential traits. Here he says that it is the essence of the human being himself. There is clearly no contradiction between these two statements, since what is essential for a being's essential traits is essential for that being itself.

7. This is a reference to the direct knowledge a human being has of God as his Creator and Lord, which he attains either innately through his *fiṭrah* or through a combination of *fiṭrah* and reason.

8. He knows that God has likes and dislikes by virtue of his own knowledge of good and evil. We can understand this by recalling that the intellect independently understands that certain actions are inherently good and praiseworthy while others are inherently evil and deplorable. When the human intellect can perceive such things, then the creator of intellect undoubtedly knows them. Furthermore, if the creator of good and evil perceives good and evil, it is only natural that he like good and dislike evil, because the converse—that God likes evil and dislikes good—is unthinkable.

9. Since we know through rational means that God likes good and dislikes evil, it is only natural to assume that he wants us to do good and to refrain from evil. Furthermore, if he has commanded us thus, then we have the ability to either obey or disobey him. In conclusion, our intellect independently knows that God likes some things and has thus commanded us to do them and dislikes some things and has thus commanded us to refrain from them.

TRADITION 1.1.35 TEACHES THE FOLLOWING:

- The intellect is more important than human beliefs, actions, and morality; is the source from which they issue; is their essence; and is what nurtures them so they increase and improve.
- A human being cannot benefit from his beliefs, actions, and morality without his intellect.

- The intellect is what adorns human beings and is a guiding light for them.
- The intellect is the sole means for us to attain three vital kinds of knowledge:
    - ◊ The first is direct, innate knowledge of God as our everlasting creator and the manager of our affairs. This type of knowledge is called *fiṭrah.*
    - ◊ The second is conceptual, theoretical knowledge, which we attain through rational means. It is knowledge of the existence of *an* everlasting creator and *a* manager of our affairs without identifying for us who he is.
    - ◊ The third is rational knowledge of good and evil and some examples of each.
- The *fiṭrah* is a product of the intellect.
- Our intellect understands that it is deplorable for a person to be ignorant of God and of what he wants of us; and that it is laudable for a person to know God and know what he wants of us.
- Since the intellect realizes that it is incapable of knowing what God likes and dislikes, it deems it necessary to seek such knowledge from God himself.

Tradition 1.1.36

عَلِيُّ بْنُ مُحَمَّدٍ عَنْ بَعْضِ أَصْحَابِهِ عَنِ ابْنِ أَبِي عُمَيْرٍ عَنِ النَّضْرِ بْنِ سُوَيْدٍ عَنْ حُمْرَانَ وَ صَفْوَانَ بْنِ مِهْرَانَ الْجَمَّالِ قَالَا: سَمِعْنَا أَبَا عَبْدِ اللَّهِ عليه السلام يَقُولُ:

ʿAlī ibn Muḥammad reported from one of his teachers from Ibn Abī ʿUmayr from al-Naḍr ibn Suwayd from Ḥumrān and Ṣafwān ibn Mihrān al-Jammāl that they both said, "We heard Abū ʿAbd Allāh [al-Ṣādiq] say:

لَا غِنَى أَخْصَبُ مِنَ الْعَقْلِ، وَ لَا فَقْرَ أَحَطُّ مِنَ الْحُمْقِ،

'There is no [cause for] sufficiency more profitable than intellect, and no poverty more lowly than foolishness.[1]

وَ لَا اسْتِظْهَارَ فِي أَمْرٍ بِأَكْثَرَ مِنَ الْمَشُورَةِ فِيهِ.

'There is no better [way to take] precaution in a matter than to consult [with others] about it.'"[2]

---

1. This sentence is nearly identical in meaning to *al-Kāfī* 1.1.25.

2. By consulting with the right person, we benefit from his intellect and experience, protect ourselves against harm, and gain confidence in our chosen course of action.

TRADITION 1.1.36 TEACHES THE FOLLOWING:

- Consultation is the best way to protect ourselves against harm and to gain confidence in our chosen course of action.

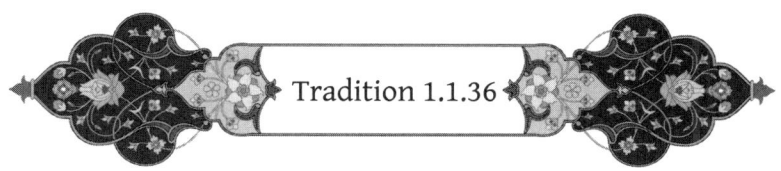

Thus ends the *Book of Intellect and Foolishness*. Praise is solely for God. May God shower his mercy upon, and extend his salutations to, Muḥammad and his family.

وَهَذَا آخِرُ كِتَابِ الْعَقْلِ وَالْجَهْلِ، وَالْحَمْدُ لِلَّـهِ وَحْدَهُ، وَصَلَّى اللَّهُ عَلَى مُحَمَّدٍ وَآلِهِ وَسَلَّمَ تَسْلِيماً.

Index

A

ʿabd 148
ʿaql. *See* intellect
ʿAmr ibn al-ʿĀṣ 189
Abraham 18
Abū al-Ḥusayn Aḥmad ibn ʿAlī al-Najāshī. *See* al-Najāshī
Abū Jaʿfar Muḥammad ibn al-Ḥasan al-Ṭūsī. *See* al-Ṭūsī
Adam xl, 8, 9, 10, 41, 143
  taught through personified concepts 9
Akhbār al-qāʾim xiii
ākhirah 47
al-Astarābādī xxiv
al-Baḥrānī xxxvi
al-Dhahabī xix
al-Dharīʿah ilā ḥāfiẓ al-sharīʿah xxxvii
al-Durr al-manẓūm min kalām al-maʿṣūm xxxvii
al-Fihrist xx
al-Hadāyā xxxvii
al-Ḥāshiyah ʿalā uṣūl al-kāfī xxxvii
al-Ḥillī xv
  popularizes Ibn Ṭāwūs categories xxxii
al-Ḥillī, Jamāl al-Dīn Ḥasan ibn Yūsuf. *See* al-Ḥillī
al-Ḥusayn ibn Rūḥ xxvi
  shuns his doorman xxvi
  threatens to shun a companion xxvi
al-Kāfī
  authenticated by Imam al-Mahdī xxiv
  authenticity of xxiii
  books of xxi
  commentaries on xxxvi
  divisions of xxiii
  Furūʿ al-kāfī xxiii
  Kulaynī's authentication of xxxv
  number of traditions in xxxvi
  Rawḍat al-kāfī xxiii
  Uṣūl al-kāfī xxiii
al-Karakī xxi
al-Kashf al-wāfī fī sharḥ uṣūl al-kāfī xxxvii
al-Khiḍr 17
al-Khulāṣah xv
al-Khurāsānī, Muḥammad Kāẓim liv
al-Kulaynī
  biography of xi
  birth of xii
  death of xx
  epithets of xii
  reputation of xviii
  students of xvii
  teachers of xiii
  testimony concrning *al-Kāfī* xxxii, xxxiii
  testimony of xxxiii
  writings of xix
allegory 8, 138
al-Majlisī xxiv, xxviii, xxxvi
al-Majlisī, Muḥammad Taqī xxi
al-Māzandarānī xxxvi
al-Mufīd xx, xxiii
al-Muqtadir xvii, xxvi
al-Murtaḍā xxiii
al-Najāshī xiii, xvi, xviii, xx, xxviii
al-Qazwīnī xxiv
al-Qāʾim 165
al-Rijāl xviii, xix, xx
al-Ṣadūq xx, xxiii, 166
al-Shalmaghānī xxvii
al-Shalmaghānī, Muḥammad ibn ʿAlī. *See* al-Shalmaghānī
al-Taklīf xxvii

al-Ta'dīb xxvii
al-Taʿlīqah ʿalā uṣūl al-kāfī xxxvii
alternation of night and day 36
al-Ṭūsī xii, xviii, xix, xx, xxiii, xxvi, xxviii
al-Tustarī xx
al-Tustarī, Muḥammad Taqī. *See* al-Tustarī
al-Uṣūl al-arbaʿumi'ah xxviii, xxix
al-Wāfī xxxvi
al-Zanjānī, Mūsā al-Shubayrī xi, xxxix
al-ʿĀmilī, Bahā' al-Dīn. *See* al-Bahā'ī
amusement 47
angels
  fallible understanding 23
  sinless 23
anger 141
army of foolishness
  adulteration of one's faith with polytheism 132
  aloofness 135
  anger 129
  announcement 133
  arrogance 129, 131
  audacity 129
  being deceived into procrastinating repentance 135
  casting God's covenant into oblivion 133
  collusion 132
  contempt for the truth 130
  covetousness 128
  cowering in fear of the enemy 132
  denial of belief 128
  desire 129, 134
  despair of God's mercy 128
  difficulty of an act 134
  disclosure of secrets 132
  disdain of his laws 135
  disobedience to whom obedience is due 131
  doing and enjoing evil 133
  doubt in what is clearly true 130
  dullness 132
  enmity 131
  evil 128
  excess 134
  exhibitionism 133
  exultance 135
  failure to recognize 132
  fatigue 134
  filth 134
  flippancy 134
  forgetfulness 130
  garrulousness 130
  greed 128, 130
  hardness of heart 129
  harshness 129
  haste 129
  hatred for all that is good 131
  haughtiness 135
  heedlessness 130
  hoarding more than is needed 134
  hostility 132
  idiocy 129, 132
  ignorance 129
  impatience 129
  indecency 134
  ingratitude 128
  iniquity 128
  iniquity in fulfilling one's duty to one's wife 133
  ire at God's decree 128
  irresponsibility 131
  laziness 135
  mendacity 131
  miserliness 135
  misery 135
  not fasting 132
  not praying 132
  obliteration of the reward for an act 134
  ostentation 133
  partiality 133
  persistence in sin 135
  poverty 130

refusal to give charity 131
severing ties 130
shamelessness 129
talebearing 133
treachery 131
tribulation 131, 134
unbelief in God 128
uncontrolled grief 130
vengeance 130
wickedness toward one's parents 133
wrong 131
army of intellect
acuity 132
adherence to all of God's laws 135
affability 135
altruism 131
attestation to belief 128
awareness 130
belief in God 128
building ties 130
circumspection 129
cleanliness 133
comprehension 129, 132
confidentiality 132
contentment 130
decency 134
dignity 134
dissimulation 133
doing and enjoining good 133
ease of an act 134
energy 135
fairness 133
fasting 132
fearfulness of God 129
forbearance 129
friendship 131
generosity 135
goodness 128
goodness toward one's parents 133
graciousness 132
grooming 133
guarding one's tongue against talebearing 133
hajj 133
happiness 134
hope in God's mercy 128
hopelessness to attain what others possess 128
humility 129, 131
increase in the reward for an act 134
indifference to the material world 129
jihad 132
kindness 129
knowledge 129
love 131
loyalty 131
magnanimity 130
mercy 129
moderation 134
modesty in dress 133
obedience to whom obedience is due 131
patience 130
prayer 132
purity of faith in God's oneness 132
recognition 132
reliance solely on God 128
remembrance 130
repentance 135
restfulness 134
restraint 129
right 131
sadness 135
satisfaction with God's decree 128
security in absentia 132
seeking forgiveness 135
sensitivity 129
silence 130
sincerity in worship 133
submission to the truth 130
supplication 135
sustenance 134
thankfulness 128
trustworthiness 131
truthfulness 131

wealth 130
well-being 131, 134
wisdom 134

B

Believer from the House of the Pharaoh 62
Black Stone 143
blessing 145
bothering others 118
Buyids xvi

C

charity 159
Computer Research Center of Islamic Studies xi
conceit 195
contemplation 80, 202
contemplation of the Qurʾān 67
contentment 101, 141
contradictory traditions liv
cosmological argument 207
covenant with God 143
covetousness 140

D

Dār al-Ḥadīth xxxviii
decency 9
devotion 9
difference between prophet and messenger 30
dignity 118
dīn. *See* devotion
discipline 155, 202
dissimulation 150
double entendre 23
doubts 26
dunyā 47

E

evidence 35
evil 208
excess 93
exultance 145

F

far-fetched hopes 81
fatigue 144
Fāṭimah al-Zahrāʾ 146
fear of God 71
financial independence 101
foolishness and its army 126
front and center of a gathering 116

G

Gabriel 8, 9
gentleness 189
Ghaffārī, ʿAlī Akbar xxxviii
God's commands
existential commands 10
legal commands 10
god vs. lord 37
good 208
greed 140
grooming 144

H

ḥadd 44
ḥaqīqah 144
ḥayāʾ. *See* decency
ḥujjah
meaning divine guide 35
hajj 143
harshness 189
heart
seat of intellect 151
seat of knowledge 190
Hishām ibn al-Ḥakam 32
hopelessness 140
humanity 112

I

ʿibād 148
Ibn Abī al-ʿAzāqir. *See* al-Shalmaghānī
Ibn al-Athīr xix
Ibn al-Sikkīt 160
Ibn Ṭāwūs xix, xx, xxviii
  categorizes traditions xxxii
Ibn ʿAsākir xvi
Imam al-Bāqir
  traditions of 1, 20, 151, 165, 179, 190
Imam al-Hādī
  traditions of 92, 160
Imam al-Ḥasan
  traditions of 30, 75, 114, 188
Imam al-Jawād
  traditions of 146
Imam al-Kāẓim
  traditions of 32, 140, 157
Imam al-Mahdī
  titles of 165
Imam al-Riḍā
  traditions of 13, 15, 144, 155, 196
Imam al-Ṣādiq
  traditions of 4, 11, 17, 21, 25, 26, 55, 92, 118, 126, 143, 148, 150, 153, 158, 167, 169, 175, 176, 180, 183, 185, 191, 195, 198, 201, 204, 211
Imam Zayn al-ʿĀbidīn
  traditions of 48, 114, 146
Imam ʿAlī
  servant of Muḥammad 149
  The Gateway to the City of Knowledge 149
  traditions of 8, 14, 48, 73, 86, 89, 98, 106, 114, 117, 122, 124, 125, 141, 146, 149, 151, 156, 159, 183, 189, 191, 193, 195, 200, 201
indicators 116
intellect
  correlation with God's love 6
  correlation with reward and punishment 6
  coupled with decency and devotion 10
  four meanings of 2
  friend of man 13
  God's most beloved creature 5
  means for worshipping God 11
intellect and its army 126
Islamic Texts Institute
  commentary and translation of *al-Kāfī* xxxviii
  mission of xi
  use of technology xxxviii
Israelites 21

J

Jesus 160
Jewish man on an island 21
Joseph 9
just ruler 117

K

Khawārij 10
Kifāyat al-uṣūl liv
Kitāb al-radd ʿalā al-qarāmiṭah xix
Kitāb al-rijāl xix
Kitāb mā qīla fī al-aʾimmah min al-shiʿr xix
Kitāb taʿbīr al-ruʾyā xix
knowing God as he has described himself 30
kufr 198
Kumayl ibn Ziyād 159

L

liver
  seat of base qualities 190
lord
  manager of human affairs 39
  manager of human development 42
  manager of human ethics 43
  manager of ideology 45
  manager of legal affairs 44

manager of the cosmos 37
Lot 50
Luqmān 69, 146
proverbs of 70
Luʿluʿat al-baḥrayn xxxvi
lying 111

M

magic 160
majority censured 58
Mary 146
may I be your ransom 126
Maʿ al-kulaynī wa kitābihi al-kāfī xxxvi
Miftāḥ al-falāḥ xii
minority praised 61
miracles 163
Mirʾāt al-ʿuqūl xxiv
Mirʾāt al-ʿuqūl fī sharḥ akhbār āl al-rasūl xxxvi
Miṣbāḥ al-uṣūl liv
Moses 17, 160
Muḥaqqiq al-Karakī. *See* al-Karakī
murajjiḥāt liv
Muʿāwiyah xxvi, 4, 11, 12, 170, 189

N

Nahj al-balāghah
letter 31 200
proverb 66 117
proverb 131 48
proverb 147 159, 189, 191
proverb 161 177
proverb 175 122
proverb 207 124, 156
proverb 211 89
proverb 274 141
proverb 295 14
proverb 424 89
proverb 456 113
sermon 130 141
sermon 192 184
sermon 193 146
sermon 201 86
need 93, 108
Noah 61

O

ostentation 144

P

Parable of the Slave-partner 45
Perennialist School 3
perfection 5
personification of human attributes 8
philosophy of religion 87
polytheists 45
poverty 176
process of deriving law 149
Prophet Joseph 9
Prophet Muḥammad
traditions of 4, 6, 25, 28, 30, 67, 70, 81, 117, 148, 149, 176, 183
prophets' intellects greater than people's 28
purity 142

Q

Qāmūs al-rijāl xx
qāʿidat al-takhyīr liv
qiṣāṣ 44
Qurʾān
2:2 175
2:30 23
2:44 57
2:114 107
2:150 77
2:163-4 36
2:170 54
2:171 55
2:261 83
2:269 31, 65, 145

3:4 175
3:7 66

3:8 103
3:49 162
3:59 41
3:85 18
3:175 194
3:190 66
3:191-5 66

4:31 172
4:59 172
4:80 172
4:165 77

5:103 62

6:21 107
6:32 47
6:37 62
6:78 23
6:98 liii
6:116 58
6:149 77
6:151 43

7:68 171
7:169 l
7: 172-3 143

8:42 xlvi, 122

9:122 l

10:39 l
10:42 55
10:58 146
10:81 162

11:6 98
11:40 62
11:89 49
11:114 172

12:4 9
12:36 9
12:42 199
12:43 9
12:58 143
12:105 66
12:106 199

13:4 42
13:19 66, 117
13 26 142
13:28 193

15:21 5

16:12 41
16:40 10
16:43 l
16:97 194

17:29 93
17:31 43

18:58 107
18:79 17

19:93 148

20:124 194

21:67 18

22:11 lii

23:96 188

24:2 141
24:12 188

25:44 56
25:67 93

26:12-16 121
26:82 140

28:31-32 162
28:76 145
28:79-80 86

29:18 121
29:34-5 49
29:43 51
29:63 60

30:24 43
30:28 44
30:39 83

31:12 69
31:18 183
31:25 59

32:16 194

34:13 61

35:28 103

37:89 23
37:136-8 49

38:4 163
38:24 61
38:29 66

39:9 66
39:17-8 32
39:28 xlvi

40:28 62
40:53-4 67
40:60 145
40:67 41

41:11 4

43:87 li

45:5 42

49:12 188

50:37 69

51:55 67
51:56 173

53:32 183

57:17 42

59:14 57

63:8 118

68:4 154

91:9 190

93: 7 103

Qurʾānic comparisons 51

R

Raḍī al-Dīn ʿAlī ibn Ṭāwūs. *See* Ibn Ṭāwūs
Rasāʾil al-aʿimmah xix
reality 87
recognition 142
reliance 141

S

ṣaḥīḥ
  according to al-Kulaynī xxxii
  according to Ibn Ṭāwūs xxxii
  meaning of xxxii
Ṣubḥī al-Ṣāliḥ xli
sadness 145
Ṣaḥīḥat Hishām ibn Sālim xxxiv
Samanids xvi
satanic insinuations 27

Sayyid Ibn Ṭāwūs. *See* Ibn Ṭāwūs
Sayyid Mūsā al-Shubayrī al-Zanjānī. *See* al-Zanjānī
secrets 143
sexual indecency 44
Shahīd al-Awwal xxi
Sharḥ furūʿ al-kāfī xxxvii
Sharḥ uṣūl al-kāfī xxxvii
Shaykh al-Bahāʾī. *See* al-Bahāʾī
Shaykh al-Kulaynī. *See* al-Kulaynī
Shaykh al-Najāshī. *See* al-Najāshī
Shaykh al-Ṣadūq. *See* al-Ṣadūq
Shaykh al-Ṭūsī. *See* al-Ṭūsī
solitude 85
sport 47
Subḥānī, Jaʿfar xii, xiii, xxx
submission 141
sufficient notice 121
Syed Hossein Nasr 3
syllogism 18

T

tadhakkur 65
takhyīr liv
talebearing 144
taqiyyah xxxii
teleological argument 207
traditions
  factors that have obscured their teachings 150
  need for deliberation 149

U

Uṣūl al-ḥadīth wa aḥkāmuhu xii, xiii
uṣūl ʿamaliyyah liv

V

variations in the night and day 37

W

wisdom 65
  simple wisdom 91
  versus material pleasures 91